SOLID MODELING
with AutoCAD
Second Edition

For AME 2.0 & 2.1

VENTANA
PRESS

SOLID MODELING
with AutoCAD
Second Edition

For AME 2.0 & 2.1

Ronald W. Leigh

VENTANA
PRESS

The AutoCAD Reference Library™

Solid Modeling With AutoCAD, Second Edition

Copyright© 1992 by Ronald W. Leigh

The AutoCAD Reference Library (TM)

Library of Congress Cataloging-in-Publication Data

Leigh, Ronald W. (Ronald Wilson)
　　Solid modeling with AutoCAD : using the advanced modeling extension release 2
　　for release 11 & release 12 / Ronald W. Leigh. — 2nd ed.
　　　p. cm.
　　Includes index.
　　ISBN 1-56604-004-3
　　1. AutoCAD (Computer file) 2. Engineering models. I. Title.
QA76.76.W56W48 1992
005.4'3-dc20　　　　　　92-25588 CIP

Book design: Karen Wysocki, Ventana Press
Cover design: Douglass Grimmett, Chapel Hill, NC
Cover illustration: Douglass Grimmett, Chapel Hill, NC
Cover photography: Peter Hutson, Raleigh, NC
Icons: John Nedwidek, Sitzer:Spuria
Editorial staff: Diana Cooper, Jessica Fields, Patricia Frederick, Linda Pickett, Pam Richardson
Production staff: Rhonda Angel, Brian Little, Karen Wysocki
Technical editor: Brian Matthews, Architectural Technology Dept. Head, Wake Technical Community College, Raleigh, NC

Second Edition　9 8 7 6 5 4 3 2 1
Printed in the United States of America

Ventana Press, Inc.
P.O. Box 2468
Chapel Hill, NC 27515
919/942-0220
FAX 919/942-1140

Limits of Liability and Disclaimer of Warranty

Trademarks

Trademarked names appear throughout this book. Rather than list the names and entities that own the trademarks or insert a trademark symbol with each mention of the trademarked name, the publisher states that it is using the names only for editorial purposes and to the benefit of the trademark owner with no intention of infringing upon that trademark.

About the Author

Ronald W. Leigh is ranked "Master Instructor" in the Drafting/CAD Technology Department, an Authorized AutoCAD Training Center, at Indiana Vocational Technical College in Fort Wayne, Indiana. He is also an AutoCAD and AutoLISP consultant.

Ronald W. Leigh
Fort Wayne, Indiana

CONTENTS

CHAPTER 5

Projects: Basic, Swept & Edge Primitives   91

CHAPTER 6

Putting the Pieces Together: Boolean Operations   111

CHAPTER 7

CHAPTER 8

CHAPTER 9

Moving & Changing Solids   199

CHAPTER 10

Analyzing the Solid: Material Properties   219

CHAPTER

Projects: Modifying & Analyzing   235

CHAPTER

Detail Drawings & Assemblies   249

CHAPTER 13

Projects: Detail Drawings & Assemblies   271

CHAPTER 14

Downstream Applications of AutoCAD AME   299

CHAPTER 15

AutoLISP & API Programs Supplied With AME   307

List of Figures in This Book

Sample Color Illustrations

Most of the color illustrations are renderings of black-and-white figures that appear throughout the book. (The last three were supplied by Autodesk and do not appear elsewhere in these pages.) They were directly photographed from a standard VGA screen. Thus, they represent exactly what you see on a color monitor.

The built-in SHADE command has been used in many of the pictures; but they haven't been touched up or rendered with any additional shading or rendering software.

INTRODUCTION

Introduction

Why Learn Solid Modeling?

It's difficult not to wax eloquent about the tremendous strides made in the area of computer-based modeling in the last few years. It seems only yesterday that physical models were a designer's only choice when attempting to gain a realistic 3D representation of an object. While many of us knew of computer-based modeling being done on large, expensive computers, the cost and learning curve were well beyond our reach.

With AutoCAD's Advanced Modeling Extension, Autodesk has delivered an inexpensive, effective way to execute a wide range of solid modeling capabilities at a relatively low cost. Not only can you create a realistic 3D representation of nearly any object, but you're now able to extract visual and mathematical information about the object's surfaces and interior as well.

Realistic 3D rendering and modeling is slowly but surely changing the way designers work—i.e., from a 2D to a 3D orientation. The day is near when design students and professionals will learn to draw in 3D, create realistic models, walk-throughs, auxiliary and section views without having to expend so much brain-power on tasks that can (and should) be automated.

In other words, designers will have more time to *design*, delegating the less creative tasks to their computers. AutoCAD's AME and associated products are an important step in making sophisticated design technology available to everyone.

Who Needs This Book?

This book presents AutoCAD's newest, most advanced 3D capability—solid modeling. To take full advantage of the projects offered here, you should already be familiar with using AutoCAD for 2D drawing. If you're not, it would be helpful for you to set this book aside and get a copy of *AutoCAD: A Concise Guide to Commands & Features* (also published by

Ventana Press) to familiarize yourself with AutoCAD's drawing, editing, display and inquiry commands in 2D.

What's Inside

Solid Modeling With AutoCAD contains reference chapters and project chapters. The reference chapters explain solid modeling concepts and procedures. Each *project* chapter presents hands-on exercises based on the material explained in the preceding *reference* chapters. This approach allows this book to serve as both reference manual and tutorial.

The projects used in the book evolved from assignments given to solid modeling classes at the Authorized AutoCAD Training Center in Fort Wayne, Indiana.

NOTE: This book is based on Versions 2 and 2.1 of the AutoCAD's Advanced Modeling Extension (AME R2, AME R2.1). If you have created solid models with AME R1, you can use those models in AME R2. However, since AME R1 was single-precision and AME R2 is double-precision, models converted from AME R1 may undergo minor changes when the model is re-evaluated in AME R2.

Hardware/Software Requirements

To use AutoCAD's solid modeling, you must have AutoCAD Release 11 or 12, including the Advanced Modeling Extension (AME). The instructions in this book assume that both AutoCAD Release 11 or 12 and AME are installed and configured on your PC-compatible hardware.

How to Use This Book

Everyone learns by doing, so you would be wise to work through each project in the hands-on chapters (Chapters 2, 5, 7, 11 and 13). Should you do *all* the projects? No and yes. The book is not built around a single project that runs from beginning to end; individual projects are largely independent of each other. Generally, you won't find it necessary to edit a drawing you completed in an earlier chapter in order to do the project for the current chapter. This allows you the freedom of selecting the exercises you feel will be of greatest help in understanding certain concepts or procedures.

On the other hand, each exercise is unique. The projects progress from easiest to most difficult and for that reason are closely tied in with the content of the preceding chapters. While there is some overlap, no two exercises aim at illustrating the same ideas. Therefore, working through all the exercises will provide the most complete exposure to the capabilities and procedures of solid modeling with AutoCAD. In addition, some explanations given in the projects are not included in any of the reference chapters (such as the material on viewport numbers and handles in Project 2A).

The one project that all the others depend on is Project 2A, which sets up a prototype drawing called SMA.DWG. This drawing is used in all the other projects, even Project 7D, which creates a prototype drawing called SMB.DWG that is easily converted from SMA. The SMA and SMB prototype drawings are both available on the companion diskette available with this book.

Do You Need the Companion Diskette?

Although this book stands alone, you may find a lot of value in the *Solid Modeling With AutoCAD* Companion Diskette. For example, the batch files and AutoLISP programs can boost your productivity considerably. These programs are designed to automate certain aspects of solid modeling and thus save time and increase output as you use AME in an actual drawing environment. The pausing scripts can serve as an introduction to or a review of basic solid modeling procedures. You may also find it instructive to compare the projects you complete with the same projects on the diskette.

See Appendix A for a brief description of the files on the companion diskette.

A Word About Color

To the layman, solid modeling often implies color, shading and a host of other special effects. Yet, as is evident throughout these pages, solid modeling has a good deal more to do with the intrinsic spatial and material properties of a solid object. In order to achieve advanced color effects using AME, drawings and models produced using AME must be exported to a software package capable of producing advanced effects such as multiple light sources, altered surface reflectivity, shading and shadows, object translucency, thousands of hues and even animation. Surface mesh information produced from AME can be exported directly to a package such as AutoShade or RenderMan in order to manipulate and refine the picture. A discussion of these products, and the use of advanced color capabilities in general, falls outside the scope of this book.

Some of the color pages in this book represent what you see when you use AutoCAD on a color monitor. The built-in SHADE command was used in many of the pictures, which were not retouched or rendered with any additional shading or rendering software.

Let's Get Started

As your desktop computer gains more and more graphics processing power at less cost, you can be certain that the people at Autodesk will be creating CAD products that address the tasks that only mainframes could do just a few years ago. While solid modeling is one of these tasks, it's nonetheless only as useful as one makes it. So, let's get started!

— Ron Leigh
Fort Wayne, IN

SOLID MODELING DEFINED

1

Solid Modeling Defined

S olid modeling is the most direct, efficient, complete and effective way engineers and designers can represent a physical object without actually *making* the object.

Although traditional 2D engineering drawing methods will be with us for a long time to come, all designers would be wise to explore the potential of solid modeling.

As we discuss the differences between solid modeling and the other two computer-aided modeling approaches (wireframe and surface), you'll gain more insight into the many advantages this method offers.

 ## Modeling Modes

A physical object can be represented as a physical model, a flat 2D (on paper) model or a computer model. While each type is useful for certain purposes, each has deficiencies, and none is complete in itself.

Physical Models

Physical models have been used for a long time with great success to represent real-world objects. Physical models are such things as a sculpture of a person, animal or thing; an architect's scaled mock-up of a new building; a chemist's "blowup" of a complex molecule; an inventor's prototype of a labor-saving device; even a full-size wax model of a car for wind tunnel testing. Such models are truly three-dimensional and can be very effective tools for communicating certain information about the real object, such as overall shape and relationships between parts.

However, when physical models are used, many practical aspects must be either left to the imagination or provided in other forms: for example, the sculpture's underlying anatomy; interior detail of the architect's model; dynamic forces within the molecule; and exact dimensions, materials and processes needed to construct the device.

In addition to these limitations, physical models can be difficult and time-consuming to create—and especially to revise.

Flat Models

Traditional, two-dimensional flat models comprise photographs and pictorial (isometric and perspective) renderings, as well as standard engineering assembly and detail drawings, including orthographic, auxiliary, sectional and plan views, elevations, cut-aways, enlargements, etc.

For decades, industry has used these 2D engineering drawings with great skill and productivity. For example, consider the Boeing 747. This highly successful aircraft is widely accepted throughout the aviation industry and even is used as the President's "Air Force One." The 747 design process was a huge engineering feat, requiring over 75,000 drawings created mostly without computer assistance. These thousands of 2D drawings were in effect the model of the airplane.

Engineers have become so good at using this method of modeling that they don't stop to focus on the mental gymnastics it requires. In the beginning, the engineer has a concept, a 3D "vision" of an object in mind. And in the end the manufacturer produces a real 3D object. But in between, in the design phase, the object is represented in only two dimensions—the standard engineering assembly and detail drawings. A lot of time and mental effort are devoted to translating the 3D ideas into 2D models, then translating the 2D models back into 3D objects. Since they begin and end in 3D, this 2D segment of the process seems terribly inefficient.

Computer Models

Computer models are mathematical models of real objects. The computer manipulates the numbers and displays the graphic image of the information contained in those numbers.

But not all computer models are 3D. If the computer representation consists merely of 2D views of an object, then it's only a model of a 2D drawing of the object, rather than a model of the object itself. Therefore, CAD (Computer Aided Design/Drafting) software that's limited to creating 2D views does not do 3D modeling, even though the views define a 3D object. True 3D computer models contain information about the object in space, not merely information about the projections of the object onto flat planes. A 3D model lets you view the "object" from any angle and extract 2D projections when needed.

True 3D computer models comprise three basic types—wireframe, surface and solid. Each type contains elements in all three dimensions—X, Y and Z. But beyond that similarity they have marked differences.

Wireframe Models Wireframe models represent an object by defining its edges. For some time, AutoCAD has been able to produce 3D wireframe models using lines, circles, arcs and polylines to represent the edges. With the appearance in Release 10 of the User Coordinate System (UCS) and Viewports, the process of wireframe modeling became much more efficient.

Since edges imply surfaces, and in turn these surfaces can imply a solid, a wireframe model provides a fairly useful description of an object. Certain information such as spatial relationships between the various features can be extracted from a wireframe model more directly than from a 2D multiview drawing.

But wireframe models also have disadvantages and limitations. Since an edge has no thickness, it cannot hide anything behind itself. In fact, a wireframe model has no real surfaces to hide anything. This means that no hidden-edge views or shaded renderings of the model can be displayed. So when you look at a wireframe model, too much information may be visible at one time. You often see more than you want to see. Edges on the far side of the object "intersect" edges on the near side, producing an optical illusion.

In some cases, wireframe models can even be ambiguous and misleading. An edge can belong to more than one surface, so one wireframe model can seem to represent more than one object, as illustrated below.

Figure 1-1: Ambiguous wireframe model.

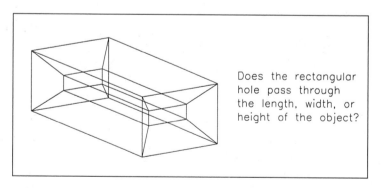

Does the rectangular hole pass through the length, width, or height of the object?

Surface Models Surface models define surfaces, including the edges of each surface. The edges can be displayed to make up a representation that looks just like a wireframe model. But since there are surfaces, the representation can also be displayed as a true surface model, with nearer surfaces hiding surfaces and edges farther from the viewer. This is referred to as a hidden-edge view. When the surfaces are "filled in," it's known as a shaded rendering and has the advantage of making the object (at least its nearer portions) easier to see. Also, using additional software, a surface model can be used to create realistic images that include multiple light sources, varying surface reflectivity, etc.

But a surface model is just an empty shell. And since surfaces have no thickness, surface models contain no information about an object's weight. In other words, surface models do not contain mass property or dynamic inertial information. Therefore, while a surface model can do a good job of showing the shape of an object, it does not define other characteristics that are important to a designer.

Solid Models   Solid models define the entire volume (3D space) that the object occupies, including all surfaces with their edges. This gives solid models the usefulness of wireframe and surface models with the addition of descriptive data about the "insides" of the object. In addition to providing more comprehensive information, solid models are relatively easy to construct.

A solid model can be displayed either in wireframe mode (edges only) or in surface mode (a hidden-edge view or a shaded rendering). But either way, it contains all the information needed to calculate surface area, volume and center of gravity. And because a solid model has a particular material assigned, analysis can also be made of its weight, moment of inertia, thermal conductivity, stress, etc. (Although Finite Element Analysis [FEA] can be performed on solid models, AutoCAD depends on third-party software for FEA, since Advanced Modeling Extension [AME] does not include this feature.)

In AutoCAD, you can create a variety of solid building blocks (primitives), including box, wedge, cylinder, cone, sphere, torus, extruded solids, revolved solids, chamfers and fillets. These basic components can be combined with each other using the three standard Boolean operations: union, difference and intersection. You can do mass properties analysis of the solid. You can revise the solid or revise any of its components. And you can extract any 2D views of the model needed for standard engineering drawings.

So solid models are the most complete of the three computer model forms. They're more like their real-world counterparts than either wireframe or surface models. In AutoCAD they're also easier to construct.

After the composite model is finished, the design can be easily revised, since the primitives making up the solid can be changed without breaking the solid down into its parts.

Using Solid Modeling

When working with a solid model throughout the design process, no time and energy are spent translating the object back and forth between 3D and 2D. The designer can focus directly on refining the 3D model. With solid modeling, the designer thinks, sketches, draws and communicates in 3D from the beginning to the end of the project.

When 2D drawings are needed, they can be produced from the 3D model. And since the computer can easily produce any views of the model, including primary and secondary auxiliary views and section views, the task of translating a 3D model to a 2D drawing is automated to a large extent.

Over time, industry will gradually adapt its procedures to make increasing use of solid modeling. The gradual shift to solid models will also affect the education requirements of engineers and drafters. For example, some aspects of descriptive geometry will always be important, but time spent mastering secondary auxiliary views and solid intersections can be better spent on other engineering concepts in the future.

AutoCAD'S Advanced Modeling Extension (AME 2.0 & 2.I)

AME grew out of another Autodesk product, AutoSolid. Those who have used both packages claim that AME is more capable and user-friendly than its predecessor.

AME is a self-contained software package, an AutoCAD Development System (ADS) application. It includes the full set of solid modeling capabilities for working with three-dimensional solids. It also includes a region modeler that allows the creation of a 2D area from closed 2D figures (circles, polylines, polygons, etc.) and Boolean operations. Solids can be created from regions, and regions can be extracted from solids.

AutoCAD's AME uses Constructive Solid Geometry (CSG) techniques but also keeps track of Boundary Representation (B-rep) information. Some of AME's algorithms were rewritten in the C language from the

Parts and Assembly Description Language (PADL) developed at the University of Rochester. As mentioned earlier, Finite Element Analysis (FEA) is not included in AME.

This book assumes you've already installed the AME program on your computer. AME must be loaded when you first enter AutoCAD's drawing editor. (The first time you load AME you must also enter your AME authorization code.)

AME can be loaded manually or automatically. In Release 12, AME loads when you first enter an AME command either at the Command prompt or from the "Model" pull-down menu. To load manually in Release 11, pick "AME" (either from the sidebar menu or the pull-down menu), then pick "Load AME." Or enter (xload "ame").

To load AME automatically, place the following line in your ACAD.LSP:

```
(defun s::startup () (xload "ame"))
```

There is good reason to load AME automatically. See the warning at the beginning of Chapter 9, "Moving & Changing Solids."

To find out the version of AME you're using, enter SOLAMEVER at the command prompt.

AME can be unloaded by entering (xunload "ame").

The AME software uses a special layer named AME_FRZ to store information about each solid. This information includes blocks that represent the solid in both wireframe and mesh form and, if the solid is a composite, information about the primitives that make up the solid. *You should not attempt to manipulate anything on this layer.* For example, suppose you accidentally thaw (using a wild card) all layers including AME_FRZ. You may see alternate wireframe or mesh blocks used to represent your solids. You should not attempt to erase these primitives or edit them in any other manner. Instead, merely freeze layer AME_FRZ.

Also, AME uses handles to identify all solid primitives and composites. Therefore you should never use the HANDLES command to turn handles off in a drawing containing a solid model.

Moving On

In this chapter, I have pointed out the key differences between solid models and other types of models, and described how solid modeling fits into the design process. I suggested that solid modeling is an effective tool that holds a lot of promise for the future of design and engineering. You will probably observe increasing use of solid modeling in many disciplines, so you would be wise to consider the place solid modeling might hold for you.

I also described AutoCAD's solid modeler, the Advanced Modeling Extension. But a general description doesn't mean much until you have actually seen AME work—or better, tried it out yourself. In Chapter 2, "Projects: Setup & Overview," we begin using AME, first setting up a prototype drawing for solid modeling, and then creating a simple solid model from which we extract an engineering drawing.

PROJECTS: SETUP & OVERVIEW

2

Projects: Setup & Overview

This chapter features two projects. Project 2A creates the prototype drawing that will be used in Project 2B and the other projects that follow. Project 2B creates a solid model of a Hold-Down Clamp. This project gives you a bird's-eye view of the overall process of solid modeling—from creation of the building blocks that make up the solid model to mass properties analysis of the object and extraction of 2D views for dimensioning.

The idea is to provide a hands-on introduction to basic solid modeling operations. Explanations of the commands and procedures used will come later. Remember that these projects will work for you only when you take the time to enter the commands at your computer.

Give Solid Modeling a Chance

If you presently view solid modeling with skepticism, you aren't alone. Solid modeling is quite different from the traditional way of doing things, so it's only natural that you should question it. But don't be discouraged—especially if this is your first exposure to solid modeling—when the newness of some of the ideas and practices becomes distracting.

Although this chapter gives you an introduction to some of the steps in solid modeling, you won't have enough input to be able to make a balanced judgment about its usefulness for your situation until you've worked more extensively with it throughout the rest of this book.

Solid modeling is better suited to certain engineering tasks than others, but the advantages and disadvantages for your type of work will not be apparent until you've worked through a variety of different examples of solid modeling.

Keystroke Instructions

In this introductory chapter, we give you specific keystroke instructions for every step (set in a contrasting typeface) as well as general instructions (set in the regular text face). In later projects, only new procedures will include complete keystroke instructions.

The prompts that appear on the screen when you enter an AutoCAD command are reproduced here. You should read them carefully because the responses given in the keystroke instructions will make better sense when you understand the prompt you're responding to. Take your time and think about what you're entering. Your goal here should be to understand the commands and procedures, not to race through the project.

Many of the commands used in these projects can be carried out more easily by using the pointer—to either select menu items or indicate locations in the drawing. Feel free to use the method that works best for you. If you aren't sure how to accomplish a step, you can always revert to the keyboard and enter each step exactly as it is printed.

About the Prototype Drawings

Each actual modeling project uses a prototype drawing. The prototype drawings are created in separate projects. (They're also available on this book's companion diskette.)

If you use the prototype drawings from the diskette, take the time to look through the projects, 2A and 7D, that create those prototypes, so you'll understand what's in the drawings. Solid modeling requires quite a bit more setup than 2D drawing in terms of Paper Space viewports (see "Model Space Versus Paper Space" in Chapter 3, "General 3D Commands: UCSs, Space & Viewing") and layers (particularly the freeze/thaw status of the various layers in each viewport). So it would be to your advantage to know how these things are set up in the prototype drawings you'll be using. Even if you have the prototype drawings on the disk, you may still find it helpful to create each prototype step by step.

Project 2A: SMA.DWG, A-Size Prototype Drawing

This project sets up the A-size prototype drawing called SMA, as shown on page16, that you will use in Project 2B and other projects.

1. Start AutoCAD and create a drawing called SMA that does not use any other prototype drawing. (SMA stands for Solid Model, A-size sheet.)

In Release 11, start AutoCAD using your usual procedure, then at the Main Menu enter 1 then enter SMA=

In Release 12, pick "New" from the FILE pull-down menu (or enter NEW at the Command prompt). Then in the dialogue box enter SMA= as the new drawing name.

(The equal sign guarantees that this drawing is not dependent on any other prototype drawing.)

You must enter Paper Space and set up Paper Space limits. Remember that Model Space and Paper Space each have their own set of limits.

2. Set TILEMODE to 0. This automatically places you in Paper Space.

>   Command: `TILEMODE [Enter]`
> New value for TILEMODE<1>: `0 [Enter]`
> Entering Paper Space. Use MVIEW to
>   insert Model Space viewports.
>   Regenerating drawing.

3. Set the corners of the limits to 0,0 and 10,7.5. Then ZOOM ALL. Leave the grid off so it doesn't conflict with the grid inside the viewports.

>   Command: `LIMITS [Enter]`
>   ON/OFF/Lower left
>   corner<0.0000,0.0000>: `[Enter]`
> Upper right corner<12.0000,9.0000>: `10,7.5 [Enter]`
>
>   Command: `ZOOM [Enter]`
> All/Center/Dynamic/Extents/Left/
> Prev/Vmax/Window/Scale (X/XP): `A [Enter]`

General Layers & Viewport-Specific Layers

In solid modeling, you work with two types of layers: *General Layers* and *Viewport-specific Layers*. General layers are the layers on which the solid model itself is created and the layers that are for items in Paper Space.

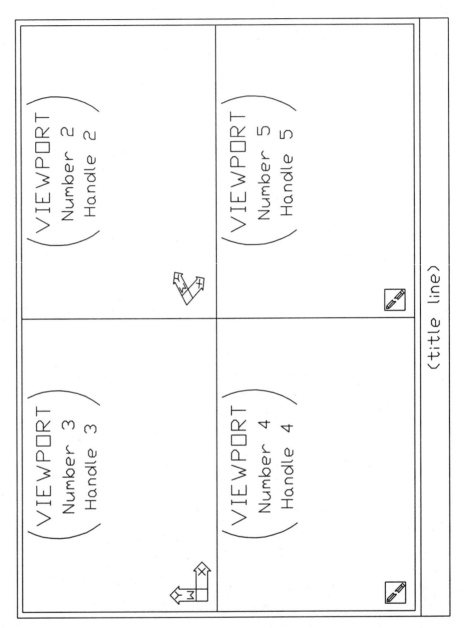

Figure 2-1: A-size prototype drawing.

Viewport-specific layers are frozen in all viewports except one so that the 2D views and the dimensions that are unique to a given view show up only in that viewport.

General Layers

Let's create the general layers first:

LAYER	COLOR	LINETYPE
0 (existing)	7 White	Continuous
SM	4 Cyan	Continuous
BORDER	6 Magenta	Continuous
VPBORDER	5 Blue	Continuous

4. Create three new layers: SM for solid model, BORDER for border and title line, and VPBORDER for viewport borders. Assign cyan (4) to layer SM; magenta (6) to layer BORDER; blue (5) to layer VPBORDER. Check to make sure these three layers are present and have the correct colors. Then make VPBORDER the current layer.

Use the pull-down menu of SETTINGS/Layer Control to obtain a dialogue box or use the following command.

```
                  Command: LAYER [Enter]
?/Make/Set/New/ON/OFF/Color/
          Ltype/Freeze/Thaw: N [Enter]
          New layer name(s): SM,BORDER,VPBORDER [Enter]
  ?/Make/Set/New/ON/OFF/Color
          /Ltype/Freeze/Thaw: C [Enter]
                       Color: 4 [Enter]
  Layer names for color 4 (Cyan)<>: SM [Enter]
?/Make/Set/New/ON/OFF/Color/
          Ltype/Freeze/Thaw: C [Enter]
                       Color: 6 [Enter]
Layer names for color 6 (Magenta)<>: BORDER [Enter]
?/Make/Set/New/ON/OFF/Color/
          Ltype/Freeze/Thaw: C [Enter]
                       Color: 5 [Enter]
```

Layer names for color 5 (Blue)<>: `VPBORDER [Enter]`
?/Make/Set/New/ON/OFF/Color/
Ltype/Freeze/Thaw: `?[Enter] [Enter]`
(Check the new layers)
?/Make/Set/New/ON/OFF/Color/
Ltype/Freeze/Thaw: `S [Enter]`
New current layer<>: `VPBORDER [Enter][Enter]`

Next, let's turn Handles on and create four Paper Space viewports. You create these viewports before creating any other entities so that their handles, which are hex numbers, will be as low as possible. This will be an advantage later when you have to name layers according to the viewport handles. Use the exact coordinates in the following instructions.

5. Turn Handles on and make four viewports.

Command: `HANDLES [Enter]`
Handles are disabled.
ON/DESTROY: `ON [Enter]`

Command: `MVIEW [Enter]`
ON/OFF/Hideplot/Fit/2/3/4/
Restore/<First Point>: `4 [Enter]`
Fit/<First Point>: `.1,.6 [Enter]`
Second Point: `9.9,7.4 [Enter]`

6. List the four viewports to check their handles.

(Write the number of your handles in the box below. Later, when you create more layers, you'll need to know these handles.)

Command: `LIST`
Select Objects: `Pick upper right viewport`
`[Enter]`

(Check the handle number and
write in the box below.)
(Handle in the Prototype drawing is 2.)

UPPER RIGHT 11

Upper Left Handle = /2	Upper Right Handle = 11
Lower Left Handle = /3	Lower Right Handle = /4

Command: `LIST`
Select Objects: `Pick upper left viewport`
`[Enter]`

(Check the handle number and
write in the box above.)
(Handle in the Prototype drawing is 3.)

Command: `LIST`
Select Objects: `Pick lower left viewport`
`[Enter]`

(Check the handle number and
write in the box above.)
(Handle in the Prototype drawing is 4.)

Command: `LIST`
Select Objects: `Pick lower right viewport`
`[Enter]`

(Check the handle number and
write in the box above.)
(Handle in the Prototype drawing is 5.)

Next, draw the border and title line.

7. Make BORDER the current layer.

Flip screen with function key F1.

Command: `LAYER [Enter]`
?/Make/Set/New/ON/OFF/Color/
Ltype/Freeze/Thaw: `S [Enter]`
New current layer<>: `BORDER [Enter][Enter]`

8. Draw the border and the space for the title line.

> Command: LINE [Enter]
> From point: 0,0 [Enter]
> To point: 10,0 [Enter]
> To point: 10,7.5 [Enter]
> To point: 0,7.5 [Enter]
> To point: C [Enter]

> Command: LINE [Enter]
> From point: 0,.5 [Enter]
> To point: 10,.5 [Enter]
> To point: [Enter]

You need to set up the view in each viewport for a typical three-view drawing (top, front and right) with an added non-orthographic view in the upper right corner. Each viewport must be assigned an appropriate viewpoint, and an appropriate UCS for dimensioning.

9. Go into Model Space and make sure you are in the World Coordinate System (WCS).

> Command: MSPACE [Enter]

> Command: UCS [Enter]
> Orig/Zaxis/3pnt/Enty/View /X/Y/Z/
> Prev/Restor/Save/Del/?<World>: [Enter]

Grid = 1 Snap = .25 PLAN VIEW	Grid = 1 Snap = .25 Vpoint = 4,-3,5 3D VIEW
Grid = 1 Snap = .25 Vpoint = 0,-1,0 FRONT VIEW	Grid = 1 Snap = .25 Vpoint = 1,0,0 RIGHT VIEW

10. Make the upper right viewport current. Set GRID at 1. Set SNAP at .25.
Create a right-front-top oblique view.

Pick upper right viewport.

Command: GRID [Enter]
Grid spacing(X) or ON/OFF/Snap/
Aspect <0.0000>: 1 [Enter]

Command: SNAP [Enter]
Snap spacing ON/OFF/Aspect/
Rotate/Style<1.0000>: .25 [Enter]

Command: VPOINT [Enter]
Rotate/Viewpoint<0.000,0.000,1.000>: 4,-3,5 [Enter]

11. Make the upper left viewport current. Set GRID at 1. Set SNAP at .25.
Make sure you have a top (plan) view.

Pick upper left viewport.

Command: GRID [Enter]
Grid spacing(X) or ON/OFF/Snap/
Aspect<0.0000>: 1 [Enter]

Command: SNAP [Enter]
Snap spacing ON/OFF/Aspect/
Rotate/Style<1.0000>: .25 [Enter]

Command: PLAN [Enter]
<Current UCS>/UCS/World: [Enter]

12. Make the lower left viewport current. Set GRID at 1. Set SNAP at .25.
Create a front view.

Pick lower left viewport.

Command: GRID [Enter]
Grid spacing(X) or ON/OFF/Snap/
Aspect<0.0000>: 1 [Enter]

Command: SNAP [Enter]
Snap spacing ON/OFF/Aspect/
Rotate/Style<1.0000>: .25 [Enter]

Command: VPOINT [Enter]
Rotate/<Viewpoint>
<0.000,0.000,1.000>: 0,-1,0 [Enter]

13. Make the lower right viewport current. Set GRID at 1. Set SNAP at .25. Create a right view.

Pick lower right viewport.

Command: GRID [Enter]
Grid spacing(X) or ON/OFF/Snap/
Aspect<0.0000>: 1 [Enter]

Command: SNAP [Enter]
Snap spacing ON/OFF ? Snap/
Aspect/Rotate/Style<1.0000>: .25 [Enter]

Command: VPOINT [Enter]
Rotate/<Viewpoint>
<0.000,0.000,1.000>: 1,0,0 [Enter]

14. Create and save a Front and Right UCS, then return to the WCS.

Command: UCS [Enter]
Orig/Zaxis/3pnt/Enty/View/X/Y/
Z/Prev/Restor/Save/Del/?<World>: X [Enter]
Rotation angle about X axis <0.0>: 90 [Enter]

Command: UCS [Enter]
Orig/Zaxis/3pnt/Enty/View/X/Y/
Z/Prev/Restor/Save/Del/?<World>: S [Enter]
?/Desired UCS name: FRONT [Enter]

Command: UCS [Enter]
Orig/Zaxis/3pnt/Enty/View/X/Y/
Z/Prev/Restor/Save/Del/?<World>: Y [Enter]
Rotation angle about Y axis <0.0>: 90 [Enter]

Command: UCS [Enter]
Orig/Zaxis/3pnt/Enty/View/X/Y/
Z/Prev/Restor/Save/Del/?<World>: S [Enter]
?/Desired UCS name: RIGHT [Enter]

Command: `UCS [Enter]`
Orig/Zaxis/3pnt/Enty/View/X/Y/
Z/Prev/Restor/Save/Del/?<World>: `[Enter]`

Viewport-Specific Layers

Now you'll create your viewport-specific layers. But before doing so, you need to consider the reason for viewport-specific layers and the difference between viewport numbers and viewport handles.

In order to extract 2D views (profiles) of your solid, you should have several profile layers set up in your prototype drawing. For example, to extract a 2D view in the viewport with handle 2, you should have layers PV-2 for visible lines and PH-2 for hidden lines. In the layer name, the P is for profile, the V or H is for visible or hidden, and the number is the viewport handle.

In order to dimension in this same viewport, you should have layer DIM2. Having designated layers for each viewport lets you turn them off in the other viewports. Having layers named according to viewport handles allows you to set up a suitable color and linetype for extracting each 2D view with the PROFILE command.

In Paper Space, viewports have both numbers and handles. Viewport numbers are decimal numbers assigned successively (starting with number 2) as viewports are created. Therefore, viewport numbers will usually be small. For example, if you have six viewports in Paper Space, they'll probably be numbered 2 through 7. You can display a viewport's number with the VPLAYER command by using the ? option. These numbers may be reassigned in subsequent editing sessions if one of the viewports has been erased.

Viewport handles, however, are hex numbers assigned to the viewports as entities. If a new viewport is created very early in a drawing, it will have a small hex number. But if a new viewport is created after a lot of other modeling or drawing has been done, the handle number will be fairly large. Unlike viewport numbers, a viewport's handle will not change across editing sessions. You can display a viewport's handle, assuming you're in Paper Space, with the LIST command.

Right now, each viewport's handle is probably the same as its number. If you created the viewports as instructed above, their numbers and handles should be as illustrated.

Upper Left Number: 3 Handle: 3	Upper Right Number: 2 Handle: 2
Lower Left Number: 4 Handle: 4	Lower Right Number: 5 Handle: 5

Because viewport handles never change, and because the SOLPROF command uses layers based on viewport handles rather than viewport numbers, you'll create viewport-specific layers with names that correspond to the viewports' handles.

15. Use VPLAYER to create the layers that will be used for extracting 2D views, including both visible (solid) and hidden (dashed) lines, and layers for dimensioning. For now, use the Newfrz (New-freeze) option to create them frozen; they will be thawed in the appropriate viewports later.

NOTE: During the SOLPROF command, AutoCAD looks for certain layer names based on the handle of the current viewport. Use the exact layer names shown in the following, unless the actual handles listed in step 6 are different than 2, 3, 4 and 5.

List of viewport layers you should create:

LAYER	COLOR	LINETYPE
PV-2	2 Yellow	Continuous
PH-2	1 Red	Hidden
PV-3	2 Yellow	Continuous
PH-3	1 Red	Hidden
PV-4	2 Yellow	Continuous
PH-4	1 Red	Hidden
PV-5	2 Yellow	Continuous
PH-5	1 Red	Hidden
DIM2	6 Magenta	Continuous
DIM3	6 Magenta	Continous
DIM4	6 Magenta	Continuous
DIM5	6 Magenta	Continous

Command: VPLAYER [Enter]

?/Freeze/Thaw/Reset/Newfrz/

Vpvisdflt: N [Enter]

New Viewport frozen layer name(s): PV-2,PH-2,PV-3,PH-3,
PV-4,PH-4,PV-5,PH-5
[Enter]

?/Freeze/Thaw/Reset/Newfrz/

Vpvisdflt: N [Enter]

New Viewport frozen layer name(s): DIM2,DIM3,DIM4,DIM5
[Enter]

?/Freeze/Thaw/Reset/Newfrz/

Vpvisdflt: [Enter]

16. Assign yellow (2) to the visible layers, red (1) to the hidden layers and magenta (6) to the dimension layers. Then assign Hidden linetype to the hidden layers. Check your layers. Besides the layers you created earlier, you should have eight profile layers (four visible, four hidden) and four dimensioning layers.

```
                        Command: LAYER [Enter]
?/Make/Set/New/ON/OFF/Color/
            Ltype/Freeze/Thaw: C [Enter]
                        Color: 2 [Enter]
   Layer names for color 2(Yellow)<>: PV* [Enter]
?/Make/Set/New/ON/OFF/Color/
            Ltype/Freeze/Thaw: C [Enter]
                        Color: 1 [Enter]
    Layer names for color 1(Red)<>: PH* [Enter]
?/Make/Set/New/ON/OFF/Color/
            Ltype/Freeze/Thaw: C [Enter]
                        Color: 6 [Enter]
 Layer names for color 6(Magenta)<>: DIM* [Enter]
?/Make/Set/New/ON/OFF/Color/
            Ltype/Freeze/Thaw: L [Enter]
        Linetype(or?)<CONTINUOUS>: HIDDEN [Enter]
        Layer names(s) for linetype
                    HIDDEN <>: PH* [Enter]
?/Make/Set/New/ON/OFF/Color/
            Ltype/Freeze/Thaw: ? [Enter][Enter]
(Check the layers. An extra Enter may
      be needed to see them all.) [Enter]
```

17. Switch to Paper Space.

```
                        Command: PSPACE [Enter]
```

18. In each viewport, thaw the layers that apply to that viewport. If needed, substitute the correct handles for the ones given below.

```
                        Command: VPLAYER [Enter]
      ?/Freeze/Thaw/Reset/Newfrz/
                        Vpvisdflt: T [Enter]
          Layer name(s) to thaw: *2 [Enter]
             All/Select/<current>: S [Enter]
       Pick upper right viewport. Pick [Enter]
      ?/Freeze/Thaw/Reset/Newfrz/
                        Vpvisdflt: T [Enter]
          Layer name(s) to thaw: *3 [Enter]
             All/Select/<current>: S [Enter]
        Pick upper left viewport. Pick [Enter]
      ?/Freeze/Thaw/Reset/Newfrz/
                        Vpvisdflt: T [Enter]
          Layer name(s) to thaw: *4 [Enter]
             All/Select/<current>: S [Enter]
         Pick lower left viewport. Pick [Enter]
      ?/Freeze/Thaw/Reset/Newfrz/
                        Vpvisdflt: T [Enter]
          Layer name(s) to thaw: *5 [Enter]
             All/Select/<current>: S [Enter]
       Pick lower right viewport. Pick [Enter][Enter]
```

You can check which layers are thawed or frozen in any viewport with the VPLAYER command. To illustrate, let's check in just one viewport.

19. Use VPLAYER to make sure that layers DIM2, PV-2 and PH-2 are thawed in viewport 2. You can tell that they're thawed if they're *not* listed. All other viewport-specific layers (profile and dimension layers) should be listed as frozen in this viewport.

```
                        Command: VPLAYER [Enter]
      ?/Freeze/Thaw/Reset/Newfrz/
                        Vpvisdflt: ? [Enter]
   Select a viewport: Pick upper right
                        viewport. Pick
   (Check and make sure that no layers
          ending with 2 are listed.) [Enter]
```

20. Turn off associative dimensioning and set other dimensioning variables suitable for an A-size drawing.

> Command: `DIMASO [Enter]`
> New value for DIMASO <1>: `0 [Enter]`

> Command: `DIMSCALE [Enter]`
> New value for DIMSCALE <1.0000>: `0 [Enter]`
> Command: `DIMZIN [Enter]`
> New value for DIMZIN <0>: `4 [Enter]`

> Command: `DIMTXT [Enter]`
> New value for DIMTXT <0.1800>: `.12 [Enter]`

> Command: `DIMASZ [Enter]`
> New value for DIMASZ <0.1800>: `.12 [Enter]`

> Command: `DIMEXO [Enter]`
> New value for DIMEXO <0.0625>: `.15 [Enter]`

All that remains is to make sure that Model Space and layer SM are current when this prototype is used.

21. Change to Model Space, make SM the current layer and make the upper right viewport current.

> Command: `MSPACE [Enter]`

> Command: `LAYER [Enter]`
> ?/Make/Set/New/ON/OFF/Color/
> Ltype/Freeze/Thaw: `S [Enter]`
> New current layer <>: `SM [Enter][Enter]`
> Pick the upper right viewport
> (handle 2).

22. In Release 12 load AME and set SOLWDENS to 4.

> Command: `(xload "ame") [Enter]`

> Command: `SOLWDENS 4 [Enter]`

23. Save the drawing.

> In Release 11 ... Command: `END [Enter]`
> In Release 12 ... Command: `SAVE [Enter]`
> `SMA [Enter][Enter]`

This completes the SMA prototype drawing. It has been set up with Project 2B in mind, but it can also be used as a basis for quickly creating other prototype drawings.

Project 2B: Hold-Down Clamp Model

In this project, we'll use the SMA prototype drawing created in Project 2A and model the Hold-Down Clamp shown on page 30. (The SMA prototype drawing is also available on the *Solid Modeling With AutoCAD* companion diskette.) See color illustrations C-1 and C-2 on page 167.

1. Start a new drawing called CLAMP, using the SMA prototype drawing.

At the Main Menu in Release 11 enter `1` then enter `CLAMP=SMA`

In Release 12, pick "New" from the FILE pull-down menu. Use SMA as a prototype drawing, and CLAMP as the new drawing name.

After you enter the drawing editor, you should be in Model Space in the upper right viewport (the crosshairs should be active in the upper right viewport), and SM should be listed in the status line as the current layer.

2. Load the Advanced Modeling Extension (AME).

> Command: `(xload "ame") [Enter]`

Or, pick "AME" then "Load AME" from either the pull-down menu or the sidebar menu.

AME is loaded automatically in Release 12 when you first enter an AME command either at the Command prompt or from the "Model" pull-down menu.

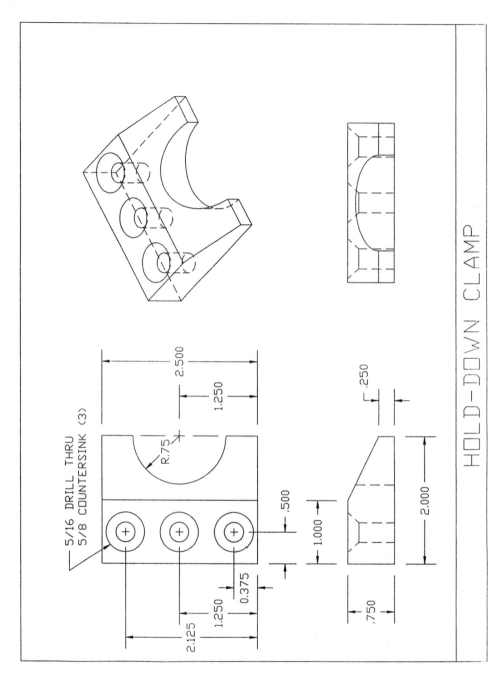

Figure 2-2: Hold-Down Clamp, dimensioned.

We will begin by creating the basic shape of the clamp from three primitives (a box, a wedge and a cylinder).

3. Create a box at 0,0,0 that is 2 x 2.5 x .75

> Command: `SOLBOX [Enter]`
> Baseplane/Center/
> <Corner of box><0,0,0>: `0,0 [Enter]`
> Cube/Length/<other corner>: `L [Enter]`
> Length: `2 [Enter]`
> Width: `2.5 [Enter]`
> Height: `.75 [Enter]`

4. Line up the view in each viewport by placing a known point in Model
Space at the center of the viewport and scaling the view full scale (the
same as Paper Space).

Pick the upper right viewport (handle 2).

> Command: `ZOOM [Enter]`
> All/Center/Dynamic/Extent/Left/
> Prev/Vmax/Window/<Scale(X/XP)>: `C`
> Center point: `1,1.25,.3 [Enter]`
> Magnification or height <>: `1XP [Enter]`

Do the same in each of the other viewports.

5. Change the box color to green.

> Command: `CHPROP [Enter]`
> Select objects: `L [Enter][Enter]`
> Change what property (Color/Layer/
> LType/Thickness)?: `C [Enter]`
> New color <BYLAYER>: `3 [Enter][Enter]`

6. List the box.

> Command: `SOLLIST [Enter]`
> Edge/Face/Tree/<Object>: `[Enter]`
> Select objects: `L [Enter][Enter]`

Notice that it is listed as a BOX, its dimensions and handle are given and it is using wireframe representation. Press F1 to return to drawing.

7. Make sure the upper right viewport is current, then create a wedge with its starting corner at 2,0,.75. The wedge should extend -1,2.5,-.5 in the X,Y,Z directions, respectively.

Pick the upper right viewport (handle 2).

<pre>
               Command: SOLWEDGE [Enter]
Baseplane/<Corner of wedge><0,0,0>: 2,0,.75 [Enter]
       Length/<other corner>: L [Enter]
                       Length: -1 [Enter]
                        Width: 2.5 [Enter]
                       Height: -.5 [Enter]
</pre>

8. Subtract the wedge from the box.

<pre>
                  Command: SOLSUB
  Source objects: Pick the box. Pick [Enter]
  Objects to subtract from them:
          Pick the wedge. Pick [Enter]
</pre>

9. List the composite.

<pre>
           Command: SOLLIST [Enter]
Edge/Face/Tree/<Object>: [Enter]
          Select objects: L [Enter][Enter]
</pre>

Notice that it is listed as a SUBTRACTION with the handles of its components also listed. Press F1 to return to drawing.

10. Create the cylinder for the clearance opening. Locate it at 2,1.25,0 with .75 radius, .75 high.

<pre>
            Command: SOLCYL [Enter]
Baseplane/Elliptical/<Center point>
                <0,0,0>: 2,1.25,0 [Enter]
          Diameter/<Radius>: .75 [Enter]
                   Height: .75 [Enter]
</pre>

11. Change the cylinder's color to red.

> Command: CHPROP [Enter]
> Select objects: L [Enter][Enter]
> Change what property (Color/Layer/
> LType/Thickness)?: C [Enter]
> New color <BYLAYER>: 1 [Enter][Enter]

Figure 2-3: Hold-Down Clamp, basic shape.

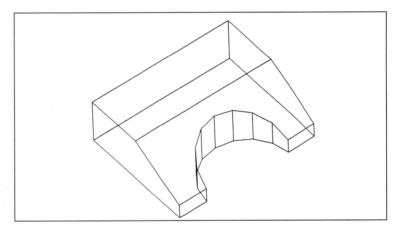

12. Subtract the cylinder from the composite.

> Command: SOLSUB
> Source objects: Pick the composite. Pick [Enter]
> Objects to subtract from them:
> Pick the cylinder. Pick [Enter]

13. Check the appearance by meshing, hiding and shading the composite.

> Command: SOLMESH [Enter]
> Select objects: Pick the composite. Pick [Enter]
>
> Command: HIDE [Enter]
>
> Command: SHADE [Enter]

If the shaded rendering does not appear satisfactory on your monitor, you may want to experiment with other settings for system variable SHADEDGE. Possible settings are 0, 1, 2 and 3.

14. Return the composite to wireframe representation.

> Command: REGEN [Enter]
>
> Command: SOLWIRE [Enter]
>
> Select objects:Pick the solid. Pick [Enter]

15. Save your drawing.

Next we'll create one countersunk hole in the middle position. It will be created from a cylinder and a cone. Then we'll copy that countersunk hole to its two other locations and subtract them from the basic shape created in the earlier composite.

16. Create a cylinder for a 5/16 drilled hole at .5,1.25,0.

> Command: SOLCYL [Enter]
>
> Baseplane/Elliptical/<Center point>
>
> <0,0,0>: .5,1.25,0 [Enter]
>
> Diameter/<Radius>: D [Enter]
>
> Diameter: .3125 [Enter]
>
> Height of cylinder: .75 [Enter]

Figure 2-4: Hold-Down Clamp, finished model with hidden edges removed.

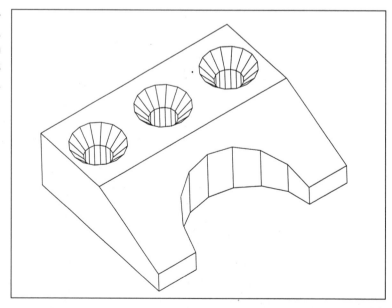

17. Create a cone for the countersink with 5/8 diameter and 82 degree included angle (the depth of the cone will be .36 in the negative Z direction).

> Command: `SOLCONE [Enter]`
> Baseplane/Elliptical/<Center point>
> <0,0,0>: `.5,1.25,.75 [Enter]`
> Diameter/<Radius>: `D [Enter]`
> Diameter: `.625 [Enter]`
> Height of cone: `-.36 [Enter]`

18. Join the cylinder and the cone.

> Command: `SOLUNION [Enter]`
> Select objects: Pick the cylinder and cone. `Pick both [Enter]`

19. Copy the countersunk hole to its other two locations, .875 apart.

> Command: `COPY [Enter]`
> Select objects: Pick the countersunk hole. `Pick [Enter]`
> <Base point or displacement>/Multiple: `M [Enter]`
> Base point: `0,0 [Enter]`
> Second point of displacement: `0,.875 [Enter]`
> Second point of displacement: `0,-.875 [Enter][Enter]`

20. Subtract the three countersunk holes from the composite.

> Command: `SOLSUB [Enter]`
> Source objects: Pick the clamp. `Pick [Enter]`
> Objects to subtract: Pick all 3
> countersunk holes. `Pick three [Enter]`

21. Check the appearance by meshing, hiding and shading the composite.

> Command: `SOLMESH [Enter]`
> Select objects: Pick the solid. `Pick [Enter]`
> Command: `HIDE [Enter]`
> Command: `SHADE [Enter]`

22. Return the composite to wireframe representation.

> Command: `REGEN [Enter]`
>
> Command: `SOLWIRE [Enter]`
>
> Select objects: Pick the composite. `Pick [Enter]`

23. Save your drawing.

Once the solid is finished, its mass properties can be analyzed. This is an easy step, accomplished with just one command.

24. Find the weight (mass) of the clamp.

> Command: `SOLMASSP [Enter]`
>
> Select objects: Pick the solid. `Pick [Enter]`

Examine the readout. The mass depends on the material assigned to the solid and the units are determined by a variable, as explained later.

> Write to a file?<N>?: `[Enter]`

Next, we will extract views from the model suitable for dimensioning. Instead of taking the time needed to dimension the clamp completely, we'll illustrate the process of setting up for dimensioning and let you place the dimensions you choose.

25. In each viewport, use the SOLPROF command to create a profile. Place hidden lines on a separate layer. (The visible and hidden lines of the profile will automatically be placed on layers PV-2 and PH-2 in the viewport having handle 2; on PV-3 and PH-3 in the viewport having handle 3, etc. These layers are already in the prototype drawing.)

> Command: `SOLPROF [Enter]`
>
> Select objects: Pick the model. `Pick [Enter]`
>
> Display hidden profile lines on
>
> separate layer<Y> ?: `Y [Enter]`
>
> Project profile lines onto a plane?<Y>: `Y [Enter]`
>
> Delete tangential edges?<Y>: `Y [Enter]`

Do the same in each viewport.

If any profile shows up in more than one viewport, check the freeze/thaw status of your layers with the VPLAYER command.

26. Select the lower right viewport, make DIM5 the current layer, then freeze layer SM.

Pick the lower right viewport (handle 5).

```
                    Command: LAYER [Enter]
?/Make/Set/New/ON/OFF/Color/
        Ltype/Freeze/Thaw: S [Enter]
      New current layer <>: DIM5 [Enter]
?/Make/Set/New/ON/OFF/Color/
        Ltype/Freeze/Thaw: F [Enter]
    Layer name(s) to freeze: SM [Enter][Enter]
```

As you can see, some of the hidden profile lines coincide with visible lines and will need to be removed.

27. Freeze all layers that contain visible profile lines.

```
                    Command: LAYER [Enter]
?/Make/Set/New/ON/OFF/Color/
        Ltype/Freeze/Thaw: F [Enter]
    Layer name(s) to freeze: PV* [Enter][Enter]
```

28. Set LTSCALE to .6.

```
                    Command: LTSCALE [Enter]
    New scale factor <1.0000>: .6 [Enter]
```

29. In each viewport, explode the profile block and erase all unnecessary hidden lines.

Pick the lower right viewport (handle 5).

> Command: EXPLODE [Enter]
>
> Pick the block. (Lines will change color.)
>
> Command: ERASE [Enter]
>
> Select objects: Pick 4 lines forming outline of part. Pick [Enter]
>
> Command: REDRAW [Enter]
>
> Command: ERASE [Enter]
>
> Select objects: Pick all other lines that will coincide with the solid lines. Pick [Enter]

Do the same in the lower left and upper left viewports, erasing hidden lines that will coincide with solid lines. (In the upper left viewport, all hidden lines are redundant, so the entire hidden line block can be erased.)

NOTE: An AutoLISP program, PROCLEAN, on the companion diskette makes this job easy. But, for now, do this operation manually.

30. Thaw the visible profile layers and explode the blocks containing the visible (solid) lines.

> Command: LAYER [Enter]
>
> ?/Make/Set/New/ON/OFF/Color/ Ltype/Freeze/Thaw: T [Enter]
>
> Layer name(s) to thaw: PV* [Enter][Enter]
>
> Pick the upper left viewport (handle 3).
>
> Command: EXPLODE [Enter]
>
> Pick block with solid lines. (Lines will change color.)

Repeat this procedure in the lower left and lower right viewports.

31. In order to create more room for dimensioning the top view, switch to Paper Space and, with ortho on, STRETCH the viewports as needed. Then return to Model Space and pan the views within the viewports as needed.

Command: PSPACE [Enter]

Turn ortho on with function key F8: [F8]

Command: STRETCH [Enter]
Select objects: C [Enter]

Window the horizontal line separating the top two viewports from the bottom two and stretch down about 1 inch.

Command: MSPACE [Enter]
Pick the upper left viewport (handle 3).

Command: PAN [Enter]
Pick two points to pan the view down to the center of the viewport.

As needed, restore the FRONT UCS and pan the view down in the lower left viewport. Do the same on the lower right viewport. (Turn SNAP on to maintain alignment of these two views.)

32. Dimension your 2D views. Before you place any dimension in a particular viewport,

(1) Switch to the appropriate UCS by restoring either the WCS or the Front or Right UCS (both of these UCSs are already in the prototype drawing).

(2) Switch to the appropriate dimension layer—DIM2, DIM3, DIM4 or DIM5.

If any of your dimensions show up in more than one viewport, check the freeze/thaw status of your layers with the VPLAYER command.

Pick the lower left viewport (handle 4).

> Command: LAYER [Enter]
>
> ?/Make/Set/New/ON/OFF/Color/
>
> Ltype/Freeze/Thaw: S [Enter]
>
> New layer name(s): DIM4 [Enter][Enter]
>
> Command: UCS [Enter]
>
> Orig/Zaxis/3pnt/Enty/View/X/Y/Z/
>
> Prev/Restor/Save/Del/?<World>: R [Enter]
>
> ?/Name of UCS to restore: FRONT [Enter]

Dimension in this viewport then repeat the above procedure in any other viewports you want to dimension.

33. Return to Paper Space, make BORDER the current layer and place the text "HOLD-DOWN CLAMP" in the box for the title line.

> Command: PSPACE [Enter]
>
> Command: LAYER [Enter]
>
> ?/Make/Set/New/ON/OFF/Color/
>
> Ltype/Freeze/Thaw: S [Enter]
>
> New current layer: BORDER [Enter][Enter]
>
> Command: TEXT [Enter]
>
> Justify/Style <Start point>: M [Enter]
>
> Middle point: 5.25,.25 [Enter]
>
> Height: .25 [Enter]
>
> Rotation angle<0>: 0 [Enter]
>
> Text: HOLD-DOWN CLAMP [Enter]

34. Save your drawing.

You can easily plot your four views of the clamp if you want to.

35. Freeze layer VPBORDER and plot your drawing.

Command: LAYER [Enter]
?/Make/Set/New/ON/OFF/Color/
Ltype/Freeze/Thaw: F [Enter]
Layer name(s) to Freeze: VPBORDER [Enter][Enter]

Use your usual plotting procedure.

Moving On

You have now set up a good prototype drawing you can use in other solid modeling projects. And you've created a relatively simple solid model and extracted the views needed for a standard detail drawing. As you worked through this last project, you were exposed to many of the commands and procedures used constantly in solid modeling.

At this point it's tempting to plunge into the details of the various solid modeling commands. But before we do that, we need to step back and make sure we know our way around in 3D. There are many general 3D skills and commands you need to understand in order to work with any type of 3D modeling. The next chapter covers three key areas: User Coordinate Systems, Paper Space and 3D viewing. If you have limited experience working in 3D, you need to learn these general 3D commands before moving on to commands unique to solid modeling.

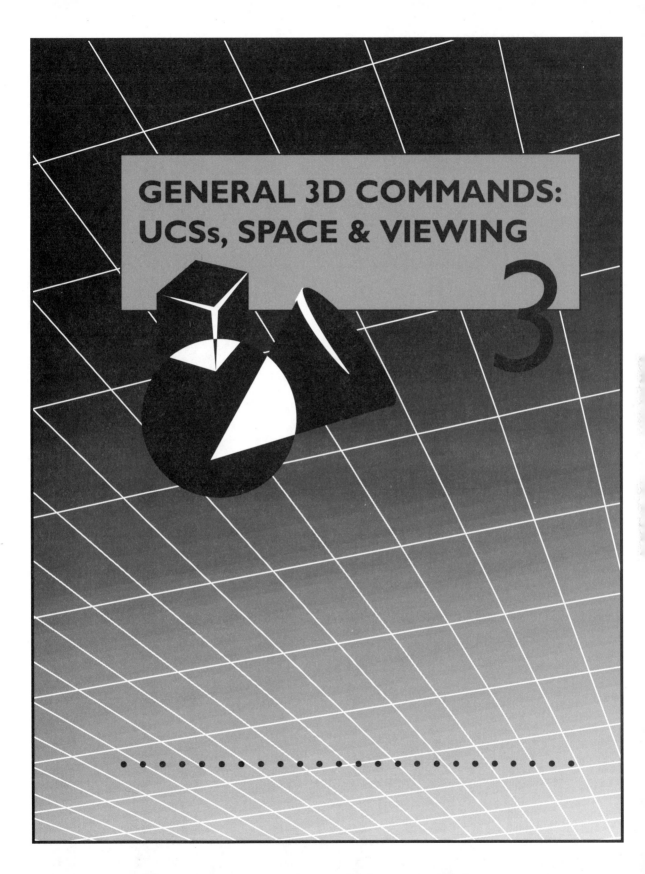

GENERAL 3D COMMANDS:
UCSs, SPACE & VIEWING

3

General 3D Commands: UCSs, Space & Viewing

Many of the commands covered in this chapter are "general," in the sense that they apply to all three types of 3D modeling—wireframe, surface and solid. Many of these commands were included in earlier releases of AutoCAD. If you've been working with wireframe or surface models, you may want to skip the sections in this chapter that cover familiar material.

If you've used AutoCAD only for 2D drawing up to this point, you need to learn, all at once, about User Coordinate Systems, 3D viewing, viewports, Paper Space and viewport-specific layer control. It is difficult to learn any of these subjects in isolation from the others, so there's no logical sequence for presenting them.

Because the overview project in the previous chapter gave you some exposure to these 3D subjects, our discussion of them here will be more meaningful. As you read about these 3D subjects, you may want to experiment with them in an actual drawing such as the Hold-Down Clamp you completed in the previous chapter.

User Coordinate Systems

A User Coordinate System (UCS) is, as you might suspect, a coordinate system (X-Y construction plane) defined by the user. Defining a UCS is simply a process of placing the X-Y construction plane at a particular location and angular orientation.

UCSs involve two commands, UCS and UCSICON, and several system variables, including UCSICON and UCSFOLLOW, which are described in separate sections that follow.

The World Coordinate System & User Coordinate Systems

The standard (default) coordinate system is called the World Coordinate System (WCS), to distinguish it from coordinate systems established by the user. The WCS is the current system when you begin a new drawing (assuming it has not been replaced by a UCS in your prototype drawing).

For most 3D drawings, you'll need to establish several UCSs with the 0,0,0 (X,Y,Z) origin located in different places and/or the axes pointing in different directions. You can set up as many UCSs as you need. There is no limit.

Complex 3D geometry would be difficult to construct if all entities had to be located from the basic X-Y construction plane in the WCS. AutoCAD lets you place an X-Y construction plane anywhere in space and orient it at any angle. This lets you place various entities in a complex configuration using simple X-Y distances in the new X-Y plane. You can easily switch between UCSs at any time during the drawing process.

Once you have defined a new UCS, all coordinates you enter and all coordinates displayed are based on this new UCS. However, coordinates preceded by an asterisk, such as *2,4,6 or @*5<30, are interpreted as WCS coordinates.

The UCS is independent of the current viewpoint (although the viewpoint can be automatically tied to the current UCS with the UCSFOLLOW variable). Only one UCS will be active at any given time, even though you may have various viewports displayed, each with a different viewpoint.

Since the UCS and the viewpoint do not necessarily coincide, you should pay close attention to the UCS icon to help you see the current orientation of the UCS. (See "The UCSICON Command" later in this chapter.)

The grid always appears on the X-Y construction plane in the current UCS. If the elevation (Z height) is set at something other than 0 (zero) (with the ELEV command), then the grid and the construction plane will appear above or below the 0,0,0 origin of the UCS. However, it's recommended that you keep the elevation at 0 (zero) and move your UCS, rather than changing elevations during the course of drawing and editing.

Remember that whenever you place entities in your drawing with the pointer, all locations will be on the X-Y construction plane, even when your current viewpoint or your current UCS makes the crosshairs appear to be somewhere above the construction plane.

When you save a drawing, the current UCS is saved with it and will automatically become the initial UCS when you begin to edit that drawing the next time.

Right-Hand Rules

The X-Y-Z axes will always be oriented in relation to each other according to a right-hand rule. When your right hand is positioned as shown below, with the thumb representing the positive X axis and the first finger representing the positive Y axis, the positive Z axis will point in the direction of the second finger.

Also, rotation around any given axis will follow another right-hand rule: When the thumb of the right hand points along the positive direction of any given axis, as illustrated in Figure 3-2, then positive rotation around that axis follows the direction of the curled fingers.

Figure 3-1: Right-hand rule for determining axis orientation.

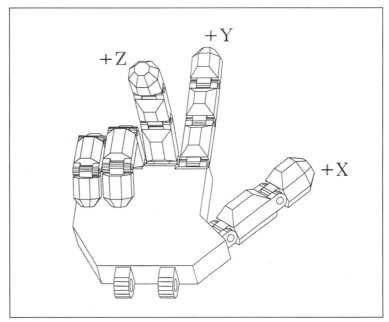

The UCS Command

The UCS command establishes, saves or recalls a User Coordinate System (UCS). All the UCS options described are also accessible in the UCS Control dialogue box, which can be brought up by entering DDUCS at the keyboard, or by selecting "Settings" then "UCS Control" from the pull-down menus.

Remember that when you're defining a new coordinate system, all input is interpreted according to the current UCS, except when preceded by an asterisk.

You will want to use immediate osnap modes to enter many of the points mentioned in the following pages.

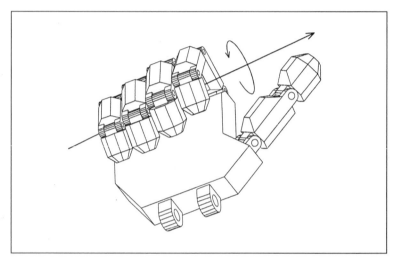

Figure 3-2: Right-hand rule for determining direction of rotation around an axis.

When prompted, enter the following:

W To switch to the World Coordinate System (WCS)—that is, to make the WCS the current coordinate system. W is always the default response in the UCS command prompt.

O Then enter the coordinates of the origin of the new UCS. This new UCS will have an origin shifted from the current coordinate system, but its X, Y and Z axes will point in the same direction as the current system.

Z A Then enter the coordinates of the origin of the new UCS (if different from the origin of the current system), then a point through which the positive Z axis will pass.

3 Then enter three points to define the new UCS: (1) the origin, (2) a point on the positive X axis and (3) a point on the positive Y half of the X-Y plane. (Once the X and Y axes are determined, the Z axis is determined by the right-hand rule.) This option, used with immediate osnap modes, is handy when you want to

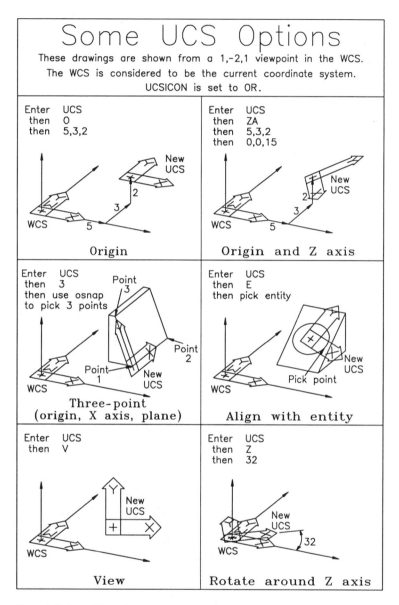

Figure 3-3: Some UCS options.

attach the new coordinate system to certain features of an object, especially if the new coordinate system will end up at an angle that is oblique to the major planes of the current UCS.

E To define the new UCS by using an entity already in the drawing. Whenever you use this option, the positive Z axis will be oriented in the same direction as when the entity was created. This forces the X-Y plane to be parallel to the X-Y plane that was current when the entity was created. However, the direction of the X and Y axes may differ.

V To adopt the current viewing direction as the direction of the negative Z axis (the origin remains unchanged).

X (or **Y** or **Z**) Then enter an angle to rotate the new coordinate system around the X (or Y or Z) axis. The origin will remain unchanged. The right-hand rule for rotation will determine the direction of the rotation.

P To return to the previous coordinate system. AutoCAD remembers the ten previous coordinate systems you have used (named or unnamed).

? To get a listing of the names and orientations of all the saved coordinate systems. The WCS is listed first. The current coordinate system is also listed and called *NO NAME* unless you have given it a name. Remember that each coordinate system is listed according to the current system.

S To save the current UCS, then enter its name (up to 31 characters). When you save a UCS, you don't save the current viewpoint.

R Then enter the name of the UCS you want to restore. The viewpoint will remain the same unless system variable UCSFOLLOW is set to 1.

D To delete the name of a saved coordinate system. You can list several names separated by commas, or use wildcards.

Whenever you create a new UCS, you can establish a plan view within that UCS by entering PLAN. Or, if you set system variable UCSFOLLOW to 1, AutoCAD will automatically establish the plan view each time you change to a new UCS.

The UCSICON Command

The UCSICON command controls the UCS icon display. The Model Space UCS icon is shown below. This icon provides information about the current coordinate system. The settings for the UCSICON command affect only the current viewport unless you use the A option explained below.

If the current coordinate system is the WCS, a W appears in the Y-arm of the icon. If the icon is positioned at the origin of the current UCS, the plus sign will be present in the icon. If the current viewpoint looks at the object from the underside (originates from a negative Z location), the box at the elbow of the icon will be missing.

Figure 3-4:
UCS icon for
Model Space.

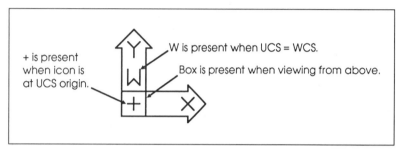

When prompted, enter the following:

A   To make all UCS icon settings that are changed during this use of the command apply to all viewports.

ON   To enable the UCS icon.

OFF   To disable the UCS icon.

OR   To place the icon at the origin of the current UCS. If this moves the icon outside the current viewport or too near the edge, the icon is displayed in the lower left corner of the viewport.

N   (for Not-at-origin) To place the icon at the lower left corner of the viewport.

The UCS icon also appears in two other forms in Model Space. When your viewing direction is parallel to the X-Y construction plane of the current UCS, the icon appears as a broken pencil in a box. When this occurs, you should change your viewing direction before trying to indicate any locations with the pointer. When you are viewing your object in perspective (see "The DVIEW Command" later in this chapter), the icon appears as a perspective cube.

Figure 3-5: Broken
pencil and Per-
spective icons.

The icon shown below indicates you're in Paper Space. The "+" and "W" and box operate the same as described above for the Model Space UCS icon.

The UCSICON system variable can be set at 0 to place the icon in the lower left corner of the viewport; at 1 to disable the icon; or at 2 to place the icon at the origin, if allowed by the current display. Each viewport, as well as Paper Space, can have its own unique setting for UCSICON. The default is 0.

The UCSFOLLOW system variable enables or disables automatic display of the plan view each time you change to a different UCS. When set to 1, AutoCAD will switch to a plan view automatically when you change UCSs. Thereafter, any viewpoint can be adopted as usual. When set to 0, the viewpoint will not change. The default is 0. This variable has no meaning in Paper Space.

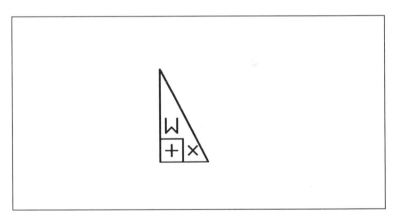

Figure 3-6: UCS
icon for Paper
Space.

Model Space Versus Paper Space

Model Space is the space in which you construct your 3D model (and is the default in the ACAD.DWG prototype drawing supplied with AutoCAD).

Paper Space is the space in which you organize different views of your 3D model and add your border, title block and certain annotations for plotting. Paper Space is primarily two-dimensional, and its limits should be set to the dimensions of the border on the sheet it will be plotted on. (See "About the Prototype Drawings" in Chapter 2, "Projects: Setup & Overview.")

Figure 3-7:
Model Space and
Paper Space.

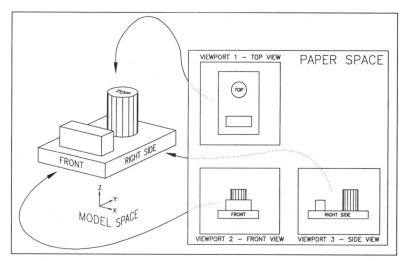

TILEMODE, MSPACE & PSPACE

Paper Space and Model Space are controlled by both the TILEMODE system variable and by the MSPACE and PSPACE commands. The relationship between the two TILEMODE settings and the two spaces can be somewhat confusing at first, but it will help if you keep in mind that there are only three possible situations:

1. TILEMODE=1 You are limited to Model Space.

2. TILEMODE=0 You establish Model Space with the MSPACE command.

3. TILEMODE=0 You establish Paper Space with the PSPACE command.

When TILEMODE is 0 and you are in Paper Space, the MSPACE command will switch to Model Space, then the PSPACE command will switch back to Paper Space.

When TILEMODE is set to 1 (On), you are in Model Space and cannot enter Paper Space. In fact, any Paper Space entities that might be in your drawing are not displayed. You can set up various viewports in Model Space with the VPORTS command. Each viewport setup (configuration) can be saved under a particular name; you can create as many configurations as you like, and switch back and forth between them at will. However, the viewports themselves behave like tiles, in that they must always be adjacent and they must never overlap or have any space between them. (Model Space was the only space available in versions of AutoCAD before Release 11.)

In contrast, when TILEMODE is 0, you can be in either Paper Space or Model Space. Switching TILEMODE to 0 places you in Paper Space, but you can switch back and forth between Paper Space and Model Space as needed with the PSPACE and MSPACE commands respectively.

You can create as many Paper Space viewports as you want with the MVIEW command; and, as in Model Space, each viewport can have a different viewpoint and magnification factor. However, Paper Space viewports are much more flexible than Model Space viewports. You can move Paper Space viewports around, scale them, stretch them, separate them, let them overlap, freeze certain layers in some viewports but not in others, etc. But you cannot save various viewport configurations, as you can when TILEMODE is 1. In other words, when TILEMODE is 0, your arrangement of viewports in Paper Space *is* your viewport configuration.

All your 3D modeling will be done in Model Space, always at full scale. Also, extraction of 2D views (section views, profile views, etc.) will be done in Model Space. You will even dimension these extracted 2D views in Model Space.

When you are "in" a viewport (that is, when you are in Model Space and your cursor is limited to a single viewport), you can switch to another viewport simply by moving the cursor arrow to that viewport and pressing the Pick button.

When you're in Paper Space, you cannot pick entities in Model Space, and vice versa. In addition, the VPORTS, DVIEW, VPOINT and PLAN commands are disabled.

AutoCAD lets you know you're in Paper Space in several ways. First, the Paper Space icon appears (if enabled). Second, the letter P appears in the status line. Third, your crosshairs run across the entire screen instead of appearing only within a single viewport.

In Model Space, you can plot from within the current viewport only. In Paper Space, you can plot the entire paper with all its viewports at once.

When you're in Model Space, drawing and editing commands affect all viewports, whereas display commands affect only the current viewport. Each individual viewport can have its own unique settings for commands such as GRID, SNAP, AXIS, VIEWRES, UCSICON, VPOINT, ZOOM, PAN and DVIEW. You can change from one viewport to another in the middle of a drawing or editing command, but not in the middle of a display command. You can build a selection set by selecting some entities in one viewport and others in a different viewport. Entities will be highlighted only in the viewport in which they're selected. While REDRAW and REGEN affect only the current viewport, REDRAWALL and REGENALL affect all viewports.

You will usually switch from one viewport to another by picking it with the pointer. However, in those cases where one viewport is entirely inside another, you may need to use Ctrl-V to switch to the desired viewport. Also, system variable CVPORT holds the number (as opposed to the handle) of the current viewport, so this provides another means of switching viewports.

Viewports in Solid Modeling

Both tiled and Paper Space viewports can be used for solid modeling. As you can see from the three possible situations listed earlier, you can work in Model Space with TILEMODE set to either 0 or 1. Even though a solid model will always be built in Model Space, should the model be built with tiled viewports (using TILEMODE=1) or Paper Space viewports (using TILEMODE=0)?

In some cases, TILEMODE=1 will be sufficient for solid modeling. There may be no need for Paper Space. Perhaps the sole purpose for creating the model is to perform mass properties analysis, or to extract information from the model for CAM or some other post-processing purpose. There may be no need to extract 2D views for dimensioning or to plot more than one view of the model. Such a solid model could easily be built in Model Space with TILEMODE=1. Several tiled viewports could be established to view the model during its construction.

However, often you may want to have several plotted views of the model or a complete dimensioned engineering drawing. In this case, it would be simpler to keep TILEMODE set at 0 throughout the entire process and switch back and forth between Model Space and Paper Space with the MSPACE and PSPACE commands. This approach is relatively simple because you're working only with the Paper Space viewport configuration.

This second approach is the one we've adopted in this book. As you recall from Projects 2A and 2B, we set up the prototype drawing so that TILEMODE is 0. When we created the Hold-Down Clamp, we never set TILEMODE back to 1 but switched back and forth between Model Space and Paper Space with MSPACE and PSPACE. When we were in Paper Space, we used the MVIEW command rather than the VPORTS command. If you need a more complete discussion of the use of the VPORTS command and viewport configurations (when TILEMODE=1), see the *AutoCAD Reference Manual* or *AutoCAD: A Concise Guide to Commands and Features*, Second Edition (published by Ventana Press).

The MVIEW Command

The MVIEW command creates viewports in Paper Space.

When prompted,

```
MVIEW
ON/OFF/Hideplot/Fit/2/3/4/Restore/ <First Point>:
```

Pick two opposite corners to create a new viewport.

Or Enter

ON Then select the viewports you want turned on. The number of viewports that can be on at one time is determined by system variable MAXACTVP.

OFF Then select the viewports you want turned off. This is not the same as erasing a viewport. When you erase a viewport, both the viewport border and the view of Model Space within the border disappear. When you turn a viewport off, the border remains and can be manipulated as usual, but no view of Model Space appears within the border.

H (for Hideplot) To designate a viewport for hidden line removal during plotting. When prompted, enter ON to turn HIDEPLOT on, or OFF to turn HIDEPLOT off, then select the viewports you want turned on or off. This command does not affect the way the model appears within the viewport on screen. To see hidden line removal on screen, use the HIDE command.

F (for Fit) To create a new viewport that fills up the entire graphics area.

2 or **3** or **4** To indicate how many viewports you want to create in one operation. You'll be prompted for either Fit or First point, then Opposite point.

If you enter 2, viewports can be divided either horizontally or vertically.

If you enter 3, you can choose to have three equal-size viewports divided vertically or horizontally, or one large and two small viewports, with the large viewport located above, below, left or right of the others.

If you enter 4, four equal-size viewports will be created.

R (for Restore) To make use of a viewport configuration previously saved in Model Space. Enter its name. Then pick the opposite corners of the window it will fit in, or enter F (for Fit) to have the viewport configuration fill the entire graphics area.

After Paper Space viewports are created, they can be moved, stretched, scaled and copied like regular entities. This allows you to place them and size them as you please. They can overlap or have a gap between; or one can be entirely enclosed within another.

The **REDRAWALL** & **REGENALL** Commands

REDRAWALL redraws all viewports and REGENALL regenerates all viewports. REDRAWALL can be used transparently (you can enter 'REDRAWALL in the middle of another command).

The VPLAYER Command

The VPLAYER command provides independent layer control in each Paper Space viewport. The layers you want to control with VPLAYER must already be thawed and on globally. If they aren't, you must use the LAYER command to thaw them or turn them on.

When prompted,

```
VPLAYER
?/Freeze/Thaw/Reset/Newfrz/Vpvisdflt:
```

Enter

? To list layer-frozen status in one viewport. Then select the viewport.

F To freeze one or more layers. Then enter the name(s) of the layers to freeze. Then you're prompted for the viewports: All (all viewports), Select (pick one or more viewports) or Current (for the current viewport).

T To thaw one or more layers. Then enter the name(s) of the layers to thaw. Then you're prompted for the viewports: All (all viewports), Select (pick one or more viewports) or Current (for the current viewport).

R To reset the default status of layers. Then enter the name(s) of the layers to reset. Then you're prompted for the viewports: All (all viewports), Select (pick one or more viewports) or Current (for the current viewport). See the V option below for changing defaults.

N (for Newfrz) To create new frozen layers in all viewports. Enter the name(s) of the new layers. Then you'll want to thaw each layer in at least one viewport so you can use it. To do this, use the T option.

V (for Vpvisdflt) To establish a layer's default status in subsequently created viewports. Then enter the layer's name(s). Enter T to set the indicated layer(s) default as thawed; F to set the default to frozen.

Each time you select one of these options, the main prompt reappears. Press Enter to return to the Command prompt.

Viewing in 3D

After any solid is created, whether it's a primitive or a composite solid, it appears on-screen in a wireframe display. AME automatically creates a block composed of lines, circles and arcs for the sole purpose of displaying the solid. (This is why you must use the SOLLIST command to list the dimensions of a solid. The LIST command will merely list the display block with its insertion point, scale factors, etc.). In order for a solid to appear solid (i.e., with hidden lines removed) or shaded, a pface mesh must be applied to the solid, using the SOLMESH command. When this is done, AME creates a block from the pmesh for display purposes. At this point, the solid has two blocks that can be used for display purposes. Either the SOLMESH or the SOLWIRE block is used, depending on which command was last applied to the solid. The current representation is given in the listing from the SOLLIST command—either "WIREFRAME" or "PMESH."

The VPOINT Command

The VPOINT command sets the location in space from which the viewing line of sight originates. The VPOINT command is disabled in Paper Space.

You can set a viewpoint with (1) X,Y,Z coordinates, (2) the compass and axes or (3) two angles that rotate the viewpoint.

1. When prompted, enter the X,Y,Z coordinates, separated by commas. The line of sight is the vector from the selected coordinates to 0,0,0. Only the direction is important, not the distance from the coordinates to 0,0,0. Thus, a viewpoint location of 1,-2,2 is identical to 5,-10,10.

2. You can also set the viewpoint by using the compass and axes, pictured on the next page. To get the compass and axes, press Enter when prompted for the viewpoint coordinates.

   To use the compass, imagine yourself above the surface of a globe at the North Pole, looking toward the center of the globe. Think of the compass as a flattened globe with the center as the North Pole, the outer circle as the South Pole and the inner circle as the equator.

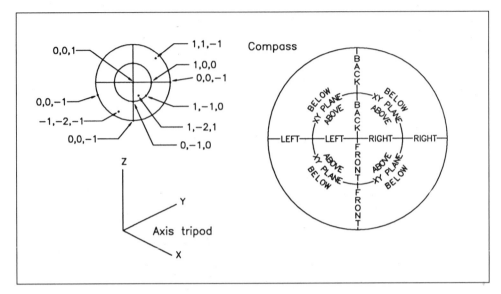

Figure 3-8: Compass and axes.

As you move the pointer around the compass, the axes show the relative positions of the positive X, Y and Z axes. Select your viewpoint by locating the appropriate point on the compass. The vector from that point to the center of the (round) globe defines the line of sight.

3. You can also set the viewpoint by using two angles (similar to spherical coordinates). When prompted, enter R (for Rotate), then enter the angle in the horizontal plane, then the angle in the vertical plane. Rotation of the line of sight begins from the positive X axis (1,0,0). The two angles you enter rotate the viewpoint around 0,0,0—first in the X-Y plane, then toward the +Z or -Z axis.

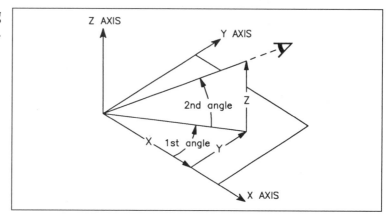

Figure 3-9: Rotating the viewpoint.

To get a viewpoint of an object that's the same as a typical isometric view, use a viewpoint of -1,-1,1 (left, front, top) or 1,-1,1 (right, front, top).

The PLAN Command

The PLAN command displays a plan view of a selected UCS. The plan view is the straight-on view of the X-Y construction plane in the current UCS. It's the same view you get when you use the VPOINT command and enter coordinates 0,0,1.

When prompted,

```
PLAN
```
<Current UCS>/Ucs/World:

Enter

      C For a plan view of the current UCS. (C is the default.)

      U For a plan view of a previously saved UCS, then enter the name of the desired UCS.

      W For a plan view of the World Coordinate System.

The xp Option of the ZOOM Command

The ZOOM command lets you enter a number followed by "xp" (which stands for "times Paper Space") to set up different scale factors in different viewports. The "xp" for a viewport can be listed with the LIST command.

(Switch to Paper Space. Then use LIST to list the viewport. The readout will show the "Scale relative to Paper Space.")

Assuming Paper Space will be plotted at full scale (1=1), and your model was created at full scale,

- When the xp number is 1.0000, the object in the viewport will be plotted at full scale.

- When the xp number is greater than 1.0000, the object in the viewport will be plotted larger than its actual size.

- When the xp number is less than 1.0000, the object in the viewport will be plotted smaller than its actual size.

For example, you may want to produce a plotting in which the first viewport is at full scale, the second is at 4:1 (4x) scale, and the third is at 1:2 (.5x) scale. In the first viewport, you would enter ZOOM, then 1xp. In the second, 4xp. In the third, 1/2xp.

The DVIEW Command

The DVIEW command provides certain special viewing capabilities not found in any other viewing commands. For example, you can dynamically rotate the object, obtain a perspective view or twist the view around the viewing direction.

Some aspects of the DVIEW command are more pertinent to solid modeling than others, so we'll include a brief explanation here of only those aspects. (For a complete description of the DVIEW command including its photography terminology, see the *AutoCAD Reference Manual* or *AutoCAD: A Concise Guide to Commands and Features*, Second Edition.)

First, you're prompted to select "preview objects." These are the objects that will dynamically rotate, providing a preview of the actual display of the objects that will reappear when you complete the command. Normally, you would select a few key features of an object—preferably straight portions, since they display more quickly than curved portions.

If you're using the DVIEW command with a single solid, you must select the entire object. Depending on the complexity of the solid, the dynamic rotation may not be satisfactory. Of course, you could press Enter to dynamically rotate the default "house," but that cancels the advantage of dynamic rotation.

After selecting the preview objects, enter the following:

CA To rotate the camera (your viewpoint) around the target. This is like walking around an object while looking at the same point. Then, using the keyboard or slider bar that appears on-screen, enter the angle up or down from the X-Y construction plane, then the angle around the Z-axis.

TA To rotate the target (the point you're looking at) around the camera. This is like turning your head. Then enter the angle up or down, then the angle left or right.

D To change your distance from the object. Assigning a distance shows the object in perspective. (Compare OFF later in this section.) This option can be handy when you want to add a perspective view to several standard orthographic views of an object.

PO To enter point coordinates for the target, then the camera.

PA To pan the display in any direction.

Z To zoom in or out. If you have entered a distance (if you are in perspective), this option lets you change the focal length of the camera lens. An average focal length would be 50. Very short focal lengths produce a lot of distortion, while very long focal lengths produce a view similar to parallel projection.

TW To twist (rotate) the view around the line of sight. This option is handy when you need to rotate the display in a viewport for an auxiliary view.

CL To clip the object, then enter B for back clipping or F for front clipping.

H To remove hidden lines in the preview objects.

OFF To turn perspective off. Compare **D**, described previously.

U To undo the previous DVIEW operation.

X To exit (complete) the DVIEW command.

The HIDE Command

The HIDE command hides (or displays in different colors) entities that are behind other entities according to the current viewpoint. Remember that a solid must be meshed (see SOLMESH) before HIDE will work.

The HIDE command remains active only until the next time the display is regenerated (using ZOOM, PAN, VPOINT, etc.). Depending on the complexity of the model, hiding may take a lot of time.

To display hidden lines in different colors, use the LAYER command to create layers with the same names as the layers on which the entities reside, using the prefix HIDDEN immediately in front of the layer name. For example, if your object lines are on layer SM in color 4 (cyan), create a layer called HIDDENSM and assign it a different color, such as 5 (blue). Then use the HIDE command. Lines on the hidden layer will retain their linetype.

Entities on turned-off layers may still obscure entities on visible layers. Solution: Freeze the layers that were off. Be aware of many other pitfalls when you're using HIDE with a complex drawing. See the tips on using the HIDE command in the *AutoCAD Reference Manual*.

The SHADE Command

Remember that a solid must be meshed (see SOLMESH) before SHADE will work.

When you enter SHADE, AutoCAD clears the current viewport and displays the percent completion while you're waiting for the shaded rendering. The more complex the object and the larger the viewport, the longer the shading takes.

Before entering SHADE, you can set system variable SHADEDGE to 0, 1, 2 or 3 to specify the type of shading.

- **0** Surfaces are shaded but edges are not highlighted. Requires a 256 color display.

- **1** Surfaces are shaded and edges are shown in the screen's background color. Requires a 256 color display.

- **2** The display looks like a wireframe with hidden lines removed. Edge colors are the colors of the entities. Works on all displays.

- **3** Surfaces are shown filled in, using the colors of the entities; edges are shown in the screen's background color. This works on all color displays.

When SHADEDGE is set to 0 or 1, a surface's color and brightness (the amount of light it reflects) is determined by its angle to the light source (considered to be coming from the viewer's line of sight). If a surface is normal (perpendicular) to the light rays, it is bright. If it is oblique to the light rays, it is dimmer. Surface brightness is also determined by the setting of the SHADEDIF system variable. By default, this variable is set at 70, which means that 70 percent of a surface's brightness comes from diffuse reflection from the light source, while 30 percent comes from ambient light. Values for SHADEDIF range from 0 to 100. The higher the number, the more contrast between normal surfaces and oblique surfaces.

You'll want to experiment with SHADEDGE and SHADEDIF to see which settings work best for objects on your particular display.

Use REGEN to return to the original display of the object.

A shaded rendering cannot be plotted, but you can save it as a slide with the MSLIDE command.

Moving On

With this general background in 3D and Paper Space, we are now ready to consider each solid modeling command in detail. The next chapter explains the commands that create solid primitives, the building blocks used in creating solid models.

You'll find that AutoCAD provides a wide variety of tools for shaping the model. These commands are very important in solid modeling, and you would do well to master the various options available with each command so you can exploit the full potential of solid modeling with AutoCAD.

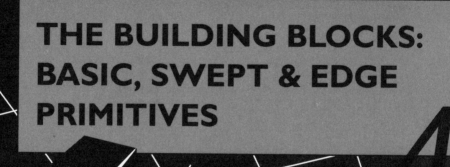

THE BUILDING BLOCKS: BASIC, SWEPT & EDGE PRIMITIVES

4

The Building Blocks:
Basic, Swept & Edge Primitives

A solid model is usually a composite solid made up of several parts called solid primitives. These primitives are the building blocks of solid modeling. This chapter, covers the commands used to create solid primitives. You'll notice they all begin with the "SOL" prefix. Primitives can be divided into three groups.

- Basic Primitives
- Swept Primitives
- Edge Primitives

Basic primitives are the classic geometric shapes: box, wedge, cylinder, cone, sphere and torus.

Swept primitives include extrusion and revolution. These are generated by moving (sweeping) an existing 2D shape, often a polyline, through either a straight or circular path.

Edge primitives include chamfer and fillet, which are modifications to the edges of existing solids. (For further details on primitives, see Chapter 8, "Modeling Strategies & Regions.")

Some commands go by two names. AutoCAD calls the second name the *alias*. You can think of an alias as a nickname or an abbreviation—a name you can use instead of the real name and get the same result. AutoCAD comes with certain alias names already assigned in its ACAD.PGP file. These can be changed and added to by altering that file. In our command descriptions later in this chapter, the corresponding default ACAD.PGP-file alias is listed in parentheses following the command name.

Remember that when you create solids or any 3D objects, you'll be able to see them better if you've set up an appropriate viewpoint with the VPOINT command. Usually you'll want to view 3D objects from the left-front-top (such as -1,-2,1) or right-front-top (such as 1,-2,1). Also, using two or three viewports, each with a different viewpoint, allows you to see your objects from several angles at once.

If you completed Project 2A, you could use the SMA prototype drawing to experiment with solids. That prototype has four viewports, each with a different viewpoint on the solid: top view, front view, right-side view and a non-orthographic view in the upper right corner.

As you create the various solids, you can use the usual methods of point entry, including all the various osnap modes. After a solid is created, many of its features are available for the osnap modes, such as the endpoints and midpoint of the edge of a solid box, or the center of the base or top of a cylinder.

After the solids are created, they can be edited with the usual editing commands.

Chapter 5, "Projects: Basic, Swept & Edge Primitives," gives you exercises in creating the primitives described in this chapter. But you may find it helpful to create each primitive as you read about it in this chapter. As each one is created, list it with both the regular LIST command and the special SOLLIST command (explained later in this chapter). You might want to jump ahead and read the section on the SOLLIST command so you can use it as you create each solid.

By the way, when you list a solid primitive with the regular LIST command, it will list as a block reference. You'll be able to tell that it is a solid rather than a regular block because "*U" will appear where the name usually appears in the listing.

Do not explode a solid primitive. If you do so accidentally, it will disappear or break down into lines, circles and ellipses. This happens because AutoCAD uses these entities to display the primitive on screen, although the primitive cannot be constructed from these elements to begin with.

Curved surfaces on certain shapes (cylinders, cones and spheres, for instance) are displayed with special lines, circles and arcs to help you see the curvature of the surface. These display lines are called *tessellation lines*.

You should not hide solids until you've applied a mesh to the solid with the SOLMESH command. If you attempt to hide a solid before it's meshed, you will get varying unexpected results. For example, if you attempt to HIDE a primitive with mostly straight edges, such as a box or wedge, it will appear that nothing has changed. But if you attempt to hide a primitive that has a curved shape, such as a sphere or torus, it may appear to hide—only because AutoCAD uses circles for the display of these primitives, and circles will hide entities behind them. However, this is not the proper way to hide a solid. In either case, you will not be able to select the solid with the pickbox until you've regenerated the display. Proper hiding requires that a mesh be applied to the solid. See the SOLMESH command later in this chapter.

The word "Baseplane" will appear at the beginning of the prompt for all six of the commands that create basic primitives: SOLBOX, SOLWEDGE, SOLCYL, SOLCONE, SOLTORUS and SOLSPHERE. The use of this Baseplane option is explained later in the section called "Baseplanes & Construction Planes."

The SOLBOX Command (Alias: BOX)

The SOLBOX command creates a solid box. The box is defined from a starting corner or center, then from its X, Y and Z dimensions—which can be positive or negative. If you use the Center option, the center will be located midway within the box *in all 3 dimensions* (at the box's center of gravity).

First, you're prompted for the starting corner or center of the box. Once that point is fixed, the box's dimensions can be entered in one of three ways.

The default method is to locate the opposite corner of the box (and thus provide all three dimensions). If the pointer is used, a rubber-band cursor will be attached to the starting corner. (When you're in plan view, this rubber-band cursor will actually be a rectangle showing you the temporary outline of the base. If you're not in plan view, the usual straight rubber-band cursor will appear.) If you entered the opposite corner of the base and the Z coordinate was zero (or omitted), you will be prompted for the height. If you started by using the Center option, "Other corner" can be any corner.

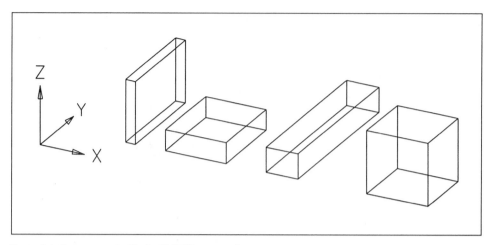

Figure 4-1: Boxes created with the SOLBOX command.

Or, when prompted for the opposite corner, you can enter L for length, then enter all three dimensions of the box separately: length (X dimension), width (Y dimension) and height (Z dimension).

Or, when prompted for the opposite corner, you can enter C for cube, then enter the dimension of one side of the cube.

The base of the box will always lie in a plane parallel to the X-Y construction plane (which may be the UCS in effect when you started the command, or the Baseplane established within the command). The edges of the box will always be created parallel to the current X, Y and Z axes of the current construction plane. If you want the box to appear at a certain rotation or angle, either set up an appropriate UCS before creating the box, use the ROTATE or SOLMOVE command after creating the box or use the Baseplane option within the command.

The SOLWEDGE Command (Alias: WEDGE or WED)

This command creates a wedge. The slanted surface of the wedge always runs from its full Z-height to a zero-height, tapering to a sharp edge as you move along the X axis.

The prompts for SOLWEDGE are almost identical to those for SOLBOX, although there is no Center option.

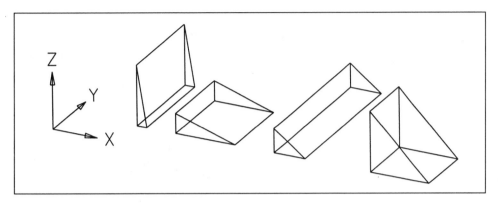

Figure 4-2: Wedges created with the SOLWEDGE command.

The SOLCYL Command (Alias: CYLINDER or CYL)

The SOLCYL command creates both round and elliptical cylinders. That is, the bases of the cylinder can be either circles or ellipses. The cylinder will always be a right cylinder (the centerline of the cylinder will be perpendicular to the base).

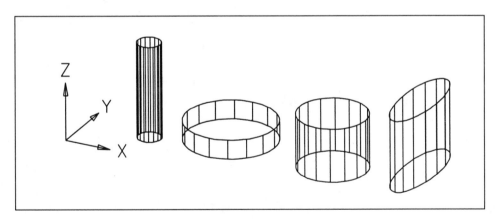

Figure 4-3: Cylinders created with the SOLCYL command.

The first prompt assumes the base will be a circle rather than an ellipse, so it asks for the center of the base. After you enter the center, you're prompted for the base radius. You can enter the radius or enter D, then the diameter (similar to the CIRCLE command). Finally you're prompted for the cylinder height, which can be positive or negative.

Instead of entering the height, you can enter C to locate the center of the other end of the cylinder. This allows you to tip the cylinder so that its base is not necessarily aligned with the current UCS or Baseplane. For example, locating the center of the other end by using spherical coordinates allows you to indicate both the length of the cylinder (the first number of the spherical coordinates) and the angular orientation of the cylinder.

To create an elliptical cylinder, enter E when prompted for the center of the base. You'll get a series of prompts similar to those in the ELLIPSE command. You can locate the two endpoints of the first axis of the ellipse, then the endpoint (or half-length) of the second axis. Or, you can enter C for center, then locate the center of the ellipse, then the endpoint of the first axis, then the endpoint (or half-length) of the second axis.

An oblique cylinder must be created as a composite solid, either by subtracting something like a box or wedge from one or both ends of a right cylinder, or by intersecting a box with a tilted cylinder. The Boolean operations of subtraction and intersection are explained later.

The SOLCONE Command (Alias: CONE or CON)

The SOLCONE command creates both round and elliptical cones. That is, the base of the cone can be either a circle or an ellipse. The cone will always be a right cone (the line from the apex to the center of the base will be perpendicular to the base). Also, the cone will always be a full cone rather than a truncated cone or frustum.

The series of prompts is identical to those for SOLCYL, except "Apex" replaces "Center of other end."

A truncated cone can be created in several different ways: as a primitive, by extruding a circle with the SOLEXT command or revolving a polyline around an axis with the SOLREV command. Or it can be created as a composite solid by starting with a cone and combining it with a box (or other object) using the Boolean operation of subtraction or intersection. Again, these commands and operations are explained later.

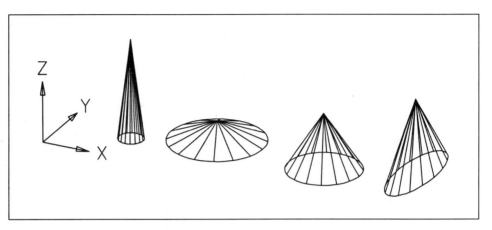

Figure 4-4: Cones created with the SOLCONE command.

The SOLSPHERE Command (Alias: SPHERE or SPH)

The SOLSPHERE command creates a sphere. You're prompted for the center of the sphere, then the radius. When you're prompted for the radius, you can enter D, then the diameter.

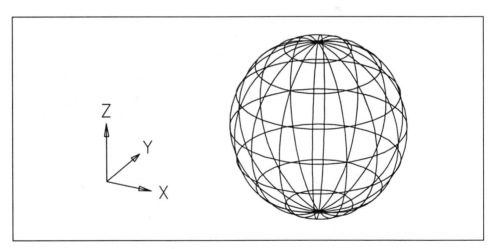

Figure 4-5: Sphere created with the SOLSPHERE command.

Wireframe representation of the sphere will resemble a globe, with circles representing latitudinal and longitudinal lines. The axis of this globe (the line from pole to pole) will always be placed parallel to the Z axis of the current UCS or Baseplane.

The SOLTORUS Command (Alias: TORUS or TOR)

The SOLTORUS command creates a torus, which is normally shaped like a donut. The torus will be created so that its straight centerline (the centerline running through the center hole, not the circular centerline running through the tube) is perpendicular to the X-Y construction plane of the current UCS or Baseplane.

First you're prompted for the center of the torus. Then you're prompted for the radius of the torus. This is the major radius, which is the distance from the center to the circular centerline of the tube. This radius can be positive or negative, but cannot be zero. When prompted for this radius, you can enter D, then the diameter.

The next prompt is for the radius of the tube. This is the minor radius and it must be positive. Here, also, you can enter D, then the diameter.

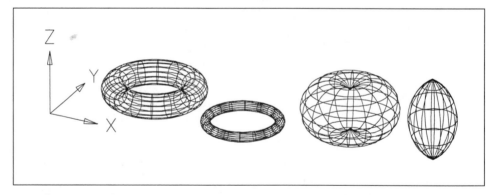

Figure 4-6: Tori created with the SOLTORUS command.

Normally the torus's radius will be greater than the tube's radius. If it's positive but smaller than the radius of the tube, the torus will have no center hole. If it's negative, a football shape is produced. Although a negative radius is allowed for the torus, its absolute value cannot be equal to or greater than the radius of the tube, since that would produce a solid with no volume (known as a null solid).

Baseplanes & Construction Planes

Each of the six preceding commands has a prompt that begins with "Baseplane." The use of this Baseplane option is explained here.

Often when creating a solid, you need to set up an X-Y construction plane appropriate for that solid. For example, the SOLBOX command always creates a box whose sides are parallel to the principal planes of the current UCS. So the appropriate UCS must be established either before you begin the SOLBOX command or at the start of the SOLBOX command by means of the Baseplane option.

Of course, it is possible to create any solid at the origin then place it in its proper location with the regular MOVE and ROTATE commands or the SOLMOVE command. However, it is often advisable to set up an appropriate User Coordinate System (UCS) either ahead of time or during the use of the solid primitive command so the solid can be originated in its proper location.

There are four different types of bases that you need to be aware of— the WCS (World Coordinate System), various UCSs (User Coordinate Systems), Baseplanes and CPs (Construction Planes).

- The WCS (World Coordinate System) can be considered the "home UCS" and is the direct or indirect base for all other UCSs. Although many solids can be constructed while in the WCS, most realistic models require the use of other UCSs. The WCS cannot be altered, and is usually the default coordinate system at the beginning of a drawing unless your prototype drawing establishes a different UCS. After establishing a different UCS, the WCS can be restored with the UCS command.

- A UCS (User Coordinate System), which can be oriented anywhere in relation to the WCS, forms the base for subsequent UCSs as well as drawing, modeling and inquiry commands. A UCS stays in effect until another UCS is established, so it can be thought of as relatively permanent. All UCSs are established with the UCS command or the SOLUCS command.

- A baseplane is a temporary UCS. A baseplane can be established at the beginning of a solid primitive command by entering B to select the Baseplane option. A baseplane can be oriented anywhere in relation to the current UCS. It forms the base for other construction planes and points created while in that command. A baseplane lasts only until you are done with the command.

- A CP (Construction Plane) is also a UCS, but it is even more temporary than a baseplane. It lasts only until the next point is entered. A CP can be established by means of the CP option at any time during a solid primitive command when a point is being requested.

The UCS allows you to set up any X-Y construction plane and save it under an appropriate name for future recall. The UCS command is explained in Chapter 3, "General 3D Commands: UCSs, Space & Viewing."

The SOLUCS command has limited usefulness. While it can be helpful in some situations, it does not control the placement of a new UCS as precisely as the 3point option of the regular UCS command. There is a brief mention of SOLUCS on page 285, after Step 9 in Project 13B.

The Baseplane and CP options are similar in the way they work. However, the Baseplane option appears as the first option in the six commands that create solid primitives (SOLBOX, SOLWEDGE, SOLCYL, SOLCONE, SOLSPHERE and SOLTORUS), and the baseplane that is established is maintained until the end of the command. In contrast, the CP option, even though it is not a listed option, is available in any of the six commands that creates solid primitives; but the UCS that is established is maintained only until the next point is entered. By establishing different UCSs with the CP option, you can work in several UCSs within one command.

The CP option is also available in other solid modeling commands that accept point entries. For example, the SOLREV command allows you to define the axis of revolution by defining two points, and the Move option of the SOLCHP command prompts for "Base point" and "Second point." You can activate CP before entering any of these points.

You can establish a baseplane at the beginning of a command, then create additional construction planes during the remainder of that command. After you enter a point in a new CP, you are returned to the baseplane, then at the end of the command you are returned to the UCS that was in effect before you started the command.

When you enter either B (for Baseplane) or CP (for Construction Plane), you are prompted to select one of the following methods of establishing the plane:

...Entity/Last/Zaxis/View/XY/YZ/ZX/<3point>:

Enter E (Entity), then select a circle, arc or polyline segment to align the temporary UCS with the selected entity.

When you select a circle, the construction plane is in the plane of the circle, the origin is at the center, and the X axis runs through the pick point.

When you select an arc, the construction plane is in the plane of the arc, the origin is at the center, and the X axis runs through the end-point of the arc nearest the pick point.

When you select a polyline, the construction plane is in the plane of the polyline, the origin is at the first vertex of the polyline, and the X axis runs through the second vertex.

Enter L (Last) to re-select the last construction plane (the construction plane established by the previous use of Baseplane or CP).

Enter Z (Zaxis), then select the origin and a point on the positive Z axis of the temporary UCS. The orientation of the X and Y axes is arbitrary.

Enter V (View), then pick a point, to select the origin of a temporary UCS whose Z axis will extend toward the current viewpoint.

Enter XY or YZ or ZX, then pick a point, to select the origin of a temporary UCS that is aligned with the XY or YZ or ZX plane of the current UCS. The X axis is pointed in the direction of the first axis in the letter pair, and the Y axis in the direction of the second. For example, if you select ZX, the X axis of the new construction plane will point in the same direction as the Z axis of the current UCS, and the Y axis of the new construction plane will point in the same direction as the X axis of the current UCS.

Enter 3 (3point, or press Enter to accept the 3point default), then select the origin, point on the positive X axis, and point in the positive Y plane of the temporary UCS.

The UCS icon is temporarily placed at the origin of the UCS to show you its orientation, even if you have set up the regular UCS icon so it is not displayed at the origin. If you use the CP option, the UCS icon returns to its former position as soon as you enter the next point. This former position might be the UCS that was in effect before you started the command, or the baseplane you selected at the beginning of the command. If you have entered B (Baseplane), the UCS and UCS icon stay there until you are done with the command, unless you use CP again to re-position it for a subsequent point.

If you know what option you want, you can go directly to it by entering: CPE, CPL, CPZ, CPV, CPXY, CPYZ, CPZX or CP3.

The SOLEXT Command (Alias: EXTRUDE or EXT)

The SOLEXT command creates a solid primitive by extruding a region, circle, polyline, polygon or 3Dpoly entity. Regions are explained in Chapter 8, "Modeling Strategies & Regions." Because a polyline can have virtually any shape, the SOLEXT command allows you to create very irregular solids. Several entities can be extruded at one time.

In order for a polyline to be extruded, it must have more than one segment, and none of the segments can cross each other. Also, if any segment lies on top of any other segment, the endpoints of both segments must also lie on top of each other. There is a limit of 500 vertices for polylines.

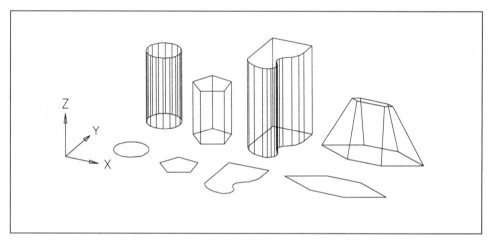

Figure 4-7: Extrusions created with the SOLEXT command.

The extrusion is always perpendicular to the entity's plane. For a circle, polyline or polygon, the plane of the entity is the plane it occupies. For a 3Dpoly entity, the plane of the entity is the X-Y construction plane in effect when it was created. The 3Dpoly entity is projected onto this plane before being extruded.

If the solid is being extruded from a polyline, SOLEXT always creates the solid as if the polyline had a zero width. If the polyline is open, it is extruded as though it were closed with a straight segment.

First you're prompted to select the object to be extruded. Then you are prompted for the height, which can be positive or negative. Finally, you're prompted for the extrusion taper angle. This angle is measured from the extrusion direction and can range from zero up to (but not including) 90 degrees. An angle of 0, which is the default, results in a solid whose top is the same size and shape as the base and whose edges are perpendicular to the plane of the entity. Any other angle tapers in the solid from the base, producing a top that's smaller than the base. If you are extruding a region, all loops will be tapered.

If the angle is too large in relation to the size of the base and the desired height of the solid, the taper from one side will meet the taper from the other side before reaching the full height.

NOTE: If a circle or polyline with arc segments is being extruded, a solid is created with an angle different than the requested angle. If you use a taper angle other than 0, you'll need to check the resulting solid rather than assuming it's what you wanted.

When you extrude a region, you are asked if you want to extrude some of the loops to heights different than the main height. If you enter Yes, you are asked to select one or more loops (press Enter to indicate when you are done selecting) and then enter the height for those loops.

This process repeats until you have indicated all sets of loops and their corresponding heights. If you enter No, all loops are extruded to the same height.

If system variable SOLDELENT is 1, the polyline will be retained after the solid is created. If it's 2, AutoCAD will ask if you want the polyline deleted. If 3, the polyline will be deleted. The default is 3 unless you've changed it in your prototype drawing.

The SOLREV Command (Alias: REVOLVE or REV)

The SOLREV command produces a solid by revolving or "sweeping" a region, circle, polyline, polygon or 3Dpoly entity around an axis. Only one entity can be revolved at a time.

In order for a polyline to be revolved, it must have more than one segment, and none of the segments can cross each other. Also, if any segment lies on top of any other segment, the endpoints of both segments must also lie on top of each other. Polylines with width are treated as if they had a width of zero. There is a limit of 500 vertices for polylines.

First you're prompted to select the object to be revolved. Then you're prompted for the axis of revolution. This axis can be indicated by picking a startpoint and endpoint, an entity, the X axis of the current UCS or the Y axis of the current UCS. If the axis you select is not already in the same plane as the object to be revolved, it will be projected onto that plane. The object to be revolved must be positioned entirely on one side of the axis (or the projected axis).

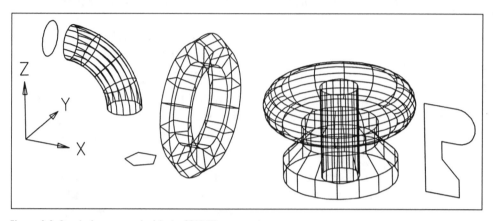

Figure 4-8: Revolutions created with the SOLREV command.

The next prompt is for the included angle. The default is a full circle. If you enter an angle less than 360 degrees, the solid will be revolved from zero degrees through that number of degrees using the right-hand rule to determine the direction of rotation. In turn, the right-hand rule is based on the positive direction of the axis of revolution. The positive direction of the axis is determined as follows: if two points were selected, the direction from the first point to the second is the positive direction. If an entity was selected, the direction from the endpoint nearest the pick point to the endpoint farthest from the pick point is the positive direction. If the X or Y axis was selected, the positive direction points toward the positive end of the axis.

When you revolve a region, you are asked if you want to revolve some loops through angles different than the main angle of revolution. If you enter Yes, you are asked to select one or more loops (press Enter to indicate when you are done selecting) and then enter the angle of revolution for those loops. This process repeats until you have indicated all sets of loops and their corresponding angles. If you enter No, all loops are revolved through the same angle.

If system variable SOLDELENT is 1, the polyline will be retained after the solid is created. If 2, AutoCAD will ask if you want it deleted. If 3, it will be deleted. The default is 3 unless you've changed it in your prototype drawing.

The SOLCHAM Command (Alias: CHAM or SOLC)

A chamfer is a beveled edge. It is actually a separate solid that's subtracted from an existing solid (in the case of an external chamfer) or joined to an existing solid (in the case of an internal chamfer). The joining or subtraction is done automatically.

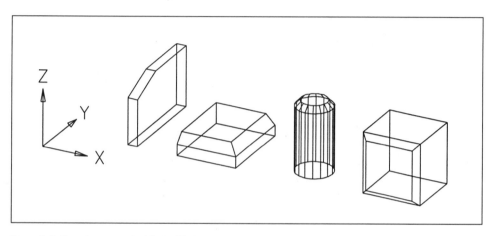

Figure 4-9: Chamfers created with the SOLCHAM command.

SOLCHAM begins by prompting you to select the base surface containing the edges you want chamfered. Since you must select a surface by one of its edges, and since each edge could belong to two different surfaces, AutoCAD highlights one of the surfaces and asks if that one is OK. If it is, simply press Enter. If it's not, enter N for next, then press Enter when the correct surface is highlighted.

Then you are prompted to select the edges. If one of the edges to be chamfered is a curved edge, you need to select the curve only once; you don't need to select each segment between display (tessellation) lines.

Finally you're prompted for the two distances. The first distance will be applied along the base surface, the second distance along the other surface at each edge.

Then AutoCAD creates the required chamfer solids, joins them to each other (if more than one edge is selected) and finally either joins them to or subtracts them from the solid being chamfered.

The SOLFILL Command (Alias: FIL or SOLF)

A fillet is a rounded edge. It's actually a separate solid that's subtracted from an existing solid (in the case of an external convex fillet) or joined to an existing solid (in the case of an internal concave fillet). The joining or subtraction is done automatically.

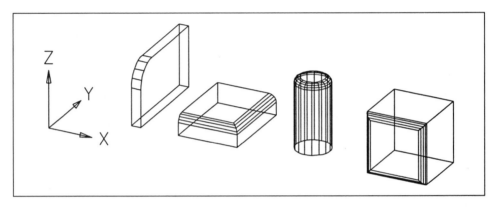

Figure 4-10: Fillets created with the SOLFIL command.

SOLFILL begins by prompting you to select the edges you want to fillet. You can select one or several edges, and the edges can be on one or several solids. If one of the edges to be filleted is a curved edge, you select the curve only once; you don't need to select each segment between display (tessellation) lines.

Then you're prompted for the radius of the fillet. When you are prompted for the radius, you can enter D, then the diameter.

Then AutoCAD creates the required fillet solids, joins them to each other (if more than one edge is selected) and finally either joins them to or subtracts them from the solid being filleted.

The SOLIDIFY Command (Alias: SOL)

The SOLIDIFY command turns thick entities into solids and flat entities into regions. A thick entity is an entity that has been assigned a positive or negative thickness with the ELEV or CHPROP command. Thick entities that can be solidified include circles, polylines, polygons, ellipses, traces and 2D solids. Entities that cannot be solidified include regions, lines, 3Dlines, 3Dfaces and 3Dpoly entities.

If a polyline has been selected, SOLIDIFY always creates the solid as if the polyline had a zero width and were closed with a straight segment.

You can select several entities at one time. Any entity that cannot be converted to a solid is highlighted, and a message appears on the screen.

If system variable SOLDELENT is 1, the original thick entity will be retained after the solid is created. If 2, AutoCAD will ask if you want it deleted. If 3, it will be deleted. The default is 3.

In order for a polyline to be solidified, it must have more than one segment, and none of the segments can cross each other. Also, if any segment lies on top of any other segment, the endpoints of both segments must also lie on top of each other.

When system variable SOLSOLIDIFY is set to 3, each thick entity will be automatically converted to a solid the first time it's selected for use in another solid command. If SOLSOLIDIFY is set to 2, AutoCAD will ask whether you want the entity turned into a solid. If it is set to 1, it merely reports that the selected entity is not a solid and was ignored by the SOLID command. In the latter case, SOLIDIFY is the proper command to turn it into a solid. The default is 2.

The SOLLIST Command (Alias: SLIST or SL)

The SOLLIST command is a specialized listing command that can be used in addition to the regular LIST command when you want to display certain information about a solid or region. Regions are explained in Chapter 8.

The regular LIST command displays a solid's space (Model or Paper), handle, location (insertion point), scale factors and rotation angle. The SOLLIST command displays a solid's name, dimensions, handle, surface area (if it has been calculated), material, representation (wireframe or mesh) and rigid-motion information. Thus, the type of information you need will determine which listing command you'll use.

All options of the SOLLIST command are covered here because you can use some of its options to check features of any primitive you've created. However, some of the most helpful aspects of the SOLLIST command pertain to composite solids, which are described later.

When prompted, enter

O (the default) for object, then select one or more solids or regions.

The first item in the listing is the type of object. If the object is a primitive, the type will be the primitive name (box, cylinder, region, etc.) and it will be followed by the primitive's dimensions in parentheses. For primitives that have different X, Y and Z dimensions (such as the box, wedge, cylinder, cone, extrusion and solidified 2D objects), the dimensions relate to the original X-Y-Z dimensions and are not affected by rotating the primitive. However, they *are* affected by scaling the primitive.

- For a box or wedge, the length, width and height are given.

- For a cylinder or cone (which can have a circular or elliptical base), the X-radius, Y-radius and height are given. If the cylinder is circular, the two radii will be equal.

- For a sphere, the radius is given.

- For a torus, the radius of the torus and the radius of the tube are given.

- For an extrusion, the number of vertices in the base, height and taper angle are given. The listing also includes the location of each vertex in relation to the polyline's beginning vertex. If the extrusion was made from a polyline with arc segments, those segments are divided into sections of 90 degrees or less and a vertex is listed at each division point. A circular base is divided into four segments.

- For a revolution, the number of vertices in the base and the included angle of revolution are given. The listing also includes the location of each vertex in relation to the start point of the axis. If the revolution was made from a polyline with arc segments, those segments are divided into sections of 90 degrees or less, and a vertex is listed at each division point. A circle is divided into four segments.

- For a region that is a solidified polyline, the listing follows the pattern of an extrusion.

- A solid formed with the SOLIDIFY command will be listed as a cylinder or extrusion.

If the solid is a composite (a combination of two or more other solids or regions) the type will be the Boolean operation (union, subtraction or intersection) which formed the composite, and the handles of the top-level objects from which it was constructed will be listed.

After the type, the solid's handle is given. Then the surface area of the solid is displayed (if the area has been calculated by the SOLAREA command or the SOLMESH command).

The listing also includes the current representation and the type of shading of the solid. The representation will be either wireframe or mesh. The shading will be either uniform or CSG.

Finally, a set of 16 numbers, which indicate the object's rigid motion (rotation), is listed.

Enter

E To display information about an edge, then select the edge.

F To display information about the plane in which the face resides. When you select a face, you'll have to select it by one of its edges. However, each edge belongs to two faces, so you must indicate which face you want. One of the faces will be highlighted. When the face you want is highlighted, press Enter to select it. Otherwise, enter N to highlight the next face. The listing includes the outward normal, which is the direction of a vector that is perpendicular to the plane and extends away from the solid. The listing also includes a point on the plane.

T To display a composite solid's CSG tree. By noticing the handles of each of the components, you can tell which ones are nested inside other components, and thus "picture" the CSG tree.

The SOLMESH Command

When prompted to select objects, pick one or more solids.

The SOLMESH command applies a PFACE entity to the surfaces of a solid. The PFACE entity is placed into a block for display purposes. It is this PFACE mesh that allows it to be displayed either shaded or with hidden lines removed. The resolution of the mesh on curved surfaces (the density of tessellation lines) is determined in part by the SOLWDENS variable.

Lines on the far side of the object are not hidden automatically by the SOLMESH command. After using SOLMESH, hidden lines are removed with the HIDE command. After the next regeneration, the hidden lines reappear but can be hidden again at any time with the HIDE command.

When a solid is meshed, remember that all edge lines are straight line segments. This means that osnap modes will operate differently than they do with a wireframe representation. For example, the CEN osnap mode will not be usable. If you need to use such osnap modes as center, quadrant or tangent, first use the SOLWIRE command to convert the solid back to wireframe representation.

The SOLWIRE Command

When prompted to select objects, pick one or more solids. The SOLWIRE command converts a meshed solid to wireframe representation. A solid can be displayed only one way at a time—either as a PFACE mesh (after using the SOLMESH command) or as a wireframe (after using the SOL-WIRE command). Keep in mind, however, that a solid that has been meshed still looks like a wireframe until you use either the HIDE or SHADE command.

A wireframe representation includes added lines, called tessellation lines, on curved surfaces. The density of these tessellation lines is determined by the SOLWDENS variable.

The SOLWDENS System Variable

The SOLWDENS system variable determines the wire density in wireframe representations in solids. It applies to new primitives or new composites formed with Boolean operations. SOLWDENS also governs mesh density for these solids when they are displayed in mesh representation.

The range of values for this variable is 1 through 12 (4 being the default). Increasing the value of SOLWDENS increases the following:

- The number of tessellation (curvature) lines in wireframe representations of solids.

- The accuracy and the number of sections in PFACE representations of solids.

- The time AutoCAD takes to mesh a solid.

- The time AutoCAD takes to perform the Boolean operations with the solid.

- The amount of RAM used for display and Boolean operations.

Obviously, there is a trade-off here; a gain in visual accuracy means a loss of speed. The *AME Reference Manual* recommends that you use a setting of 6 or higher "sparingly, if at all."

Moving On

The commands we've described in this chapter create the solid primitives that form the fundamental building blocks of solid modeling. Many shapes can be fashioned from these primitives alone. Now it's time to use these commands. In the next chapter we use each of the primitive commands (and most of their options) to create a wide variety of shapes.

PROJECTS: BASIC, SWEPT & EDGE PRIMITIVES

5

Projects: Basic, Swept & Edge Primitives

This chapter contains three projects that will give you experience using the various primitives described in the previous chapter. The primitives you create will use the SMA prototype drawing from Chapter 2, "Projects: Setup & Overview." Eventually, you will mesh and shade the simple projects.

Project 5A: Using Basic Primitives

There are six basic primitives, as shown on the next page. In this project you'll create several of each. After creating each primitive, list it with both LIST and SOLLIST. Also, mesh and shade each group of primitives, then return them to wireframe representation.

1. Start AutoCAD. Using the SMA.DWG prototype drawing, create a new drawing called PRIM-BAS.

   At the Release 11 Main Menu, enter 1 then `PRIM-BAS=SMA`

   In Release 12, pick "New" from the FILE pull-down menu. Use SMA as a prototype drawing.

2. Create the following layers and assign them the colors indicated.

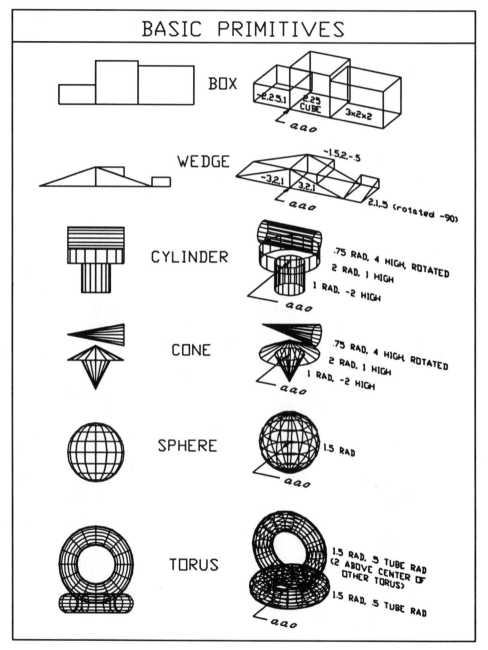

Figure 5-1: Basic primitives.

Layer	Color
PRIM-BOX	Red (1)
PRIM-WEDGE	Yellow (2)
PRIM-CYL	Green (3)
PRIM-CONE	Cyan (4)
PRIM-SPHERE	Blue (5)
PRIM-TORUS	Magenta (6)

3. Make the PRIM-BOX layer current. Freeze all other layers you just created.

```
LAYER [Enter]
S [Enter]
PRIM-BOX [Enter]
F [Enter]
PRIM* [Enter][Enter]
```

4. In Model Space, in the upper right viewport (handle 2),[1] set up a viewpoint of 1,-2,1.

Pick upper right viewport (handle 2).

```
VPOINT [Enter]
1,-2,1 [Enter]
```

5. Center the view in each viewport around 1,.5,1 using half scale.

```
ZOOM [Enter]
C [Enter]
1,.5,1 [Enter]
.5xp [Enter]
```

Do the same in each viewport.

---

[1] If your handles are different, use the handles you recorded in Project 2A in Chapter 2.

6. In Release 11, load AME.

   ```
   (xload "ame") [Enter]
   ```

   Or, pick "AME" then "Load AME" from the sidebar or pull-down menu.

   In Release 12, AME is loaded automatically when you first enter an AME command either at the Command prompt or from the "Model" pull-down menu.

7. In the upper right viewport (handle 2), create a cube at 0,0,0 that is 2.25 on each side.

   Pick the upper right viewport (handle 2).

   ```
   SOLBOX [Enter]
   0,0,0 [Enter]
   C [Enter]
   2.25 [Enter]
   ```

8. List the cube with both LIST and SOLLIST.

9. Create a box starting at 0,0,0 that is -2 x 2.5 x 1. Then list it.

   ```
   SOLBOX [Enter]
   0,0,0 [Enter]
   L [Enter]
   -2 [Enter]
   2.5 [Enter]
   1 [Enter]
   ```

10. Create a box at 2.25,0,0 that is 3 x 2 x 2. Then list it.

    ```
    SOLBOX [Enter]
    2.25,0,0 [Enter]
    @3,2,2 [Enter]
    ```

11. Mesh the three boxes, shade them, then return them to wireframe representation.

> SOLMESH [Enter]
>
> Pick all three boxes. [Enter]
>
> SHADE [Enter]

(If the shaded image does not appear satisfactory, you may want to experiment setting variable SHADEDGE to a different number. The possible numbers are 0, 1, 2 and 3.)

> REGEN [Enter]
>
> SOLWIRE [Enter].
>
> Pick all three boxes. [Enter]

12. Thaw layer PRIM-WEDGE and make it current, then freeze layer PRIM-BOX.

13. Use the SOLWEDGE command to create the four wedges described below. List and shade them, then return them to wireframe representation.

(a) Create a wedge starting at 0,0,0 that is 3 x 2 x 1.

(b) Create a wedge starting at 0,0,0 that is -3 x 2 x 1.

(c) Create a wedge starting at 3,2,0 that is 2 x 1 x .5.
Rotate the wedge -90° around 3,2.

(d) Create a wedge starting at 0,0,0 that is -1.5 x 2 x -.5.

Using immediate osnap modes, move it to the location shown in Figure 5-1.

14. Thaw layer PRIM-CYL and make it current, then freeze layer PRIM-WEDGE.

15. Use the SOLCYL command to create the three cylinders described below. List and shade them, then return them to wireframe representation.

    (a) Create a cylinder starting at 0,0,0 with radius 2 and height 1.

    (b) Create a cylinder starting at 0,0,0 with radius 1 and height -2.

    (c) Create a cylinder starting at 2,0,1.75 with radius .75. Use the "Center of other end" option and enter @4<180<0 so this cylinder will be oriented as shown in Figure 5-1.

16. Thaw layer PRIM-CONE and make it current, then freeze layer PRIM-CYL.

17. Use the SOLCONE command to create the three cones described below. List and shade them, then return them to wireframe representation.

    (a) Create a cone starting at 0,0,0 with radius 2 and height 1.

    (b) Create a cone starting at 0,0,0 with radius 1 and height -2.

    (c) Create a cone starting at 2,0,1.75 with radius .75. Use the "Apex" option and enter @4<180<0 so this cone will be oriented as shown in Figure 5-1.

18. Thaw layer PRIM-SPHERE and make it current, then freeze layer PRIM-CONE.

19. Use the SOLSPHERE command to create the sphere described below. List and shade it, then return it to wireframe representation.

    (a) Create a sphere centered at 0,0,0 with radius 1.5.

20. Thaw layer PRIM-TORUS and make it current, then freeze layer PRIM-SPHERE.

21. Use the SOLTORUS command to create the two tori described in (a) and
(b) below. List and shade each of them, then return them to wireframe
representation.

(a) Create a torus centered at 0,0,0 with radius 1.5 and tube radius .5.

(b) Restore the UCS called FRONT. Create a torus centered at 0,2,0 with
radius 1.5 and tube radius .5.

22. Restore the WCS.

```
UCS [Enter][Enter]
```

23. In Paper Space, on BORDER layer, place the "BASIC PRIMITIVES" text in
the title line (.25 high).

24. END your drawing.

Project 5B: Using Swept Primitives

In this project, we'll create both kinds of swept primitives—extrusions and
revolutions—as shown in Figure 5-2. After creating each primitive, you
should list it with both LIST and SOLLIST. Also, mesh and shade each
primitive and return it to wireframe representation.

1. Start AutoCAD and create a new drawing called PRIM-SWE that uses the
SMA.DWG prototype drawing.

2. Create the following layers and assign them the colors indicated.

Layer	Color
PRIM-BLOCK	Red (1)
PRIM-SPLINE	Yellow (2)
PRIM-MOLDING	Green (3)
PRIM-DONUT	Cyan (4)
PRIM-PULLEY	Blue (5)
PRIM-SHAFT	Magenta (6)

3. Make PRIM-BLOCK the current layer. Freeze all the other layers you just created.

```
LAYER [Enter]
S [Enter]
PRIM-BLOCK [Enter]
F [Enter]
PRIM* [Enter][Enter]
```

4. In Model Space, in the upper right viewport (handle 2),[2] set up a viewpoint of 2,-2,1.

```
MSPACE [Enter]
```

Pick upper right viewport (handle 2).

```
VPOINT [Enter]
2,-2,1 [Enter]
```

---

[2] If your handles are different, use the handles you recorded in Project 2A in Chapter 2.

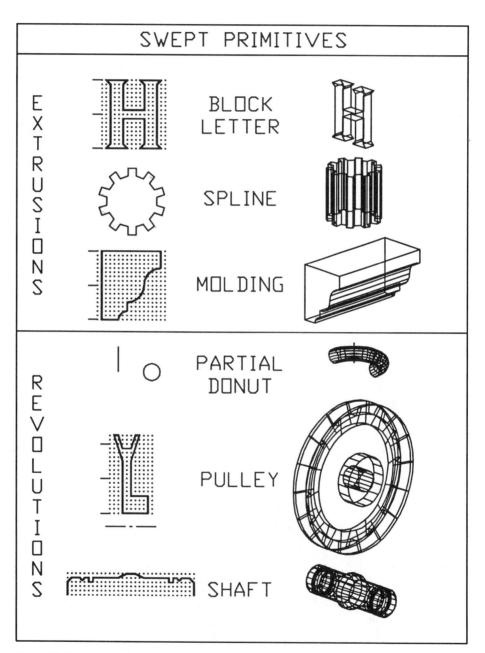

Figure 5-2: Swept primitives.

5. Center the view in each viewport around 0,0,1, using full scale.

```
ZOOM [Enter]
C [Enter]
0,0,1 [Enter]
1xp [Enter]
```

Do the same in the other viewports.

6. In Release 11, load AME.

```
(xload "ame") [Enter]
```

7. Restore the UCS called FRONT. (It already exists in the prototype drawing.)

8. In the lower left viewport (handle 4), use PLINE to create the outline of the block letter H shown in Figure 5-2. Start with the lower left corner of the letter at 0,0. The letter is 2 inches tall (the grid marks are at 1/8 inch increments). You can draw this outline easily by setting snap at .125.

9. Use SOLEXT to extrude the polyline .375 in the Z direction (no taper).

```
SOLEXT [Enter]
Pick polyline [Enter]
.375 [Enter]
0 [Enter]
```

10. In the upper right viewport (handle 2), mesh and shade the primitive, then return it to wireframe representation.

11. Restore the WCS.

12. Thaw layer PRIM-SPLINE and make it current, then freeze layer PRIM-BLOCK.

13. In the upper left viewport (handle 3), create the outline of the spline, centered at 0,0. The inner diameter of the spline is 1.5, the outer diameter is 2.0. The spline has 10 teeth, each .24 wide. Turn the outline into a polyline with PEDIT (AutoCAD should display "39 segments added").

14. Use SOLEXT to extrude the spline 2 inches in the Z direction (no taper). Mesh and shade the spline, then return it to wireframe representation.

15. Restore the UCS called FRONT.

16. Thaw layer PRIM-MOLDING and make it current, then freeze layer PRIM-SPLINE.

17. In the lower left viewport (handle 4), use PLINE to create the outline of the molding shown in Figure 5-2. Start with the lower left corner of the outline at 0,0. The molding is 2.00 inches tall and 1.75 wide (the grid marks are 1/8 inch apart).

18. Move the polyline 2 inches in the Z direction.

19. Use SOLEXT to extrude the molding 4 inches in the negative Z direction (no taper). Mesh and shade the molding, then return it to wireframe representation.

20. Thaw layer PRIM-DONUT and make it current, then freeze layer PRIM-MOLDING. (Keep the FRONT UCS current.)

21. In the lower left viewport (handle 4), draw a circle at 1,0 that has a radius of .25. Draw a line from 0,0 to 0,1.

22. Use SOLREV to revolve the circle around the line 180°.

SOLREV [Enter]

Pick the circle [Enter]

E [Enter]

Pick the line near its bottom end.

180 [Enter]

23. Mesh and shade the donut, then return it to wireframe representation.

24. Thaw layer PRIM-PULLEY and make it current, then freeze layer PRIM-DONUT.

25. In the lower left viewport (handle 4), use PLINE to draw the outline of the top half section of the pulley. Place the lower left corner of the section at 0,0. The grid marks are spaced 1/8 inch apart. Place the axis line 3/8 inch below the lower edge of the pulley section.

26. Use SOLREV to revolve this section outline around the axis. Mesh and shade the pulley, then return it to wireframe representation.

27. Thaw layer PRIM-SHAFT and make it current, then freeze layer PRIM-PULLEY.

28. In the lower left viewport (handle 4), use PLINE to draw the outline of the top half of the shaft. Place the left end of the polyline at -2,0. The grid marks are spaced 1/8 inch apart.

29. Use SOLREV to revolve the polyline around its two endpoints. Mesh and shade the shaft, then return it to wireframe representation.

30. Restore the WCS.

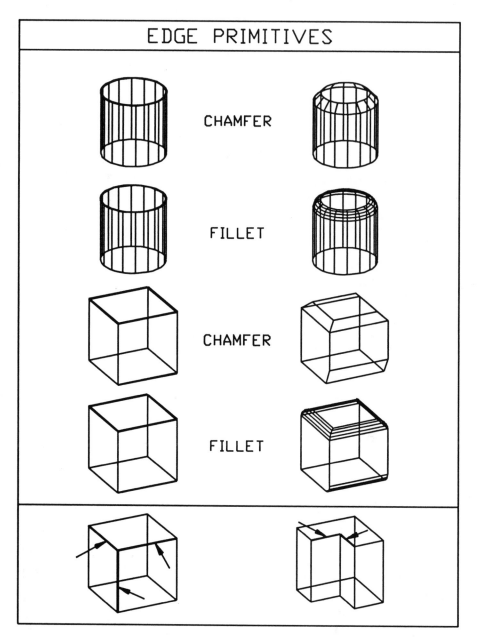

Figure 5-3: Edge primitives.

31. In Paper Space, on BORDER layer, place the "SWEPT PRIMITIVES" text in the title line (.25 high).

32. END your drawing.

Project 5C: Using Edge Primitives

In this project, we will chamfer and fillet a few primitives, as shown on the previous page. We will also note some of the limitations of the SOLCHAM and SOLFILL commands.

1. Start AutoCAD and create a new drawing called PRIM-EDG that uses the SMA.DWG prototype drawing.

2. In Model Space, in the upper right viewport (handle 2),[3] set up a viewpoint of -1,-2,1.

```
MSPACE
```

Pick upper right viewport (handle 2)

```
VPOINT [Enter]
-1,-2,1 [Enter]
```

3. Center the view in each viewport around 0,0,.5 using a 2:1 scale.

```
ZOOM [Enter]
C [Enter]
0,0,.5 [Enter]
2xp [Enter]
```

Do the same in the other viewports.

---

[3] If your handles are different, use the handles you recorded in Project 2A in Chapter 2.

4. If you are using Release 11, load AME.

```
(xload "ame") [Enter]
```

5. Create a cylinder at 0,0 with radius .5 and height 1. Use SOLLIST to list it. It will be listed as a cylinder.

6. Chamfer the top edge of the cylinder with a .125 x 45° chamfer.

```
SOLCHAM [Enter]
```

Pick top circular base. (If necessary, enter N until the proper edge is highlighted before pressing [Enter] to accept the highlighted base.)

Pick the same edge to be chamfered. [Enter]

```
.125 [Enter]
```
```
.125 [Enter]
```

7. Use SOLLIST to list it. A chamfer has been created on an outer edge and then subtracted from the cylinder, so the composite will be listed as a subtraction.

8. Use SOLSEP to separate the composite. Now the top primitive will list as a chamfer, while the original cylinder will list again as a cylinder.

The same shape could be created in a single primitive by revolving a polyline that already has the .125 x 45° chamfer on the top corner.

9. Erase the chamfer, then enter REDRAWALL.

10. Fillet the top edge of the cylinder with a .125 radius.

```
SOLFILL [Enter]
```

Pick the top circular edge. [Enter]

```
.125 [Enter]
```

11. Inspect this composite with the SOLLIST and SOLSEP commands as you did with the chamfer. Then erase both the fillet and the cylinder.

The same shape could be created in a single primitive by revolving a polyline that already has the .125 fillet on the top corner.

12. Create a 1-inch cube at -.5,-.5,0.

13. Chamfer the lower front edge using .125 on the horizontal surface and .25 on the vertical surface.

```
SOLCHAM [Enter]
```

Pick the bottom as the base by picking the bottom-front edge. (If necessary, enter N until the proper edge is highlighted before pressing [Enter] to accept the highlighted base.) Pick the same edge to be chamfered. [Enter]

```
.125 [Enter]
```

```
.25 [Enter]
```

14. Chamfer the top four edges. After selecting the top as the chamfer base, you can pick all four edges before pressing [Enter]. Enter .125 for both chamfer distances. (If you chamfer these top edges individually, or two at a time, the result will be the same. This is not true for fillets, however.)

15. Undo until you are back to the cube.

16. Fillet the bottom front edge with a .125 radius.

17. Fillet the four top edges with a .125 radius. It's important to pick all four edges at once to avoid an improper fillet at the corner. After picking all four in one operation, you may want to try filleting the top four edges in two or more operations, to see what AutoCAD does.

18. In Paper Space, on BORDER layer, place "EDGE PRIMITIVES" in the title line and END the drawing.

Keep in mind that internal as well as external edges can be chamfered or filleted. When an internal edge is chamfered or filleted, the primitive (chamfer or fillet) is unioned with the object being chamfered or filleted rather than subtracted from it.

Some of the edge configurations will not chamfer or fillet properly, as illustrated on the bottom of the drawing. For example, the three converging edges on the cube cannot be chamfered correctly by the SOLCHAM command. However, they can be filleted with the SOLFILL command. The two top edges on the L-shaped extrusion can neither be chamfered nor filleted properly. You can try them in order to see the results produced.

Moving On

You have created a lot of primitives in this chapter. But in real solid modeling you'll rarely be able to complete a solid model by using just one primitive. You'll need to combine primitives in various ways. When you do this, you open up a whole new realm of possibilities.

The next chapter explores three standard methods, known as Boolean operations, used to combine primitives and form composite solids. Learn these operations well; they are at the heart of solid modeling.

PUTTING THE PIECES TOGETHER: BOOLEAN OPERATIONS

6

Putting the Pieces Together:
Boolean Operations

The primitive solids described in Chapter 4 are used as basic building blocks to create more complex solids. These complex solids are called composite solids because they're composed of two or more solids or primitives. They are also called Booleaned solids because Boolean operations are used to create them. The process of building composite solids from primitives using Boolean operations is known as Constructive Solid Geometry (CSG).

Primitive solids can be combined into composite solids using three standard Boolean operations—union, difference and intersection. These operations and the AutoCAD commands that accomplish them are described in this chapter.

Although we focus on 3D solids in this chapter, the three Boolean operations can be applied to regions as well, since a region can be thought of as a solid with a Z-dimension of 0. Regions are discussed more fully in Chapter 8, "Modeling Strategies & Regions."

Since Boolean operations apply more naturally to mathematics (set theory, in particular) than they do to the real world of physical objects, both mathematical and physical examples will be given in the explanations that follow. Venn diagrams with shaded areas are frequently used to illustrate Boolean operations, so they too will be used to illustrate the three operations. Keep in mind, however, that we'll be attempting to illustrate three-dimensional operations using two-dimensional Venn diagrams. The Venn diagrams apply more directly to regions than to 3D solids.

After using the commands described below, if you find that the final display does not reflect the actual state of the solids, redraw the screen (by entering REDRAW or by pressing function key F7 twice).

The Union Operation

Union is the process of *joining* one or more original solids to form a new solid. Union is not the same as addition, as explained below.

One mathematical illustration would be as follows:

> Given set A (1, 2, 3, 4) and set B (7, 8, 9, 10), the union of A and B would be (1, 2, 3, 4, 7, 8, 9, 10).

A second mathematical illustration is as follows:

> We begin with set C (11, 12, 13, 14, 15) and the overlapping set D (14, 15, 16, 17, 18). The union of C and D would be (11, 12, 13, 14, 15, 16, 17, 18). Notice that numbers 14 and 15 appear only once in the union.

In this second illustration, we joined two sets, each with five members; but the resulting set has only eight members. When you union two sets, you're concerned with the individual members of the sets, not with the *size* of the sets. Therefore, the union operation is not like addition. In addition, we would ask, "How large is the first set?" and "How large is the second set?" We would then determine the sum of the two sets. But with union, we're interested in individual members; if a member appears in both sets it's included only once in the unioned set.

In Boolean terms, a union of two sets results in a set that includes every member that was in at least one of the original sets. As applied to solids, a union includes every bit of volume that was included in at least one of the original solids.

Although in the real world your original solids would not overlap, some of your computer solids will overlap (depending on how you define them), causing part of one solid's volume to merge with part of another solid's volume. However, the union operation joins the original solids in such a way that there's no duplication of volume. Therefore, the total resulting volume can be equal to or less than the sum of the volumes in the original solids.

The two Venn diagrams on the following page illustrate joining.

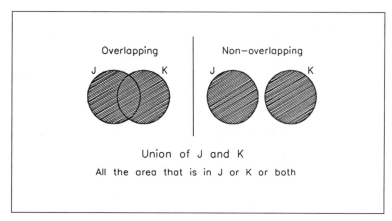

Figure 6-1: Union,
Venn diagram.

A physical illustration of joining would be welding two rectangular blocks of metal together (ignoring the actual welds).

The SOLUNION Command (Alias: UNION or UNI)

SOLUNION is the command that performs the union operation.

SOLUNION prompts you to select objects. You can select more than two solids at once. The solids you select can be overlapping (having common volume), adjacent (no common volume and no gap between) or nonadjacent (with a gap between). Normally, you would not select nonadjacent solids unless you planned to form them into a contiguous unit later using an operation such as union or difference. SOLUNION works in a similar manner on regions.

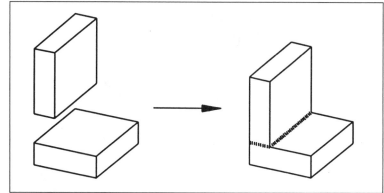

Figure 6-2: Union,
illustrated by a
weldment.

Difference

The Difference, or Subtraction, Operation

Difference is the process of forming a composite solid by starting with one solid and removing from it any volume that it has in common with a second solid. In some cases, several solids will be subtracted from several other solids.

If the entire volume of the second solid is contained within the first solid, the entire second solid is removed. But if only part of the volume of the second solid is contained within the first solid, then only *that* part (where the two solids duplicate each other) is subtracted.

A mathematical illustration of subtraction would be as follows:

Given set E (30, 31, 32, 33, 34, 35) and set F (34, 35, 36), the subtraction of set F from set E would result in the set (30, 31, 32, 33).

Notice that even though we're subtracting a set with three members from a set with six members, the resulting set has four members. As was the case with union, subtraction is not concerned with the size of the sets, but rather with their individual members. In Boolean terms, subtraction includes only those members that belong to the first set but do not belong to the second set. As applied to solids, subtraction includes only those bits of volume contained within the first solid (or group of solids) that are not contained within the second solid (or group of solids).

The two Venn diagrams below illustrate subtraction.

Figure 6-3:
Difference,
Venn diagram.

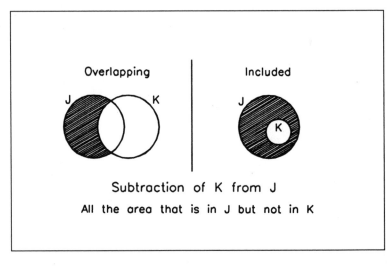

A physical illustration of subtraction is drilling a hole in a block of metal.

Figure 6-4:
Difference,
illustrated by a
drilled hole.

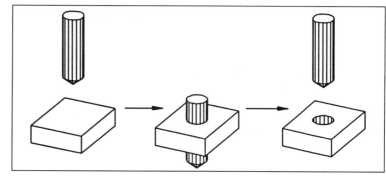

The SOLSUB Command (Alias: SUBTRACT, SUB, DIFFERENCE, DIFF or DIF)

The SOLSUB command performs the difference or subtraction operation.

SOLSUB prompts you to select the source objects (the solids from which you will subtract other solids). You can select one or several solids as source objects. If you select more than one, they're automatically unioned.

Then you're prompted to select the objects to subtract from the source object. Here again, you can select one or several. If you select several, they're automatically unioned before they're subtracted from the source solid.

If any null solids (solids with no volume) are created, the process is aborted. SOLSUB works in a similar manner on regions.

Intersection

The Intersection Operation

Intersection is the process of forming a composite solid from only the volume that is common to (duplicated in) two or more original solids.

One mathematical illustration of intersection would be as follows:

Given set G (51, 52, 53, 54, 55) and set H (53, 54, 55, 56, 57), the intersection of these two sets would result in the set (53, 54, 55).

A second mathematical illustration of intersection would be as follows:

Given set G (51, 52, 53, 54, 55), set H (53, 54, 55, 56, 57) and set I (24, 34, 44, 54, 64), the intersection of these three sets would result in the set (54) because 54 is the only number common to all three original sets.

In Boolean terms, intersection includes only those members that belong to all the original sets. As applied to solids, intersection includes only the bits of volume common to all the original solids. The two Venn diagrams below illustrate intersection.

Figure 6-5:
Intersection, Venn
diagram.

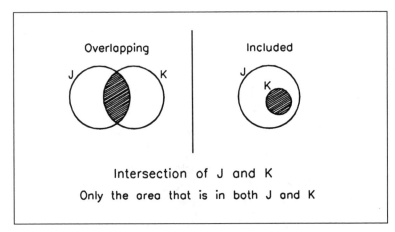

Since only duplicate volume is included, and since we're including duplicate volume rather than removing it, there are no physical illustrations of common volume. Nevertheless, intersection is a very valuable tool in fashioning realistic solid models—as you'll see later in the projects.

The SOLINT Command (Alias: INTERSECT or INT)

The SOLINT command performs the intersection operation. SOLINT prompts you to select objects. If any null solids are created, the process is aborted. SOLINT works in a similar manner on regions.

Separation of Solids

Composite solids can be separated or taken apart. Separation has the effect of undoing the last Boolean operation. Separation can be performed repeatedly until the composite solid is broken down into all the primitives from which it was composed.

The SOLSEP Command (Alias: SEPARATE or SEP)

SOLSEP prompts you to select the composite solid or region you want to take apart. You can select several solids to be disassembled at once. If a primitive is selected, it's ignored. If the composite was created with a series of Boolean operations, the composite is disassembled only one step, not all the way back to the starting primitives.

Cutting Solids

Sometimes you need to cut a solid (primitive or composite), for either construction or display purposes. The SOLCUT command lets you set up a cutting plane and then either slice a solid forming two separate parts, or cut away part of the solid. The cut is always made along a flat plane. You cannot create a three-quarters cutaway view or a staggered section view with SOLCUT.

The SOLCUT command begins by prompting you to select one or more solids.

Then you are prompted to indicate the cutting plane. If you have already established an appropriate UCS before beginning SOLCUT, use the XY option, then accept the default (0,0,0) for the point on the plane.

If you have not already established an appropriate UCS, you can establish one using the same procedures you use with the Baseplane or CP options.

Finally, you are prompted to select one side of the plane or the other and thus indicate which portion will be retained (perhaps by osnapping to a feature on the desired portion). Or, you can enter B to indicate that you want both portions retained.

AutoCAD uses a large box and the intersection and subtraction operations to create these portions. When you retain only one portion of the solid, AutoCAD intersects the original solid with a box that engulfs that portion and has one surface coincident with the cutting plane.

When you retain both portions, AutoCAD duplicates the original solid and the large box, then forms one portion by means of intersection and the other by means of subtraction. Thus, there are several cautions you should observe in the use of the SOLCUT command.

First, in most cases, it is not very efficient to shape a solid by performing a series of cuts.

Second, suppose you cut a composite into two portions, retain both, and then decide you want the two portions re-united into one. You should not union them. If you do, you will end up with more than twice as many primitives as needed. Instead, erase one portion, then separate the other portion with SOLSEP, then erase the large box. (Or, of course, if the cutting operation was recent, you can UNDO back to your original object.)

Third, when you use SOLCUT on a composite that has primitives wholly on the discarded side of the cutting plane (or wholly on either side of the plane when retaining both portions), those primitives will have no function in the new composite. To simplify your model you can delete them with the SOLCHP command.

The CSG Tree

Each composite solid can be thought of as being assembled according to its CSG tree. Understanding a little about the CSG tree will help you assemble and disassemble composite solids and interpret the SOLLIST command, which can list a composite solid's CSG tree.

Each composite solid is dependent not only on the primitives it includes but upon which Boolean operations were applied to which primitive and in which order. The CSG tree is a record of the Boolean operations, the primitives used in each of the operations and the order of the operations. The tree is actually upside down, with the single, finished solid at the top and all its various "pieces" at the bottom. (Just as it's preferable to think of DOS's "Tree-Structured Directories" as root structures, it's also preferable to think of a CSG tree as a root structure.)

For example, the CSG tree for the simplified corner bracket shown on the top of the following page begins at the lowest level with two solid boxes and two cylinders. At the middle level, the two boxes are joined, and the two cylinders are joined. At the top level, the cylinders are subtracted from the boxes.

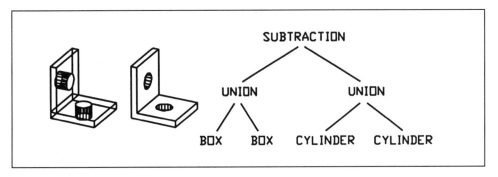

Figure 6-6: One possible CSG tree for the corner bracket.

This same composite solid could be constructed differently, as illustrated in the CSG tree below. Here, the lowest level is the same because the same primitives are used to start with, but the process is slightly different. At the middle level, one cylinder is subtracted from one box, and the other cylinder from the other box. At the top level, the two boxes-with-holes are joined. The result is the same, but the CSG tree is different.

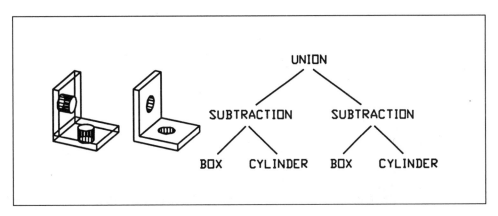

Figure 6-7: Alternate CSG tree for the corner bracket.

Even though many of the commands used to compose solids allow you to select more than two solids at once, as far as the CSG tree is concerned each fork has only two branches. In other words, the tree is structured as though solids are always operated on in pairs. For this reason, the simple operation of joining four primitives (selecting all four primitives at one time) would result in the CSG tree with three levels shown on the next page. AME balances the tree automatically.

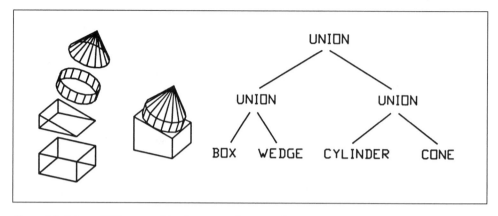

Figure 6-8: Balanced CSG tree resulting from one union operation.

On the other hand, if two of the primitives were joined, then the resulting solid joined to a third primitive, then the resulting solid joined to a fourth primitive, the CSG tree would look like this.

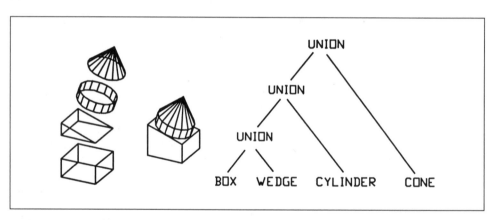

Figure 6-9: Unbalanced CSG tree resulting from three union operations.

The SOLPURGE Command

Solid modeling files tend to be quite large, and solids that are manipulated in the drawing editor require a lot of memory. The SOLPURGE command can be used on both solids and regions to help reduce the amount of memory and disk space required.

When prompted, enter

> **E** (for Erased) To recover memory still occupied by secondary entities associated with a solid you have erased. If a large number of solids has been erased, this can take a while.

> **M** To free AME memory. Then enter A to free memory for all solids, or S to select certain solids. Information about each solid is retained in AutoCAD memory so AME can reconstruct the information it needs when the solid must be manipulated. This reconstruction can take time. When you finish working with one solid or a group of related solids, you can use this option to speed up AME's performance in working on the next solid(s).

> **B** To purge Bfile information and reduce your drawing size.

> **P** To purge mesh information on certain solids, then select the solids. If a solid was in mesh representation when selected for this option, it is returned to wireframe representation.

> **2** To purge the 2D tree (for regions only). This will ensure that the CSG tree structure of a composite region is in the simplest form. If a number of Boolean operations have been performed on the region, its CSG tree can probably be simplified considerably. This simplified tree makes subsequent editing of the region easier.

If you want to conserve disk space, you can also END the drawing, load it into the drawing editor again, then END again. Doing this once or twice can significantly reduce the size of the drawing file.

Moving On

We've discussed the three Boolean operations—union, difference and intersection—and the AutoCAD commands that perform these operations. Now it's time to use these commands.

The next chapter begins with a unique project that allows you to test your understanding of Boolean operations. Then the following projects create several simple but realistic models. Each exercise emphasizes different aspects of modeling and Boolean operations.

PROJECTS: BOOLEAN OPERATIONS

7

Projects: Boolean Operations

This chapter presents projects that use the Boolean operations explained in Chapter 6. We'll start with a project that uses some of the simpler primitives, such as the box, wedge and cylinder, and end with one that involves more flexible primitives such as extrusions and revolutions.

Like the projects in Chapter 2, "Projects: Setup & Overview," these contain general instructions for each step. However, keystroke instructions are omitted for simple 2D commands and for 3D commands after they've been introduced and used a few times.

Project 7A: Predicting the Results of Boolean Operations

This project is not like the others. It's a sketching project designed to reinforce what you learned about the Boolean operations described in the previous chapter.

The following figure illustrates four groups of solids, each with three views: front, oblique (right-front-top) and right-side. Sketch the results of each Boolean operation listed below using the view(s) needed to make the sketch clear. After you've completed your sketches, create groups of solids similar to those pictured. Perform each operation so you can compare your sketches with the actual results. If you use the SMA.DWG prototype drawing, you'll already have the views you need.

Sketch the Boolean operations listed in the following groups:

Wedge & Cylinder

Union of the wedge and cylinder.
Subtraction of the cylinder from the wedge.
Subtraction of the wedge from the cylinder.
Intersection of the wedge and cylinder.

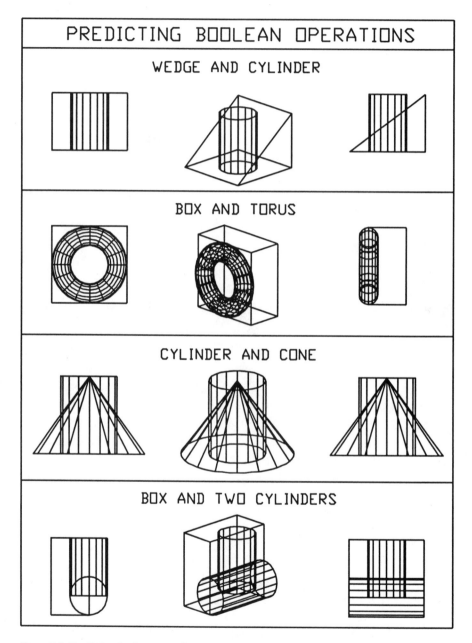

Figure 7-1: Predicting Boolean operations.

Box & Torus

Union of the box and torus.
Subtraction of the torus from the box.
Subtraction of the box from the torus.
Intersection of the box and torus.

Cylinder & Cone

Union of the cylinder and cone.
Subtraction of the cylinder from the cone.
Subtraction of the cone from the cylinder.
Intersection of the cylinder and cone.

Box & Two Cylinders

Union of the two cylinders (ignore the box).
Subtraction of the horizontal cylinder from the vertical cylinder (ignore the box).
Subtraction of the box and horizontal cylinder from the vertical cylinder.
Intersection of the box and both cylinders.

Project 7B: Skully Model

In this project, we'll create a solid model of the Skully, as shown on the next page.

The Skully uses the prototype drawing created in Project 2A. In making the Skully, we'll use all three Boolean operations. We'll model the Skully but will not attempt to extract 2D views for dimensioning. (See color illustrations C-3, C-4 and C-5 on pages 168-69).

Remember that you can use the LIST command or the SOLLIST command after any step to check on the solids.

I. Create a new drawing called SKULLY that uses SMA as a prototype.

At AutoCAD's Main Menu in Release 11, enter 1 then SKULLY=SMA

In Release 12, pick "New" from the FILE pull-down menu (or enter NEW at the Command prompt). Use SMA as a prototype drawing.

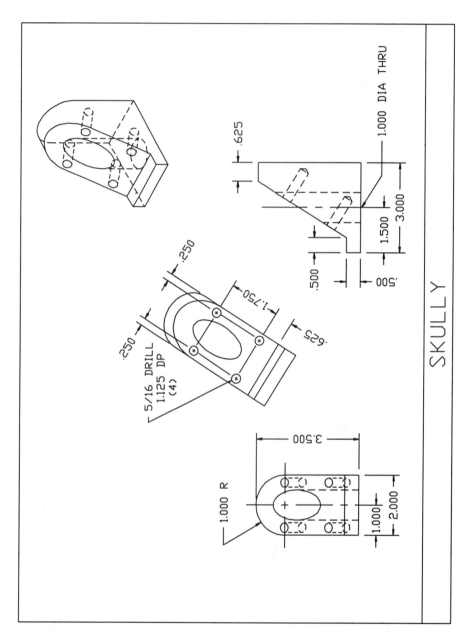

Figure 7-2: Skully, dimensioned.

2. Switch to Paper Space and make BORDER layer current.

```
PSPACE [Enter]
LAYER [Enter]
S [Enter]
BORDER  [Enter][Enter]
```

3. Use the TEXT command to place "SKULLY" in the title line (.25 high).

4. Switch to Model Space and make viewport 2[1] (upper right) current.

```
MSPACE [Enter]
```

Pick the upper right viewport (handle 2).

In order to get the largest possible view of the Skully in each viewport, we center the view and use 3/4 scale in each viewport. Based on the dimensions of the Skully and the fact that we'll place its lower left corner at 0,0,0, the center of each viewport should be at 1,1.5,1.5.

5. Place the point 1,1.5,1.5 at the center of viewport 2, and scale the viewport at 3/4.

```
ZOOM [Enter]
C [Enter]
1,1.5,1.5 [Enter]
.75xp [Enter]
```

6. Pick each of the other viewports, and center the view using the same procedure.

---

[1] If your handles are different, use the handles you recorded in Project 2A in Chapter 2.

First we'll create a shallow box for the bottom part of the Skully.

7. In Release 11, load AME.

    ```
    (xload "ame") [Enter]
    ```

    In Release 11, pick "AME" then "Load AME" from either the sidebar menu or the pull-down menu.

    AME is loaded automatically in Release 12 when you first enter an AME command either at the Command prompt or from the "Model" pull-down menu.

8. Make the upper right viewport current. Also make layer SM current.

    Pick the upper right viewport (handle 2).

    ```
    LAYER [Enter]
    S [Enter]
    SM [Enter][Enter]
    ```

9. Starting at 0,0,0, create a box that is 2 x 3 x .5.

    ```
    SOLBOX [Enter]
    0,0,0 [Enter]
    L [Enter]
    2 [Enter]
    3 [Enter]
    .5 [Enter]
    ```

Figure 7-3: Shallow
box for the bottom
of the Skully.

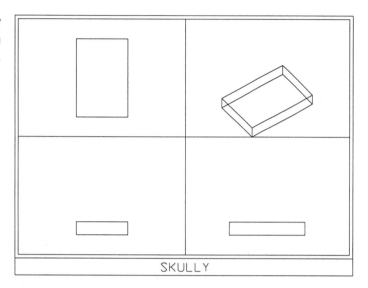

SKULLY

To create the rounded top of the Skully, we'll create a tall box and a cylinder, then join them.

10. Starting at 0,.5,.5, create a box that is 2 x 2.5 x 2.

```
SOLBOX [Enter]
0,.5,.5 [Enter]
L [Enter]
2 [Enter]
2.5 [Enter]
2 [Enter]
```

Figure 7-4: Tall box and cylinder for the body of the Skully.

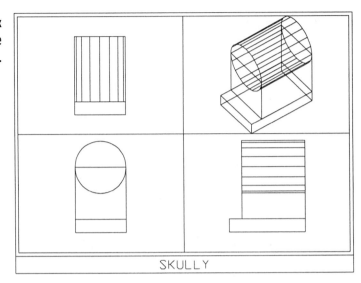

SKULLY

11. Create a 1-inch radius cylinder, centered at 1,.5,2.5, that extends 2.5 in the Y direction.

```
SOLCYL [Enter]
1,.5,2.5 [Enter]
1 [Enter]
C [Enter]
@0,2.5 [Enter]
```

12. Join the tall box and the cylinder.

```
SOLUNION [Enter]
```

Pick the tall box and the cylinder.

```
[Enter]
```

NOTE: Project 7B-Alternate illustrates another way to complete some of the remaining steps (using the SOLCUT command to create the slanted surface and the Baseplane option to locate the cylinder and cone for the drilled holes). Since project 7B-Alternate starts with the same 12 steps you have just completed, you can save yourself some work by saving your drawing now under the name SKULLY-A.

In order to create the slanted surface, we will create a wedge. Creating the wedge will be a two-step procedure, since we'll have to create it and then rotate it into position. (We could instead rotate the UCS first. Either procedure is about the same amount of work.)

13. Starting at 0,3,.5, create a wedge that is 2.5 x 2 x 4.

```
SOLWEDGE [Enter]
0,3,.5 [Enter]
L [Enter]
2.5 [Enter]
2 [Enter]
4 [Enter]
```

14. Rotate the wedge -90° around its own startpoint.

```
ROTATE [Enter]
L [Enter][Enter]
0,3 [Enter]
-90 [Enter]
```

Figure 7-5: Wedge
before rotation.

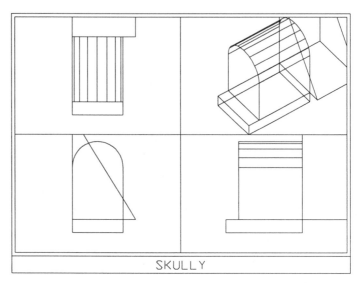

SKULLY

15. Intersect the box-cylinder composite and the wedge.

SOLINT [Enter]

Pick the box-cylinder composite and the wedge.

[Enter]

Of course, it would have been possible to create this slanted surface by subtracting a different wedge from the box-cylinder composite. Either procedure works well.

16. Union this new composite with the shallow base created earlier.

SOLUNION [Enter]

Pick the base and the composite.

[Enter]

At this point, we should check the appearance of our model by meshing it and then using the HIDE and/or SHADE command.

17. Mesh the solid.

```
SOLMESH [Enter]
```

Pick the solid.

```
[Enter]
HIDE [Enter]
SHADE [Enter]
```

18. Return the solid to wireframe representation.

```
REGEN [Enter]
SOLWIRE [Enter]
```

Pick the solid.

```
[Enter]
```

Next we create the large center hole and subtract this hole from the composite.

19. At 1,1.5, create a 1-inch diameter cylinder that is 3.5 inches tall.

```
SOLCYL [Enter]
1,1.5 [Enter]
D [Enter]
1 [Enter]
3.5 [Enter]
```

20. Subtract the cylinder from the composite.

```
SOLSUB [Enter]
```

Pick the composite.

```
[Enter]
```

Pick the cylinder.

```
[Enter]
```

Figure 7-6: Skully, main body, hidden edges removed in isometric view.

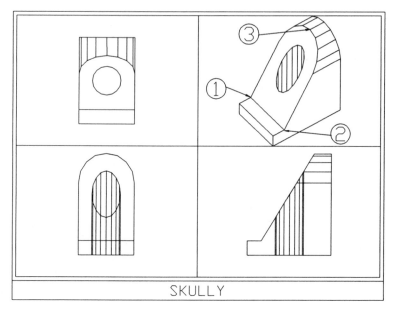

Finally, we create the four drilled holes on the slanted surface.

21. Set up and save a UCS on the slanted face of the Skully, using the 3point option and osnap to locate the 3 points.

```
UCS [Enter]
3 [Enter]
ENDP [Enter]
```

Pick point 1.

```
ENDP [Enter]
```

Pick point 2.

```
ENDP [Enter]
```

Pick point 3.

```
UCS [Enter]
S [Enter]
SLANT [Enter]
```

22. Create a 5/16-inch diameter cylinder at .25,.625 that extends 1.125 in the negative Z direction.

SOLCYL [Enter]

.25,.625 [Enter]

D [Enter]

5/16 [Enter]

-1.125 [Enter]

23. In the upper right viewport (handle 2), zoom in tightly (ZOOM Window) on the bottom end of the cylinder, then REGEN the viewport.

24. To represent the drill point, create a .1-inch-high cone at the end of the cylinder. Use osnap to attach this cone to the center of the cylinder.

SOLCONE [Enter]

CEN [Enter]

Pick bottom end of the cylinder.

D [Enter]

5/16 [Enter]

-.1 [Enter]

25. Join the cylinder and the cone. You can pick them individually with the pickbox or jointly with a crossing window. If you use a crossing window, be careful not to include anything other than the cylinder and the cone.

SOLUNION [Enter]

Pick the cone and the cylinder.

[Enter]

26. Return to the previous display (ZOOM Previous).

27. Array the drilled hole.

> ARRAY [Enter]
>
> Pick the drilled hole.
>
> [Enter]
>
> R [Enter]
>
> 2 [Enter]
>
> 2 [Enter]
>
> 1.75 [Enter]
>
> 1.5 [Enter]

28. Return to WCS.

29. Subtract the four drilled holes from the main composite.

> SOLSUB [Enter]
>
> Pick the slanted composite.
>
> [Enter]
>
> Pick the four drilled holes.
>
> [Enter]
>
> (If the drilled holes are hard to pick, try windowing the entire solid.)

30. Check the appearance by meshing the composite, then hiding and/or shading it.

This completes the modeling of the Skully. We will not attempt to extract 2D views or set up auxiliary views until a later project.

31. Return the solid to wireframe representation, and SAVE your drawing.

Project 7B-Alternate: Another Way to Model the Skully

In this project we complete the Skully using two methods that differ from the ones we used in Project 7B. We create the slanted surface with the SOLCUT command, and we use the Baseplane option to locate the cylinder and cone that form the four drilled holes.

The first 12 steps are identical to the first 12 steps of Project 7B.

If you did as we suggested in Project 7B, you will have a drawing called SKULLY-A that you can edit and then begin with step 13 below. Make sure that you are in Model Space, layer SM is current, the upper right viewport is current and AME is loaded.

13. Use the SOLCUT command to create a cutting plane through the composite (the tall box and cylinder). The cutting plane will be at an angle of 58 degrees above horizontal, so its Z-normal (vector perpendicular to the plane) will be at 32 degrees below horizontal. Retain only the back portion.

    SOLCUT [Enter]

    Pick the composite (tall box and cylinder). [Enter]

    Z [Enter]

    Osnap to point 1 or 2 in Figure 7-6 (or use coordinates 0,.5,.5).

    @1<90<-32 [Enter]

    Osnap to a point on the back portion (right-rear) of the composite (or enter 0,10).

14. Union this cut composite with the shallow base.

15. Mesh the solid, and hide or shade it to check its appearance. Then return it to wireframe.

Next we will create the large center hole and subtract this hole from the composite.

16. At 1,1.5 create a 1-inch diameter cylinder that is 3.5 inches tall.

17. Subtract the cylinder from the composite.

Finally, we create the four drilled holes on the slanted surface.

18. Create a 5/16-inch diameter cylinder at .25,.625 that extends 1.125 in the negative Z direction. (Use the Baseplane option.)

```
SOLCYL [Enter]

B [Enter]
```

Pick the three points shown in Figure 7-6: [Enter]

```
.25,.625 [Enter]

D [Enter]

5/16 [Enter]

-1.125 [Enter]
```

19. In the upper right viewport, zoom in tightly on the bottom end of the cylinder, then REGEN the viewport.

20. To represent the drill point, create a .1-inch-high cone at the end of the cylinder. (Use the Baseplane option.)

```
SOLCONE [Enter]

B [Enter]

E [Enter]
```

Pick the cylinder's bottom circle.

```
0,0 [Enter]

D [Enter]

5/16 [Enter]

.1 [Enter]
```

21. Union the cylinder and the cone.

22. Return to the previous display (ZOOM Previous).

23. Set up a UCS on the slanted surface (use the 3point option) and array the drilled hole to its three other locations. The array will have 1.75 spacing between rows and 1.5 between columns.

24. Return to WCS.

25. Complete the Skully by subtracting the four drilled holes from the main composite.

26. You may also want to check the appearance of the Skully by meshing it and hiding or shading it. Then return the solid to wireframe and SAVE your drawing.

NOTE: Although the Baseplane option is convenient in certain situations, the above procedure shows why it is more efficient to plan ahead and set up a UCS. We had to establish this slanted plane once during step 20 and again during step 23. And if we want to go back to this plane to check distances, add other features or set up a view for dimensioning, we will have to establish the plane more than twice. So it is simpler in the long run to set up a UCS ahead of time and save it under an appropriate name to be restored when needed, as we did in Project 7B.

Project 7C: Cover Plate Model

In Chapter 6, "Putting the Pieces Together: Boolean Operations," I mentioned that there are no real-world examples illustrating the Boolean operation of intersection, yet intersection is very useful in creating solid models. This project demonstrates the usefulness of intersection. In this project, we create a model of the Cover Plate, as shown. We'll use the SMA prototype drawing. (See color illustration C-6 on page 169)

Remember that you can use the LIST command or the SOLLIST command after any step to check on the solids.

1. Create a new drawing called COVER that uses SMA as a prototype.

2. Make sure you're in Paper Space, on BORDER layer.
    ```
    PSPACE [Enter]
    LAYER [Enter]
    S [Enter]
    BORDER [Enter][Enter]
    ```

3. Place the text "COVER" in the title line (.25 high).

    We'll have only three views of the Cover—two orthographic and one isometric. So we'll erase one of the viewports and enlarge two of the other viewports.

4. With ortho on, stretch the middle horizontal edges of the viewports (the edges that separate the two top viewports from the bottom two) up to within 1.5 inch of the top border. (Refer to Figure 7-8.)

5. Erase the upper right viewport. Then REDRAW the screen.

6. Switch to Model Space. Make the lower right viewport (handle 5)[2] current, and establish an isometric viewpoint of 1,-1,1. Make sure you're in WCS.
    ```
    MSPACE [Enter]
    ```

---

[2] If your handles are different, use the handles you recorded in Project 2A in Chapter 2.

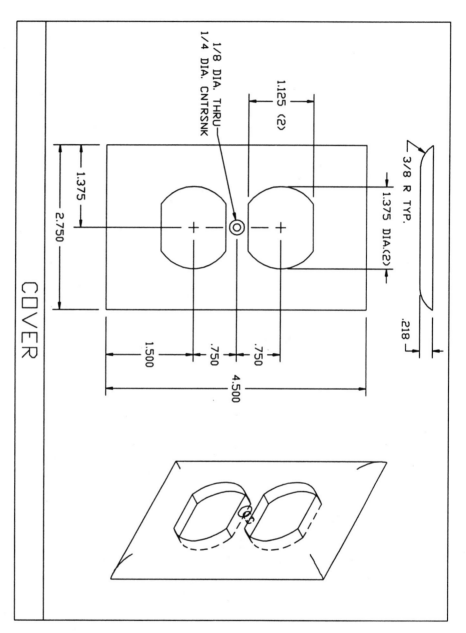

Figure 7-7: Cover dimensioned.

Pick the lower right viewport (handle 5).

```
VPOINT [Enter]
1,-1,1 [Enter]
UCS [Enter][Enter]
```

The center of the *bottom edge* of the plate will be placed at 0,0,0. Since the overall height is 4.5, and this height will be oriented in the Z-direction, the center of the model will end up at 0,0,2.25. Center the view in each viewport around this point and make each viewport full scale.

7. Center this viewport around 0,0,2.25, full scale, and save the view under the name "ISO."

```
ZOOM [Enter]
C [Enter]
0,0,2.25 [Enter]
1xp [Enter]
VIEW [Enter]
S [Enter]
ISO [Enter]
```

8. Center the views in the other viewports using the same center and the same Paper Space ratio.

To create the main body of the cover, we'll create two polylines, extrude them into solids, then intersect them. (The polylines will be constructed first as lines and arcs, then joined into a polyline.)

9. Make layer SM current.

10. In the upper left viewport (handle 3), create the straight lines that will make up part of the first polyline.

Pick the upper left viewport (handle 3).

```
LINE [Enter]
```

```
-1.375,0 [Enter]
1.375,0 [Enter][Enter]
LINE [Enter]
-1.0344,-.218 [Enter]
1.0344,-.218 [Enter][Enter]
```

11. Create the arcs that will join the ends of the straight lines.

```
ARC [Enter]
ENDP [Enter]
```

Pick the right end of the lower line.

```
E [Enter]
ENDP [Enter]
```

Pick the right end of the upper line.

```
D [Enter]
0 [Enter]
ARC [Enter]
ENDP [Enter]
```

Pick the left end of the lower line.

```
E [Enter]
ENDP [Enter]
```

Pick the left end of the upper line.

```
D [Enter]
180 [Enter]
```

12. Convert these two lines and two arcs into a polyline.

```
PEDIT [Enter]
```

Pick the upper line.

```
Y [Enter]
```

J [Enter]

Pick the other line and the two arcs.

[Enter]

(AutoCAD should report, "3 segments added to polyline")

X [Enter]

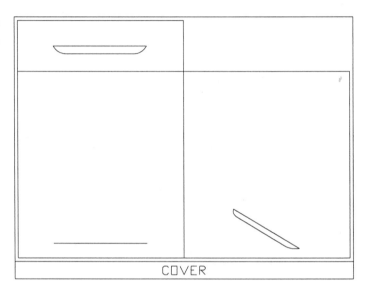

Figure 7-8: Polyline before extrusion.

COVER

13. Load AME (Release 11 only).

(xload "ame") [Enter]

14. Extrude the solid up 4.5 in the Z direction.

SOLEXT [Enter]

Pick the polyline.

[Enter]

4.5 [Enter]

0 [Enter]

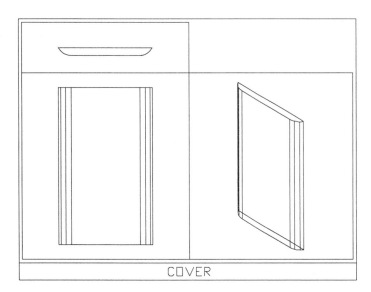

Figure 7-9:
Extrusion of
polyline.

CODVER

15. Move this solid out of the way to make room to create another extrusion.

```
MOVE [Enter]
L [Enter][Enter]
0,-1 [Enter][Enter]
```

Now we need to create the second polyline and extrusion, but we'll have to use a vertical UCS. The prototype drawing already has a UCS called "RIGHT" that will work fine.

16. Make the lower right viewport (handle 5) current.

17. Set the VPOINT at 1,0,0.

```
VPOINT [Enter]
1,0,0 [Enter]
```

18. Center the view in this viewport using the same center and Paper Space ratio as before.

19. Restore the UCS called "RIGHT."

```
UCS [Enter]
R [Enter]
RIGHT [Enter]
```

20. Draw a line from 0,0 to 0,4.5.

21. Draw another line from -.218,.3406 to -.218,4.1594.

22. Connect these lines with arcs using a procedure similar to the one in step 11.

23. Convert these two lines and two arcs into a polyline.

24. Restore the "ISO" view that was saved earlier.

```
VIEW [Enter]
R [Enter]
ISO [Enter]
```

25. Move this polyline 1.375 in the negative Z direction.

26. Extrude the polyline 2.75 in the Z direction (no taper).

Figure 7-10: Second
extrusion.

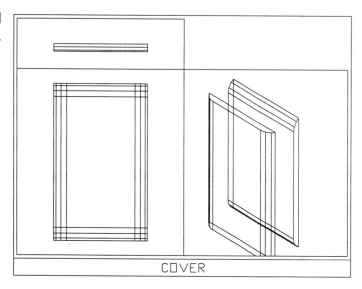

COVER

27. Return to WCS.

28. Move the first extruded solid back into position.

> MOVE [Enter]
>
> Pick the first solid.
>
> [Enter]
>
> 0,1 [Enter][Enter]

29. Intersect these two solids. You can pick them with a crossing window or separately, perhaps in the lower left viewport (handle 4).

> SOLINT [Enter]
>
> Pick both solids.
>
> [Enter]

Now we need to form the solid that will be used later to form the two receptacle holes. This solid will be formed from the intersection of a cylinder and a box.

30. Restore the UCS called "FRONT."

31. Create a cylinder at 0,1.5 with a diameter of 1.375 and a height of .25.

```
SOLCYL [Enter]
0,1.5 [Enter]
D [Enter]
1.375 [Enter]
.25 [Enter]
```

32. Create the box that will be intersected with this cylinder. It must be 1.125 high.

```
SOLBOX [Enter]
C [Enter]
0,1.5,.125 [Enter]
L [Enter]
2 [Enter]
1.125 [Enter]
.25 [Enter]
```

33. Intersect the cylinder and the box.

Figure 7-11: Box and cylinder before intersection.

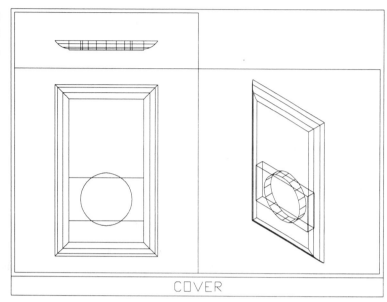

34. Copy this new composite up 1.5 in the Y direction.

35. Subtract both receptacle solids from the main body to form the receptacle holes.

Finally, we must create the countersunk hole in the middle of the cover.

36. Create a cylinder at 0,2.25 that is .125 diameter and .218 high.

37. Zoom in and create a cone at 0,2.25,.218 that is .25 diameter and .125 high in the negative Z direction.

38. Union the cylinder and the cone.

39. Zoom previous and return to WCS.

40. Subtract the cylinder-cone composite from the main solid.

41. Mesh the solid and check its appearance with HIDE and/or SHADE.

42. Return the solid to wireframe representation.

43. Return to Paper Space and SAVE your drawing.

Project 7D: SMB.DWG, B-size Prototype Drawing

We will create a B-size prototype from the A-size prototype we created in Project 2A. SMB.DWG is also available on the *Solid Modeling With AutoCAD* companion diskette.

1. Create a new drawing called SMB that uses SMA as a prototype.

2. Make sure you are in Paper Space. (If not, enter PSPACE.)

Increase the limits to 16 x 10 then set up a view suitable for stretching the border and viewports.

3. Reset the limits, leaving the lower left corner at 0,0 but changing the upper right corner to 16,10.

4. ZOOM All, then ZOOM .8x.

5. Set snap at .25 and turn ortho on. (This will make it easier to do some of the following stretching operations without having to type in all the numbers listed below.)

We use four stretching operations to enlarge both the border and the viewports.

6. Stretch the right vertical edge of the border and the right vertical edges of the two right viewports to the right by 6 inches.

```
STRETCH [Enter]

C [Enter]

9,-1 [Enter]

11,8 [Enter][Enter]

0,0 [Enter]

6,0 [Enter]
```

Figure 7-12:
Stretching right
vertical edges.

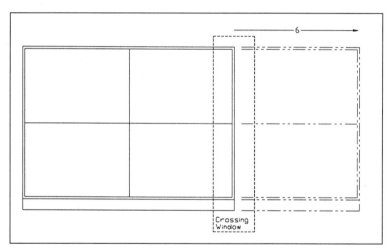

7. Stretch the middle vertical edges of the four viewports to the right by 3 inches.

```
STRETCH [Enter]

C [Enter]

4,-1 [Enter]

6,8 [Enter][Enter]

0,0 [Enter]

3,0 [Enter]
```

Figure 7-13:
Stretching middle
vertical edges.

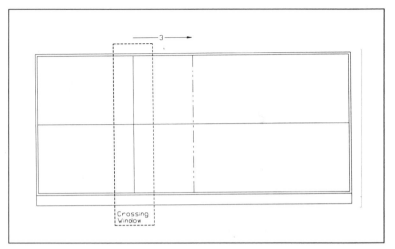

8. Stretch the top horizontal edge of the border and the top horizontal edges of the two top viewports up by 2.5 inches.

9. Stretch the middle horizontal edges of the four viewports up by 1.25 inches.

10. ZOOM All.

11. In Model Space, use ZOOM Center to center the view in each viewport around 2,2,1, using full scale (1xp). Then make the upper right viewport current.

12. SAVE the drawing.

This completes the SMB prototype drawing. We can now use it when we model the Level Body.

Project 7E: Level Body Model

Our model of the Level Body, as shown, will be placed on the SMB proto-type drawing created in Project 7D. (See color illustration C-7 on page 170.)

Remember that you can use the LIST command or the SOLLIST command after any step to check on the solids.

1. Begin a new drawing called LEVEL using SMB for the prototype.

The drawing will have three orthographic views of the level body and one oblique (nearly isometric) view in the upper right corner. Since both top and front views will show the full length of the level but the right view will show an end view, we need to adjust the size of the four viewports.

2. Make sure you are in Paper Space, on BORDER layer.

3. Stretch the middle vertical edges of the four viewports to the right by 3 inches.

```
STRETCH [Enter]
C [Enter]
7,3 [Enter]
9,8 [Enter][Enter]
0,0 [Enter]
3,0 [Enter]
```

4. Place the text "LEVEL BODY" in the title line (height .25).

We begin building the main body of the level by drawing a polyline in the upper left viewport (handle 3)[3] then extruding it to form a solid. The bottom of the level will be centered at 0,0,0 so we center all the views

---

[3] If your handles are different, use the handles you recorded in Project 2A in Chapter 2.

around 0,0,.5. The three orthogonal views will be full scale, but the isometric view will be 3/4 scale.

5. Switch to Model Space and make the upper left viewport current.

    ```
    MSPACE [Enter]
    ```

    Pick upper left viewport (handle 3).

6. Set up an appropriate view that is centered on 0,0,.5 and is full scale.

    ```
    ZOOM [Enter]
    C [Enter]
    0,0,.5 [Enter]
    1xp [Enter]
    ```

7. Center views in the lower left (handle 4), lower right (handle 5) and upper
    right (handle 2) viewports. In 4 and 5, use the same center and scale as in
    3. In 2, set the viewpoint at 6,-6,5; then center the view using the same
    center as the other viewports but with a scale of .75xp.

8. Return to the upper left viewport (handle 3), make layer SM current and
    draw a polyline representing the outline of the level body. To avoid enter-
    ing numbers, set the SNAP to .125 and use the pointer.

    Pick upper left viewport (handle 3).

    ```
    LAYER [Enter]
    S [Enter]
    SM [Enter][Enter]
    PLINE [Enter]
    -3.625,.375 [Enter]
    3.625,.375 [Enter]
    A [Enter]
    ```

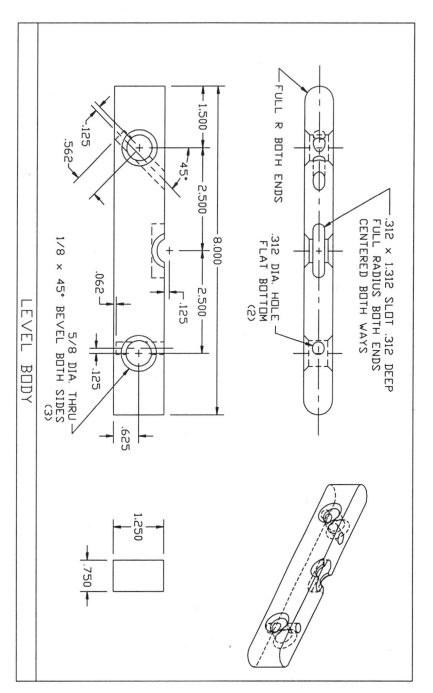

Figure 7-14: Level, dimensioned.

```
3.625,-.375 [Enter]
L [Enter]
-3.625,-.375 [Enter]
A [Enter]
CL [Enter]
```

9. Load AME (Release 11 only).

```
(xload "ame") [Enter]
```

Figure 7-15: Polyline for main body, before extrusion.

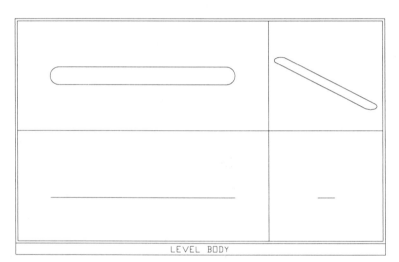

```
LEVEL BODY
```

10. Extrude the polyline into a solid that's 1.25 high.

```
SOLEXT [Enter]
```
Pick the polyline.
```
[Enter]
1.25 [Enter]
0 [Enter]
```

11. Change the color of the solid to green.

```
CHPROP [Enter]
L [Enter][Enter]
```

```
C [Enter]
3 [Enter][Enter]
```

The level has three viewing holes for the three bubbles that will be added later during assembly. These viewing holes are 5/8-inch diameter and have a 1/8-inch bevel on each side (to increase visibility of the bubble). We will create a viewing hole solid by revolving a polyline around the Y axis, then place copies at all three locations, then subtract them from the main body.

12. In the upper left viewport (handle 3) zoom up on the center of the solid.

13. Draw a polyline representing the shape of the viewing hole. To avoid entering all the numbers, reset the SNAP to .0625 and use the pointer.

```
PLINE [Enter]
0,-.375 [Enter]
@.4375,0 [Enter]
@-.125,.125 [Enter]
@0,.5 [Enter]
@.125,.125 [Enter]
@-.4375,0 [Enter][Enter]
```

Figure 7-16:
Polyline for viewing hole, before revolution.

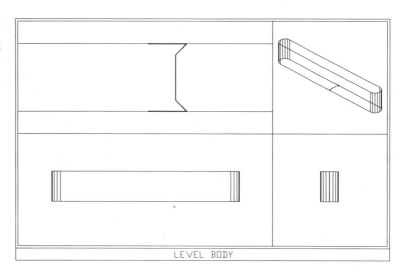

14. Revolve this polyline around the Y axis to create the viewing hole solid.

    SOLREV [Enter]

    Pick polyline.

    [Enter]

    Y [Enter][Enter] (accept "full circle")

15. ZOOM back to a full view (ZOOM Previous).

16. Move the viewing hole solid to the top location.

    MOVE [Enter]

    L [Enter][Enter]

    0,0,1.375 [Enter][Enter]

17. Copy the top viewing hole solid to the left position.

    COPY [Enter]

    L [Enter][Enter]

    -2.5,0,-.75 [Enter][Enter]

Figure 7-17: Level body with viewing hole solids in position.

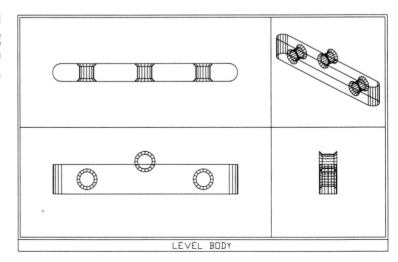

LEVEL BODY

18. Copy the top viewing hole solid to the right position.

19. Subtract the three viewing hole solids from the main body.

> SOLSUB [Enter]

> Pick the main body.

> [Enter]

> Pick the 3 viewing hole solids.

> [Enter]

Before we create any more objects, let's check the appearance of the level so far.

20. Switch to Paper Space, zoom in tightly on the level in the upper right viewport (handle 2), switch back to Model Space and select viewport 2 if it's not already current.

21. Mesh the solid.

> SOLMESH [Enter]

> Pick the solid.

> [Enter]

> HIDE [Enter]

> SHADE [Enter]

22. Return the solid to wireframe representation.

> REGEN [Enter]

> SOLWIRE [Enter]

> Pick the solid.

> [Enter]

23. Switch to Paper Space, ZOOM All then switch back to Model Space.

Figure 7-18:
Level body.

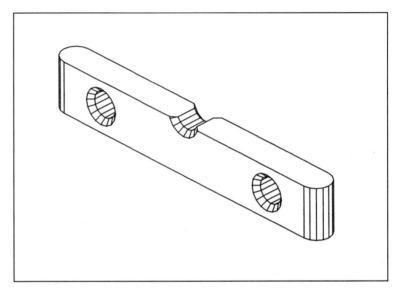

Now we create the blind holes in which the bubbles will be assembled.

24. In the upper left viewport (handle 3), create a .312 cylinder for the right blind hole.

Pick upper left viewport (handle 3).

```
SOLCYL [Enter]
2.375,0,.0625 [Enter]
D [Enter]
.312 [Enter]
1.5 [Enter]
```

25. Set up and save an appropriate UCS, then create a 5/16-inch cylinder for the left blind hole.

```
UCS [Enter]
O [Enter]
-2.5,0,.625 [Enter]
```

```
UCS [Enter]
Y [Enter]
45 [Enter]
UCS [Enter]
S [Enter]
SLANT [Enter]
SOLCYL [Enter]
.125,0,-.5625 [Enter]
D [Enter]
.312 [Enter]
2 [Enter]
```

26. Return to WCS and zoom in on the center of the level.

27. Create the milled slot for the top bubble.
```
PLINE [Enter]
-.5,.156,1.25 [Enter]
@1,0 [Enter]
A [Enter]
@0,-.312 [Enter]
L [Enter]
@-1,0 [Enter]
A [Enter]
CL [Enter]
SOLEXT [Enter]
L [Enter][Enter]
-.312 [Enter]
0 [Enter]
```

28. ZOOM Previous, pick the lower left viewport (handle 4), and change the two holes and the slot to red.

29. Subtract the two holes and the slot from the main body.

30. Mesh the solid and check appearance with HIDE and/or SHADE.

31. Return the solid to wireframe representation and SAVE your drawing.

Moving On

Using procedures similar to those illustrated in these projects, you can model a seemingly unlimited number of different objects. Nevertheless, everyone encounters objects that puzzle them. In some cases, you may wonder how the object can be modeled at all. In other cases, you may see two or more ways to model it and wonder which is the most efficient.

The next chapter gives you some suggestions for modeling types of objects you haven't worked with yet. It also provides a few basic guidelines for deciding which of two modeling approaches is best.

Sample Color Illustrations

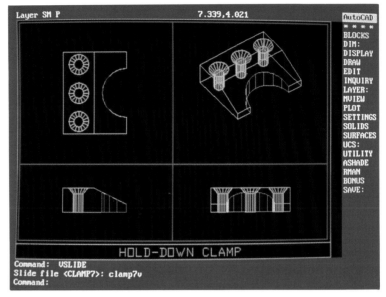

C-1: Hold-Down Clamp, wireframe (from Chapter 2).

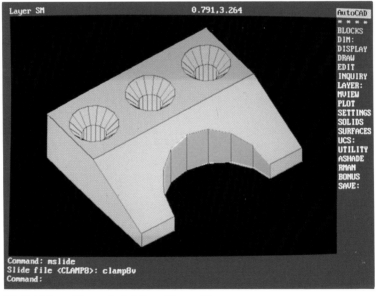

C-2: Hold-Down Clamp, shaded (from Chapter 2).

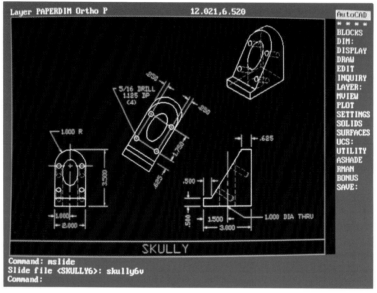

C-3: Skully, dimensioned (from Chapter 7).

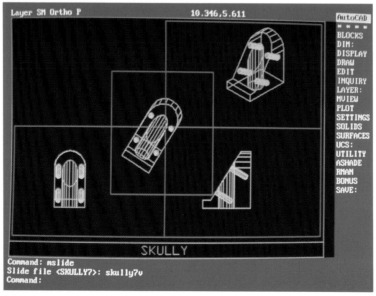

C-4: Skully, wireframe (from Chapter 7).

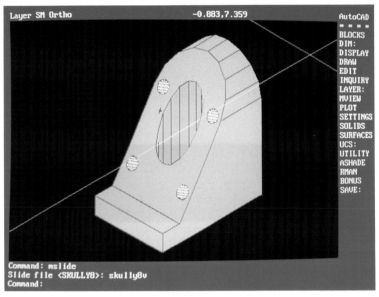

C-5: Skully, shaded (from Chapter 7).

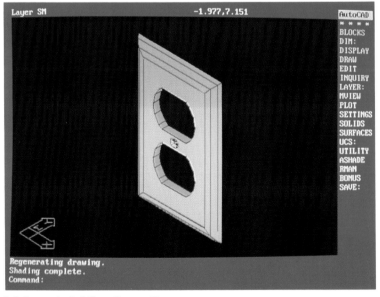

C-6: Cover, shaded (from Chapter 7).

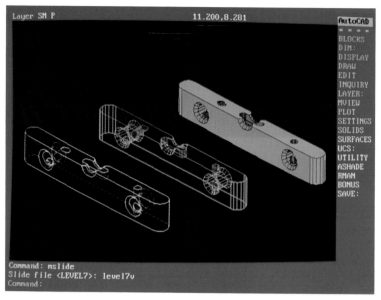

C-7: Level, profile, wireframe and shaded (from Chapter 7).

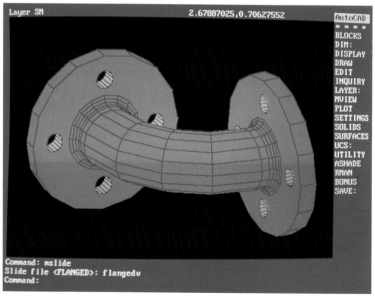

C-8: Flanged Elbow, shaded (from Chapter 8).

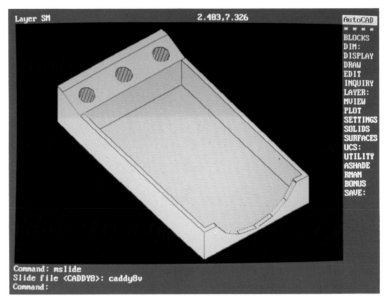

C-9: Paper Caddy, shaded (from Chapter 13).

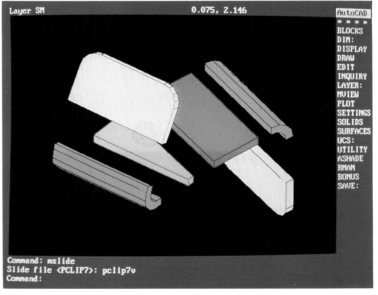

C-10: Positioning Clip, exploded primitives (from Chapter 13).

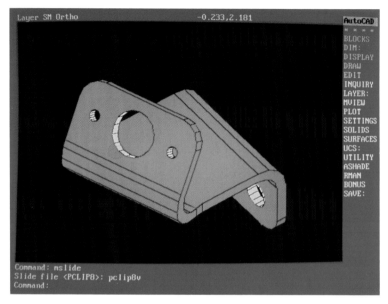

C-11: Positioning Clip, shaded (from Chapter 13).

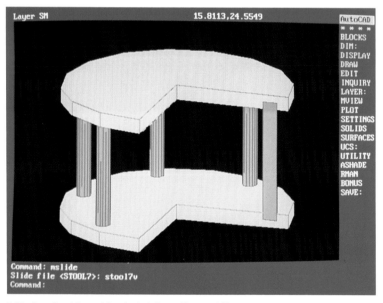

C-12: Step Stool Assembly, shaded (from Chapter 13).

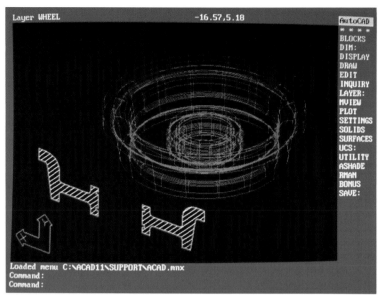

C-13: Trolley Wheel, wireframe and section (drawing supplied by Autodesk, Inc.).

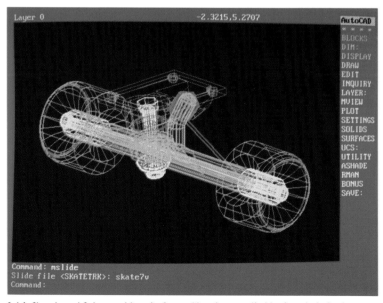

C-14: Skateboard Subassembly, wireframe (drawing supplied by Autodesk, Inc.).

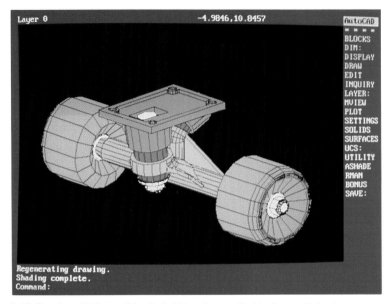

C-15: Skateboard Subassembly, shaded (drawing supplied by Autodesk, Inc.).

MODELING STRATEGIES & REGIONS

8

Modeling Strategies & Regions

The Power of Primitives

For purposes of comparison, we will group the ten primitives into three categories.

Classic Geometric Primitives	Swept Primitives	Edge Primitives
Box	Extrusion	Chamfer
Wedge	Revolution	Fillet
Cylinder		
Cone		
Sphere		
Torus		

Classic Geometric Primitives

Consider the power of these six primitives. With the box, wedge, cone and cylinder you can create a variety of shapes (in addition to the regular "boxy" shapes that come to mind immediately) by adopting extreme ratios between the various dimensions.

A box can be either a cube or a regular solid (all three dimensions in the same general range), a thin plate (one dimension much smaller than the other two) or a long narrow box (one dimension much larger than the other two).

A wedge can be either a regular wedge (all three dimensions in the same general range), a right-triangular plate (the Y dimension much smaller than the other dimensions), a long, narrow taper (the X or Z dimension much larger than the others) or a long nontapering shape (the Y dimension much larger than the others).

A cylinder can be a regular cylinder (diameter and height in the same general range), disk (height much smaller than diameter) or rod (diameter much smaller than height). In addition, it can be an elliptical cylinder, disk or rod. Similarly, a cone can be a regular, very flat or long needle cone.

The sphere and torus are not quite as flexible as the other classic primitives. The sphere is limited to one shape, since it has only one dimension. The torus can be an "apple" (self-intersecting torus) or a "football" (negative-radius torus), but these shapes are probably better created with revolutions.

Swept Primitives

The extrusion and revolution primitives are even more flexible than the classic primitives. In fact, simple 2D shapes can be extruded or revolved to duplicate nearly any 3D shape that can be created with the classic primitives. All sorts of boxes, wedges and cones can be created through extrusion; all sorts of cones, spheres and tori can be created through revolution. The elliptical cone is the only shape that is beyond the capability of extrusion and revolution.

In addition, extrusions and revolutions can use complex 2D shapes to produce solids that would require many Boolean operations if they were created from classic primitives. For example, consider the swept primitives pictured in Project 5B. In most cases, producing these same solids from classic primitives would require from 5 to 12 primitives and a number of Boolean operations. Therefore, you will often find it's more efficient to use a single extrusion or revolution in place of numerous classic primitives.

Edge Primitives

Although the chamfer and fillet are called primitives in the AutoCAD literature, they are never expected to stand alone as primitives; they're always combined with another solid. Their principal advantage is their convenience in certain circumstances rather than their flexibility.

Efficient Modeling

There is seldom just one right way to create a solid model. However, as a general rule, the method that allows you to keep the number of primitives as small as possible is the best. As illustrated with the Cover Plate and Level Body in the previous chapter, this means that you will often want to use swept primitives (extrusions and revolutions).

There are times, however, when you would be wise to use several classic primitives instead of a single swept primitive. If portions of a model are likely to be revised, then using classic primitives and the SOLCHP command to alter the size or position of one part of the model would be easier than re-forming the polyline that was extruded or revolved. For example, consider the Hold-Down Clamp in Chapter 2, "Projects: Setup & Overview." This clamp has a .75 radius clearance opening. When this clamp was modeled, three primitives were used to form the blank (box, wedge and cylinder). The same blank could have been formed from just two primitives if a polyline that included the .75 radius were extruded. However, altering the size or position of the clearance hole in the extrusion is much more cumbersome than altering the size or position of a cylinder. (See the SOLCHP command in the next chapter.)

Creating the Shapes

While a great many individual shapes (some quite complex) can be created with the primitives just described, a seemingly unlimited number of more complex shapes can be created when Boolean operations are applied to these primitives.

This section explores a number of modeling problems that have not already been illustrated in earlier chapters. Several are solved using two different modeling methods, for comparison. You'll find some comments about the various methods below.

In each of the following examples, the viewpoint is -1,-2,1. The primitives are shown on the left; the composite made from those primitives is illustrated on the right. Notice that we're using a large number of swept primitives and relatively few classic primitives, in order to show you the power and flexibility of extrusions and revolutions.

For the sake of clarity, most of the primitives are shown "exploded," or slightly out of their normal positions. In order to create the composite, the primitives need to be moved into position before the listed Boolean operation is applied.

Hex Head Cap Screw

Nearly the entire cap screw is modeled by revolving a polyline. The only purpose for the hexagonal extrusion is to place the six flats on the head. The threads on this cap screw are not true spiral threads, since it would be impractical to model them with AutoCAD.

In actual practice, there is seldom a need to model threads, knurls or very small fillets and chamfers.

Flanged Elbow

This solid has no straight edges; nevertheless, it's relatively simple to model. The main body of the elbow is made entirely of revolutions. (See color illustration C-8 on page 170.)

Elliptical Torus (Approximation)

The 12 segments shown in the drawing form three-quarters of a full elliptical torus.

The regular torus cannot be used to create an elliptical torus because it's always circular. In fact, AutoCAD is not able to construct a true elliptical torus but can create a close approximation of one. Remember that AutoCAD's ellipse is not a true ellipse—it is made of 16 arc segments. On the one hand, it only approximates an ellipse; but on the other hand, it's possible to use its segments as centerlines for solids created by revolution. By constructing an ellipse as a centerline of the torus's tube, a circle (or any other shape) can be revolved to form the segments which when unioned approximate an elliptical torus.

CAUTION: When you perform Boolean operations on a large number of revolutions—particularly if those revolutions include curved or complex shapes—AutoCAD takes a long time to perform the operations.

Spline Sweep (Approximation)

The solid shown in the drawing is an approximation, not a true spline sweep (which would involve a figure swept along a true spline). A true spline is a planar curve whose segments are not limited to circular arcs. Splines include conic sections (ellipses, parabolas, hyperbolas) or irregular curves (curves that must be dimensioned incrementally, because they are not rule-generated or formula-generated curves like conic sections).

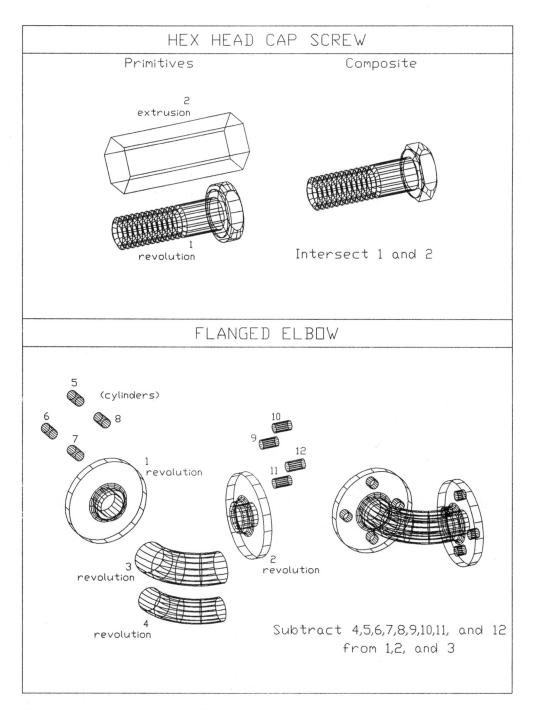

Figure 8-1: Hex head cap screw and flanged elbow.

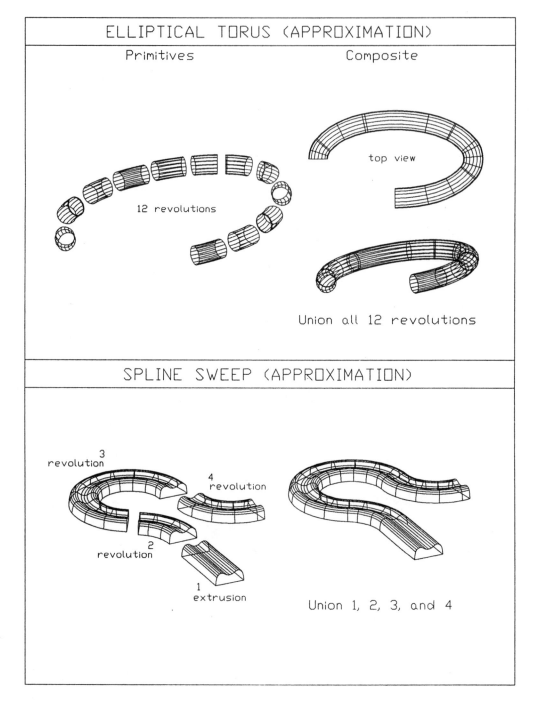

ELLIPTICAL TORUS (APPROXIMATION)

Primitives   Composite

top view

12 revolutions

Union all 12 revolutions

SPLINE SWEEP (APPROXIMATION)

3
revolution

4
revolution

2
revolution

1
extrusion

Union 1, 2, 3, and 4

Figure 8-2: Elliptical torus and spline sweep.

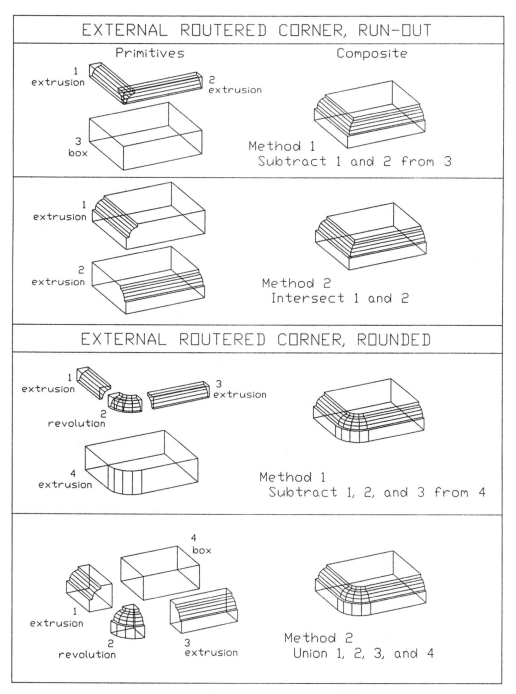

Figure 8-3: External routered corners.

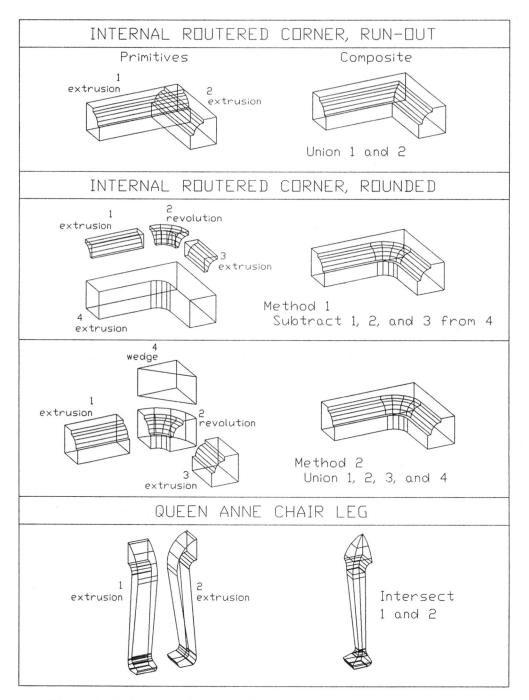

Figure 8-4: Internal routered corners and Queen Anne chair leg.

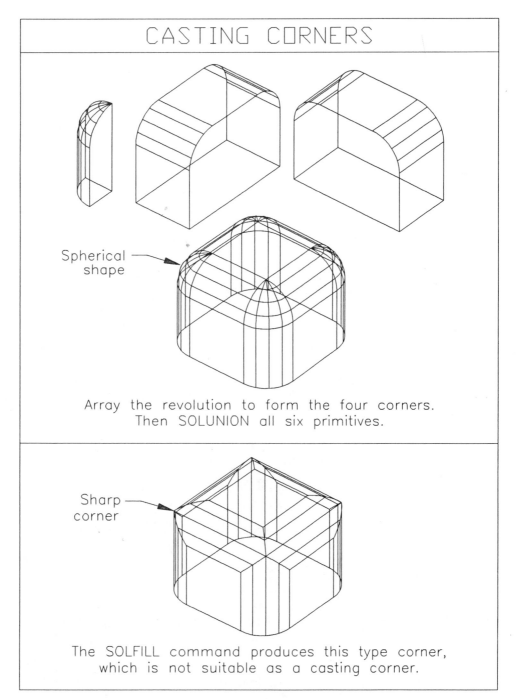

CASTING CORNERS

Spherical shape

Array the revolution to form the four corners.
Then SOLUNION all six primitives.

Sharp corner

The SOLFILL command produces this type corner,
which is not suitable as a casting corner.

Figure 8-5: Casting corners.

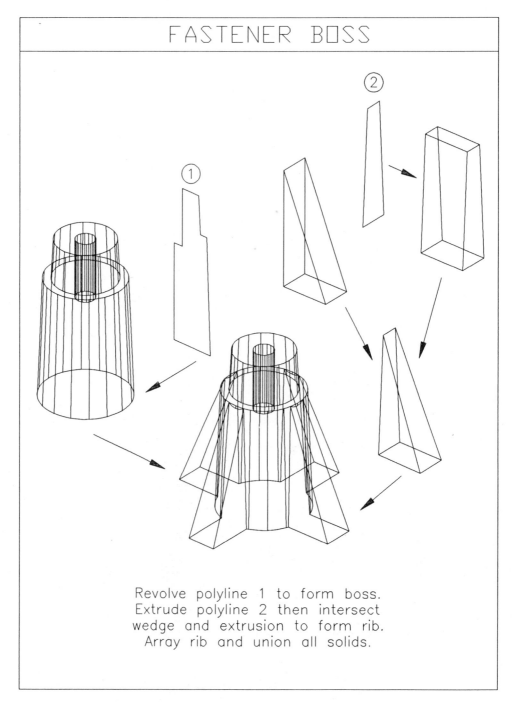

FASTENER BOSS

Revolve polyline 1 to form boss.
Extrude polyline 2 then intersect
wedge and extrusion to form rib.
Array rib and union all solids.

Figure 8-6: Fastener boss.

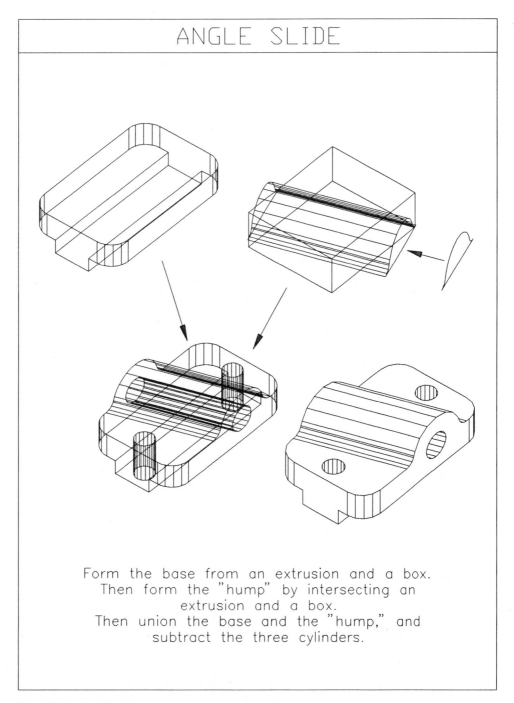

ANGLE SLIDE

Form the base from an extrusion and a box.
Then form the "hump" by intersecting an
extrusion and a box.
Then union the base and the "hump," and
subtract the three cylinders.

Figure 8-7: Angle slide.

AutoCAD's polyline is limited to sections made up of straight lines and circular arcs, so a polyline cannot be a spline.

Remember also that AutoCAD's ellipse is not a true ellipse because it's made up of 16 circular arc segments (no portion of a true ellipse is circular). Also, AutoCAD's Fit-curve option in the PEDIT command produces circular arcs, and the Spline option in the PEDIT command produces a series of straight line segments. This means that AutoCAD can produce only approximations of true splines, as defined above. However, to the degree that a true spline can be approximated by a polyline, true spline sweeps can be approximated.

The only two swept solids currently available in AutoCAD are the extrusion and the revolution. These solids are generated by moving a polyline or circle through a straight line and a circular arc, respectively. This means that in order to create a close approximation of a true spline sweep, you would have to approximate the spline by using a large number of extrusions or revolutions. This, however, is impractical, since it takes AutoCAD such a great amount of time to perform Boolean operations on a large number of revolutions—particularly if they are revolutions of curved or complex figures.

External Routered Corner, Run-out

Method 1 is probably the method that would come to mind first, particularly if you think of this shape as being created by a router on a large block of wood. When you use a router, you're subtracting wood, so you might think automatically of subtraction as the way to create this shape. And, of course, subtraction will work very well, as method 1 illustrates. However, notice that method 2 uses only two primitives.

Method 2 would probably not be considered immediately by most machinists or woodworkers—for two reasons. First, it involves the Boolean intersection operation, which has no counterpart in the real physical world. Second, it appears at first glance to be a wasteful procedure, since it requires two large blocks. But these are computer-generated blocks, which are in abundant supply, so material waste is not a factor here. The method used to create a solid model is not always parallel to the actual procedure that will be used to manufacture the object.

There's another consideration that might determine which method is the better choice. If the overall length or width of this object were revised, the method 1 solid would be easier to revise than the method 2 solid, because it's easier to change the extrusion's height and the box's dimension with the SOLCHP command than to change the extrusion's shape.

As is usually the case, there's no single method that will always be the best way to model this shape. In many cases, method 2 might be preferred; but in certain circumstances, method 1 may be the most appropriate way to achieve what you want.

External Routered Corner, Rounded

The first and second methods require the same number of primitives, take about the same amount of work to create the primitives and are equally easy to revise.

Internal Routered Corner, Run-out

Both of the internal routering problems shown in Figure 8-4 on page 184 (run-out and rounded) would be beyond the scope of the SOLCHAM or SOLFILL command, even if we were using the simpler edge configuration created by SOLCHAM or SOLFILL. To produce even a simple internal chamfer or fillet, you would have to use techniques similar to those shown in Figure 8-4.

Regarding the internal routered corner with the run-out, only one method is shown in Figure 8-4, because any other method requires too many primitives and Boolean operations. If this object were to be manufactured through a material removal process (such as milling or routering) rather than a molding process, it would typically be made from separate mitered parts. However, to model it from mitered parts would involve four primitives and two separate Boolean steps. Notice that the 45 degree mitered effect is achieved automatically by the union operation.

Internal Routered Corner, Rounded

Both methods require the same number of primitives, about the same amount of work to create the primitives and the same amount of time and effort to revise.

Queen Anne Chair Leg

This example is included to show that relatively complex shapes can often be made from a minimum of primitives and Boolean operations.

Casting Corners

Castings typically have rounded edges and spherical shapes at the corners. The SOLFILL command can produce the rounded edges, but cannot produce the spherical corners. If six seems like quite a few primitives for such a simple shape, consider the fact that the SOLFILL command generates a total of nine primitives to produce the shape at the bottom of the drawing, which still lacks spherical corners.

Fastener Boss

This fastener boss is part of a larger plastic mold. A 3 degree draft has been used on all external parts to facilitate removal from the mold. The draft is included in the polylines that form the basis for the revolution and the extrusion. (The extrusion is not tapered, only the polyline from which it is created.)

Angle Slide

This composite is created from seven primitives. After forming the "hump" extrusion, you may be tempted to use the SOLCUT command to chop off each end with a cutting plane. However, that would create two extra primitives, whereas the method shown requires only one extra primitive.

Solids With Irregular Surfaces

AutoCAD's standard mesh commands plus the smoothed meshes can produce approximations of irregular curved surfaces. The 3DMESH and PFACE commands can produce approximations of irregular surfaces, defined vertex by vertex. However, AutoCAD presently has no convenient means of creating solids from these surface approximations.

Despite all its advantages, one of the disadvantages of using Constructive Solid Geometry as the primary basis of solid modeling is its difficulty in dealing with irregular surfaces. Those who specialize in the design of objects with irregular surfaces would be better off with a solid modeler based primarily on Boundary Representation rather than CSG.

Thin Shells

AME does not model thin shells well, particularly thin shells with curved sections. A thin shell results when one object is subtracted from another that is nearly the same size, or from extruding or revolving a polyline or region with long narrow sections. Even the low- or mid-range settings of the SOLWDENS variable that allow other solids to mesh acceptably may not work properly with thin shells.

Regions Explained

Regions look very much like cross sections of a 3D object. (See the following illustrations.) A region is actually a 2D area defined by an outer perimeter and possibly containing inner perimeters called loops (holes of any shape). Since you can perform certain solid operations on regions (Boolean operations and solid editing), you can think of a region as a solid that has zero-thickness in the Z-direction. A region is confined to a single plane, but that plane can be placed at any angle and any location in space.

The outer and inner perimeters are called loops since they are continuous. Every region will have an outer loop, and may have one or more inner loops. A region that has inner loops is a composite region. Loops belonging to a composite region will always occupy the same plane and will never cross each other. Every inner loop will be entirely contained within the outer loop and will not intersect any other inner loops.

Regions can be extruded or revolved, using SOLEXT or SOLREV, to generate solids. In an extrusion, various loops can be extruded to different heights or depths. Similarly, in a revolution, various loops can be revolved at different positive or negative angles. When an inner loop (that was subtracted from the outer loop) is extruded or revolved in the opposite direction from the outer loop, the result is a portion of the composite solid that is unioned to the composite rather than subtracted from it. This is illustrated in the Bending Jig, Figure 8-9.

When you create a region from scratch (rather than extracting it from a solid), each loop is created from a continuous 2D entity or series of 2D entities such as polylines (including ellipses and polygons), circles, arcs, donuts, traces or even 2D solids. Then they are solidified into a region with the SOLSOLIDIFY command, or become a region automatically when Boolean operations are applied. After one or more regions are created, they can be edited with Boolean operations and solid editing commands.

AME cross-hatches regions. The default cross hatching is the "U" (User-defined) style with lines 1.000 apart at 45 degrees. This is based on the defaults in the hatching variables:

SOLHPAT = "U"
SOLHSIZE = 1.000
SOLHANGLE = 45

Normally you would set up these variables before you form regions. If you have already formed a region and are not satisfied with the hatching, you will need to SOLSEP the object, reset the hatching variables, then reform the composite region. However, if one of the primitives in a composite region is modified with the SOLCHP command, the hatching of that region will follow the current settings of the hatching variables when it is reevaluated (either when you use E inside the SOLCHP command or as you exit the command). So if you know you are going to edit the region with SOLCHP, make sure the hatching variables are currently set the way you want them.

Working with regions does not give you any greater capacity to construct other types of 2D areas. Whatever you create by manipulating regions can also be created by manipulating standard 2D entities such as circles and polylines. In particular, the person who is adept at working with polylines may wonder why anyone would bother with regions. However, in certain circumstances the process may be simpler or more intuitive with regions than with standard 2D entities. Also, the SOLEXT and SOLREV commands allow you to create solids from regions in a straightforward manner, and the SOLSECT command can extract a region directly from a solid.

Although certain commands allow you to select regions and solids at the same time, regions and solids are never mixed. For example, if you use the SOLUNION command and include four solids and two regions, the four solids will be unioned to each other and the two regions will be unioned to each other, but solids will not be unioned to regions. Furthermore, the two regions must lie in the same plane to be unioned. Regions must also lie in the same plane for the other two Boolean operations, subtraction and intersection.

A region has a CSG tree just as a solid does. After being manipulated with the solid commands, a region's CSG tree can be simplified by using the 2dtree option of the SOLPURGE command.

To analyze a region, use the SOLAREA and SOLMASSP commands.

Sample Region

Here are three sample regions. Each sample shows three things:

1. The 2D entities used to construct the region, in plan view.

2. The region itself, in plan view.

3. An extrusion of the region, in oblique view.

Even though regions can be created from a wide variety of 2D objects, these samples are all constructed from circles and polylines.

You may want to try creating these regions yourself. If you do, remember to use SOLPURGE to simplify the 2dtree of your region before you extrude it.

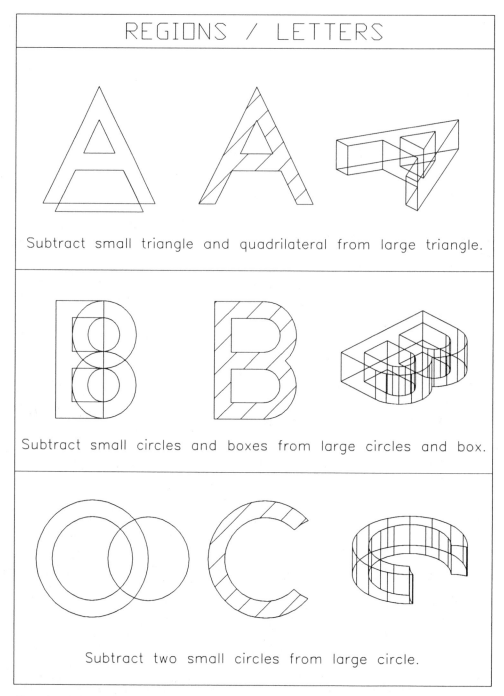

REGIONS / LETTERS

Subtract small triangle and quadrilateral from large triangle.

Subtract small circles and boxes from large circles and box.

Subtract two small circles from large circle.

Figure 8-8: Subtraction in Regions, using letters as examples.

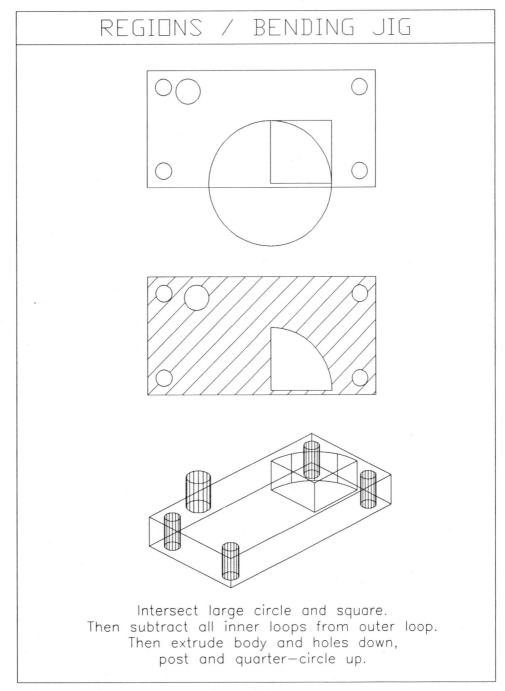

REGIONS / BENDING JIG

Intersect large circle and square.
Then subtract all inner loops from outer loop.
Then extrude body and holes down,
post and quarter—circle up.

Figure 8-9: Bending jig using examples of intersection and subtraction.

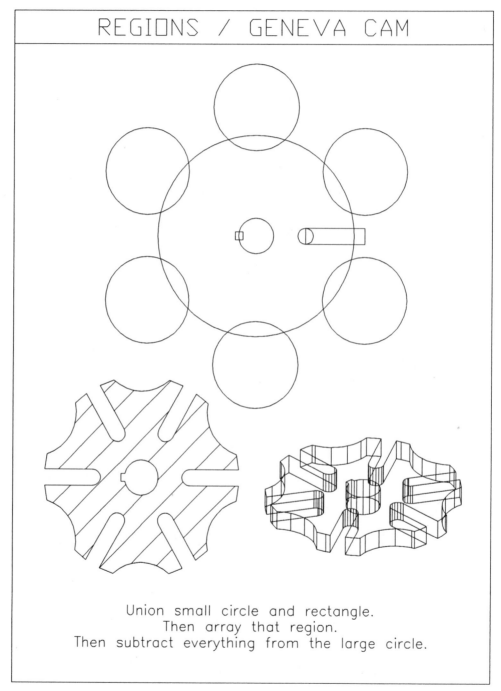

REGIONS / GENEVA CAM

Union small circle and rectangle.
Then array that region.
Then subtract everything from the large circle.

Figure 8-10: Geneva cam using examples of union and subtraction.

Moving On

We hope you got the idea from this chapter that swept primitives are very powerful and that using this method is often the "technique of choice." But no matter which type of primitives or Boolean operations you use, there will always be times when you need to modify a design.

The next chapter describes two powerful tools for editing solids, the SOLMOVE and SOLCHP commands.

MOVING & CHANGING
SOLIDS

9

Moving & Changing Solids

I t's often necessary to move and rotate solid primitives or composites. Sometimes it's easiest to do this with the regular MOVE and ROTATE commands, setting up temporary UCSs as needed. In other situations it may be easier to use the SOLMOVE command.

WARNING: Since solids and regions are represented on screen by blocks made up of lines, arcs, etc., it is possible to edit these blocks with such commands as MOVE, COPY, ARRAY, etc. If you have just entered a drawing containing solids but have not yet loaded AME, there is the danger that the editing process will corrupt the handles of the solids represented by these blocks. Thus, it is wise to load AME at the beginning of every editing session when you are working with solids and regions. AME can be loaded automatically, as explained at the end of Chapter 1, "Solid Modeling Defined."

Also, be careful when you place solids in named blocks to manipulate as part of a group of objects. Those solids will not regain their identity as solids until the block is exploded. If you run SOLPURGE and select the "Erased" option, those blocks would be unable to function again as solids.

The SOLMOVE Command (Alias: MOV)

The SOLMOVE command lets you perform several different operations. You can translate or rotate a solid, reposition the temporary Motion Coordinate System (MCS) icon, or reposition both the icon and the solid.

One advantage of the SOLMOVE command is that you can rotate objects without having to set up an appropriate UCS. The ROTATE command lets you rotate objects *only* around an axis that's perpendicular to the current X-Y construction plane. In contrast, the SOLMOVE command lets you rotate objects around any of the three axes in its temporary MCS.

Another advantage of the SOLMOVE command is that it lets you snap to the edges and faces of solids. Although you cannot use osnap modes while you're using the SOLMOVE command, you can snap the MCS icon and the selected object(s) to the edges or faces of other objects. Thus, you might want to think of SOLMOVE as providing a new kind of SNAP—solid SNAP.

After entering the SOLMOVE command, you're prompted to select the objects you want to move or rotate. After you select one or more objects, the special MCS icon appears, in all viewports, at the origin of the current UCS, and you're prompted to enter a "Motion description." The prompt reappears repeatedly, allowing you to perform a number of moves.

Here's how the MCS icon and the motion description codes work.

The MCS Icon

MCS (Motion Coordinate System) is a temporary coordinate system. The MCS icon shows the orientations of the MCS's X, Y and Z axes. The icon appears on the screen while the SOLMOVE command is in effect, to help you enter the correct motion commands. Notice that the icon has a single arrow on the X axis, a double arrow on the Y axis and a triple arrow on the Z axis.

Figure 9-1: MCS icon.

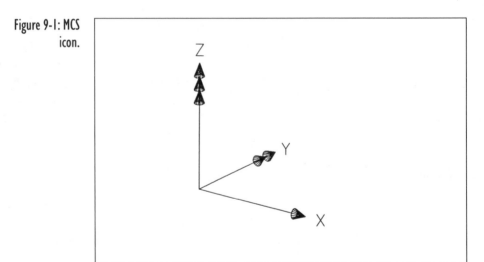

If you're using only one viewport, or if the MCS icon is not visible in some of your viewports, you may need to use the right-hand rule (see Chapter 3, "General 3D Commands: UCSs, Space & Viewing") to determine whether an axis is pointing toward you or away from you. In many situations, two of the icon arrows will be full length (or nearly full length), while the third arrow will be short or perhaps appear to have no length at all. If that's the case, you may not be sure whether the third arrow is pointing toward you or away from you. You can use the two longer arrows along with the right-hand rule to determine where the third arrow is pointing.

Since the MCS icon can be oriented many different ways within the current UCS, and can be reoriented while you're using the SOLMOVE command, remember to check the MCS icon for the MCS's current orientation before you enter your next motion description code.

Motion Description Codes

You can display a summary of the letters used in motion description codes by entering ? in response to the "Motion description" prompt. Letters can be entered in uppercase or lowercase.

SOLMOVE: Moves and Rotates a Solid About the Motion Coordinate System (MCS)

OPTIONS	MOTION DESCRIPTION
Translate along MCS axis	
TX	Translate along X axis
TY	Translate along Y axis
TZ	Translate along Z axis
Rotate solid about MCS axis	
RX	Rotate about X axis
RY	Rotate about Y axis
RZ	Rotate about Z axis
Reorient MCS icon	
E	Set axes to Edge
F	Set axes to Face
U	Set axes to current UCS
W	Set axes to WCS

Align object and MCS

AE	Align with Edge
AF	Align with Face
AU	Align with current UCS
AW	Align with WCS

Restore original situation

O	Restore MCS and Solid to original location

When you're prompted for the motion description, you have four groups of response choices:

- Move (translate or rotate) only the object in relation to the MCS's current position by using codes T and R.

- Move *only the MCS icon* in relation to any solid or in relation to the current UCS or WCS by entering codes E, F, U or W.

- Align *both the MCS icon and the object* with any solid or the current UCS or WCS by using codes AE, AF, AU or AW.

- Use code 0 to *restore the object and the MCS icon to the positions they were in* before you started the SOLMOVE command.

Moving Only the Object To translate an object, enter T, then the axis (X, Y or Z), then the distance (positive or negative). For example, to translate an object two units in the positive X direction, enter TX2 in response to the "Motion description" prompt.

You can enter several translations, separated by commas. For example, to translate an object one unit in the negative Y direction and half a unit up in the positive Z direction at the same time, enter TY-1, TZ.5. When you do several translations, you can do them in any order and still end up with the same result. Remember to check the orientation of the MCS icon before entering your motion description.

NOTE: If the MCS icon has been aligned with one of the objects being moved (by using codes E or F), the MCS icon will move with that object.

To rotate an object, enter R, then the axis of rotation (X, Y or Z), then the angle (positive or negative). For example, to rotate an object 45 degrees around the Z axis, enter RZ45. You can enter several rotations separated by commas. To rotate 90 degrees around the X axis then rotate 30 degrees around the Y axis, enter RX90,RY30. Whether the angle is positive or negative is determined by the right-hand rule for rotation (see Chapter 3).

Unlike translations, when you do several rotations, you must be careful of the order. Doing two or more rotations in one order will produce different results than doing the same rotations in another order. Always check the orientation of the MCS icon before entering your motion description.

NOTE: If the MCS icon has been aligned with one of the objects being moved (by using codes E or F), the MCS icon will move with the objects.

You can translate and rotate at the same time. For example, TZ1.5,RZ180 would translate an object up one and a half units in the positive Z direction, then rotate it 180 degrees around the Z axis.

Moving Only the MCS Icon You can move the axes icon in relation to any solid or the current UCS or the WCS. When you move the icon with one of the single letter codes in the following descriptions (E, F, U, W), only the icon moves. Any objects you have selected are not moved.

- Enter E to attach the icon to the midpoint of the edge of a solid. Then select the edge. This edge can be on the solid(s) you selected earlier or on any other solid.

- Enter F to attach the icon to the face of a solid. Then select that face by selecting one of its edges. AutoCAD will change the highlighting on one of the faces that belongs to that edge. If that's the face you want, press Enter to accept it. If it's not the face you want, enter N (for Next), then press Enter to accept it. This face can be on one of the solids you selected earlier or on any other solid.

- Enter U to orient the icon at the origin of the current UCS.

- Enter W to orient the icon at the origin of the WCS.

As you move objects with the SOLMOVE command, you may find that the display becomes sketchy in some viewports due to pixels being turned off as the objects are moved. However, while you're in the SOLMOVE command, you can use 'REDRAWALL (note the apostrophe) at any time to redraw all viewports.

Moving Both the MCS Icon and the Object   You can add A (for Align) to the front of any of the four codes described above (AE, AF, AU, AW) in order to move the objects along with the icon.

Sample Moves

The sample moves that follow are intended to illustrate how using the SOLMOVE command compares with using the regular AutoCAD editing commands.

You would be wise to construct the wedges and cylinders shown in the following samples and work through each step. The viewpoint (VPOINT) in each of the illustrations is -2,-3,1. The wedges are 2 x 1.5 x 1 (rotated -45 degrees) and the cylinders are 1.5 diameter, .5 high. The wedges are rotated so that their slopes are truly oblique rather than merely inclined surfaces.

Sample One: Centering the Cylinder on the Slope

With MOVE and ROTATE (use immediate osnap modes throughout):

1. MOVE the cylinder from the center of its base to the midpoint of the top edge on the slope.

2. Create a vertical UCS lined up with the three endpoints on the triangular side of the wedge.

3. ROTATE the cylinder around the top corner of the wedge so its base is flush with the slope. (Osnap to the bottom corner of the slope to indicate the rotation angle.)

4. Restore WCS.

5. MOVE the cylinder halfway down the slope. (The basepoint and second point of displacement will be the endpoint and midpoint of the sloping edge.)

With SOLMOVE:

I. Enter SOLMOVE and select the cylinder.

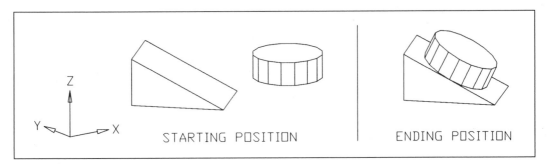

Figure 9-2: Repositioning the cylinder with SOLMOVE.

2. Place the MCS icon on the base of the cylinder. (Enter E and pick the bottom edge of the cylinder.)

3. Align both icon and cylinder with the slanted edge of the slope (enter AE and pick the near slanted edge). At this point, the cylinder is 90 degrees "off."

4. Rotate the cylinder -90 degrees around the X axis of the MCS, and translate the cylinder .75 in the negative X direction (enter RX-90,TX-.75). Notice that the icon moves with the cylinder because it was attached in step 2.

NOTE: If you know the distance the cylinder needs to be moved to center it on the slope, step 4 works well. However, if you do not know the distance, an alternate procedure would work better. In step 4, rotate the cylinder but do not translate it. Exit SOLMOVE. Then use MOVE to center the cylinder halfway across the slope. (The basepoint and second point of displacement will be the endpoint and midpoint of either the top or bottom edge of the slope.)

Sample Two: Inverting the Wedge Onto the Cylinder

With MOVE and ROTATE (use immediate osnap modes throughout):

1. Create a vertical UCS lined up with the three endpoints on the triangular side of the wedge.

2. Use ROTATE to invert the wedge so that its slope is now on the bottom. (Use the Reference option of the ROTATE command.)

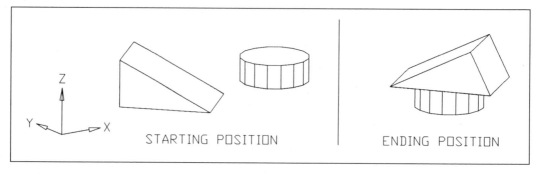

Figure 9-3: Repositioning the wedge with SOLMOVE.

3. Restore WCS.

4. MOVE the wedge from the midpoint of one of its bottom edges (on which it is now resting) to the center of the cylinder.

5. Center the wedge on the cylinder. (MOVE it from the midpoint of one of its edges to the endpoint of the same edge.)

With SOLMOVE:

1. Enter SOLMOVE and select the wedge.

2. Place the MCS icon on the slope of the wedge. (Enter F and pick the near edge of the slope; enter N until the desired face is indicated.)

3. Align both icon and wedge with the top of the cylinder. (Enter AE and pick the top edge of the cylinder.)

4. Rotate the wedge 180 degrees around the X axis. At the same time, translate the wedge .75 in the negative X direction and 1.118 in the negative Y direction (enter `RX180`, `TX-.75`, `TY-1.118`). Notice that the icon moves with the wedge because it was attached to it in step 2.

NOTE: If you know the distance the wedge needs to be moved to center it on the cylinder, step 4 works well. However, if you do not know the distance, a procedure similar to the alternate procedure explained in Sample One would work better.

When simple moves or rotations are required, the MOVE or ROTATE commands might be easier to use. When one oblique surface is involved, the SOLMOVE command might be the preferred command; but as shown, MOVE and ROTATE work very well too. However, when you need to move a solid from one oblique plane to a different oblique plane, the SOLMOVE command definitely does it more efficiently.

SOLCHP (Alias: SCHP or CHPRIM)

Solids and regions can be modified (as units) in many ways with the regular AutoCAD editing commands. Both primitives and composite solids can be moved, copied, rotated, scaled and arrayed. They cannot be stretched.

Composite solids and regions can be changed internally with the SOLCHP command. SOLCHP stands for solid change primitive.

SOLCHP: Used to Change and View Primitives in Solids

OPTIONS	DESCRIPTION
Color	Change color of primitive
Delete	Delete primitive from CSG tree
Evaluate	Recompose solid
Instance	Make copy of primitive
Move	Move primitive
Next	Select next primitive
Pick	Pick a primitive

OPTIONS	DESCRIPTION
Replace	Replace primitive with a solid (composite or primitive)
Size	Change dimensions of primitive
X	Exit the SOLCHP command

SOLCHP begins by prompting you to select a solid or region. Then you're prompted to select a primitive. You can either pick a primitive with the pointer or press Enter to begin cycling through the primitives one at a time. Each successive primitive is highlighted as it's selected.

A prompt appears with several options, each of which is explained below. After you complete one of these options, the same prompt reappears so you can make several modifications in one use of the command.

Enter

N (Next) To select the next primitive. You can repeat this option until the primitive you want to work with is highlighted. N is the default.

P (Pick) To pick a different primitive with the pointer (without having to cycle through all the primitives with the Next option). If the location of the primitive makes it difficult to pick with the pointer, you can always pick it with the Next option explained above.

C (Color) To change the color of the selected primitive. If system variable SOLRENDER is set to CSG, this color change will be visible in the composite solid. If SOLRENDER is set to Uniform, the color of the main composite will prevail, regardless of the color assigned to any primitives.

D (Delete) To remove the primitive from the CSG tree and make it a detached primitive. You're then asked if you want to retain this detached primitive. If you answer N, the detached primitive is erased from the drawing. If you answer Y, the detached primitive is still in the drawing but not part of the composite solid. If you're planning to make other modifications before exiting SOLCHP, use the E (Evaluate) option at this point to update the image. Upon exiting from the command, you may need to redraw the screen in order to see a retained primitive.

R (Replace) To replace the selected primitive with a different solid. The primitive is actually detached from the solid (removed from the CSG tree). Then you're prompted to select the replacement solid, which can be a primitive or solid. Finally you're asked if you want to retain the detached primitive. If you're going to make other modifications before exiting SOLCHP, you may want to use the E (Evaluate) option at this point to update the image. Solid primitives can be replaced only with solids. Regions can be replaced only with regions.

S (Size) To change the size of the primitive. The subsequent prompts depend on the type of primitive. For example, if the primitive is a box, you're prompted for the X, Y and Z dimensions. If it's a cone, you're prompted for radius and height. If the primitive was created by extruding or revolving a polyline, and you tell AutoCAD you want to change its shape, that polyline will be available (shown in a different color) after exiting SOLCHP. You can then rebuild the primitive, re-enter SOLCHP and replace the old version with the new. If you're going to make other modifications before exiting SOLCHP, you may want to use the E (Evaluate) option at this point to update the image.

M (Move) To relocate the primitive within the composite solid. Then you're prompted for the base point and displacement of the move. If you're going to make other modifications before exiting SOLCHP, you may want to use the E (Evaluate) option at this point to update the image.

I (Instance) To reproduce this primitive as a detached solid. The new copy of the primitive will be in the same location as the original. The original primitive is retained as part of the composite solid. You can then use the detached copy in a replacement operation, or use it in an entirely different composite solid. Upon exiting the command, you may need to redraw the screen in order to see the new primitive.

E (Evaluate) To recompose the solid from its modified CSG tree. You'll find that you need to use this option after changes such as move, size or replacement have been made. Of course, the composite solid is rebuilt when you exit SOLCHP, but this option updates the composite solid while you're still in SOLCHP, in preparation for making additional modifications.

✗ To exit the SOLCHP command.

Variables & the SOLVAR Command

The variables that govern AME can be changed with the SOLVAR command or entered directly at the command prompt. They cannot be changed with the SETVAR command.

Like the solid modeling commands, the variables have abbreviations and aliases defined in the ACAD.PGP file. However, when you enter a variable name at the command prompt, you must use its full name.

The SOLVAR command operates much like the regular SETVAR command. After entering the command, you're prompted for the name of the variable you want to change. To obtain a list of the variables and their current settings, enter ? when prompted for the variable name. There are 22 SOLVAR variables.

The variables are explained below according to their categories.

Display

• SOLWDENS (SOLid Wire DENSity). Determines the number of curvature (tessellation) lines in wireframe displays and the number of faces in mesh displays. Values range from 1 through 12. The number of tessellation lines on cylinders and cones is four times the value of SOLWDENS. In other words, the SOLWDENS setting determines the number of tessellation lines per quadrant. The number of tessellation lines on spheres and tori uses a different formula.

The higher the setting, the more accurate the mesh and the more time and RAM are required for AutoCAD to generate it. Therefore, the AME Reference Manual recommends that you seldom use settings above 6.

• SOLDISPLAY (SOLid DISPLAY). Sets the display type default for subsequently created solids to either wireframe or mesh representation. It is normal to set the display in wireframe mode. The type of display can then be changed with the SOLWIRE and SOLMESH commands.

• SOLRENDER (SOLid RENDER). Determines whether the colors used to display composites will be the colors of the primitives or the color of the composite. (The composite color is the color assigned to the layer that was current when the composite was formed; the color explicitly assigned by the COLOR command before the composite was formed; or the color assigned by the CHPROP command after the composite was formed.) This variable governs the display of composites whether they're in wireframe or mesh, hidden or shaded. The two available color schemes are CSG and Uniform. CSG uses the colors of the individual primitives, while Uniform uses only the color of the composite. When you reset SOLRENDER, the change takes effect the next time the composite is changed to wireframe or mesh representation.

- SOLAXCOL (SOLid AXis COLor). Determines the color of the MCS icon that appears when you use the SOLMOVE command or the Size option of the SOLCHP command. Choose an integer value from 1 to 8.

Modeling Operations

- SOLDELENT (SOLid DELete ENTity). When an original nonsolid entity is used to create a solid (such as when SOLEXT or SOLREV uses a circle or polyline to create an extrusion or revolution, or when SOLIDIFY converts a thick 2D entity), this variable determines whether the original entity will be deleted.

    If SOLDELENT = 1, the circle or polyline is not deleted.

    If SOLDELENT = 2, you're asked whether or not to delete it.

    If SOLDELENT = 3, it's automatically deleted.

- SOLSOLIDIFY (SOLid SOLIDIFY). Determines whether nonsolid objects that are eligible to be solidified will be solidified when selected for certain modeling operations (such as Boolean operations). For example, if you use the SOLUNION command and select a box and a circle that has been assigned thickness, the setting of this variable will govern how the thick circle is handled. Only those objects that can be solidified by the SOLIDIFY command (see Chapter 4, "The Building Blocks: Basic, Swept & Edge Primitives") can be solidified during other operations.

    If SOLSOLIDIFY = 1, nonsolids are not solidified.

    If SOLSOLIDIFY = 2, you're asked if you want each one solidified.

    If SOLSOLIDIFY = 3, nonsolids are automatically solidified.

Units

Certain commands, such as SOLAREA and SOLMASSP, display information in specific units. In other words, length is given in centimeters, inches, etc. Area is given in square centimeters, square inches, etc. And the same is true with volume, mass, etc. (This is not the case with such commands as SOLLIST and DIST, which displays a distance in pure units.) The various units available are listed in the ACAD.UNT file. This file is quite extensive, including among other things 40 length units and 32 volume units. To find out all the various units that are available and their abbreviations, you can display the file at the DOS prompt by entering MORE <ACAD.UNT.

The unit variables listed below will accept abbreviations. If you enter the full name of a unit (such as "millimeter") when assigning a unit to one of the variables below, then the full name will be used in the displayed information. If you enter an abbreviation, that abbreviation will be used. Any abbreviations you enter must be listed in the ACAD.UNT file.

- SOLLENGTH (SOLid LENGTH). Sets length units such as millimeters or inches. When you change the length units you're asked if you also want to automatically change the area and volume units. Length, area and volume should usually be set to the same units.

NOTE: When you change length units, you're implying that the real-world size of the object has changed, not that the magnitude of the object's dimensions has changed. For example, suppose your current length unit is inches, and you create a cube that is one inch on all sides. When you change length units to millimeters, the length of the sides on the cube remains at 1 rather than suddenly changing to 25.4 millimeters. The change in length units signifies that the real-world object represented by your model is now smaller because the units are smaller.

- SOLAREAU (SOLid AREA Units). Sets area units to such values as square millimeters or square inches.

- SOLVOLUME (SOLid VOLUME). Sets volume units to such values as cubic millimeters or cubic inches.

- SOLMASS (SOLid MASS units). Sets the mass units to such values as gram, kilogram, pound or ton.

Materials & Mass Properties Analysis

- SOLMATCURR (SOLid MATerial CURRent). Determines the default material that will be assigned to newly created solids. Read only. Use the Set option of the SOLMAT command to change to a different default material. Use the Change option of the SOLMAT command to change the material assigned to an existing solid.

- SOLDECOMP (SOLid DECOMPosition direction). Sets the decomposition direction used for mass properties calculations to either X, Y or Z. The most accurate results will be obtained when the direction of decomposition is set in such a way that the profile of the object is the smallest when viewed in the direction of decomposition. For example, if the object to be analyzed is narrow in both the X and Z dimensions but long in the Y dimension, then set SOLDECOMP to Y. (See the SOLMASSP command.)

- SOLSUBDIV (SOLid SUBDIVision level). Determines the number of subdivisions used for the mass properties calculations done by the SOLMASSP command.

When s stands for the setting of SOLSUBDIV, the formula for the number of subdivisions is $(2^s + 1)^2$.

SOLSUBDIV = 1	3 x 3 grid	9 subdivisions
SOLSUBDIV = 2	5 x 5 grid	25 subdivisions
SOLSUBDIV = 3	9 x 9 grid	81 subdivisions
SOLSUBDIV = 4	17 x 17 grid	289 subdivisions
SOLSUBDIV = 5	33 x 33 grid	1,089 subdivisions
SOLSUBDIV = 6	65 x 65 grid	4,225 subdivisions
SOLSUBDIV = 7	129 x 129 grid	16,641 subdivisions
SOLSUBDIV = 8	257 x 257 grid	66,049 subdivisions

If you're modeling large objects with small features, you'll need to set SOLSUBDIV higher than otherwise.

Increasing the SOLSUBDIV setting increases the accuracy of the calculation, but a higher setting also increases the time required to do the calculation. In general, each time you increase the SOLSUBDIV setting by 1, you increase the number of subdivisions by a factor of roughly 3 or 4. Each time you increase the setting by 2, you increase the subdivisions by a factor of roughly 10 or 15. This means that if using SOLMASSP on a certain composite requires 8 seconds calculation time, it may require 30 seconds when SOLSUBDIV is set one level higher, and close to 2 minutes when SOLSUBDIV is set two levels higher. See the SOLMASSP command in the next chapter.

Extracting 2D Views

- SOLSECTYPE (SOLid SECtion TYPE). Determines the contents of block created by the SOLSECT command to represent the outline of the section. When SOLSECTYPE = 1, block contains lines, arcs, etc. When 2, block contains polylines. When 3, block contains regions.

- SOLHPAT (SOLid Hatch PATtern). When the SOLSECT command is used to create a cross section, the SOLHPAT variable determines the hatch pattern that will be used. Enter none if you do not want the section hatched. The file ACAD.PAT determines valid responses. SOLHPAT also determines the hatch pattern used in regions.

- SOLHSIZE (SOLid Hatch SIZE). When the SOLSECT command is used to create a cross section, SOLHSIZE specifies the size of the hatch pattern by applying a scale factor to the basic hatch pattern definition. It also determines the size of the hatch pattern used in regions.

- SOLHANGLE (SOLid Hatch ANGLE). When the SOLSECT command is used to create a cross section, SOLHANGLE specifies the angle of the hatch pattern according to the current UCS. It also determines the angle of hatch patterns in regions.

Miscellaneous Variables

- SOLAMEVER (SOLid AME VERsion). Displays the Release number of AME currently in use. Read only.

- SOLPAGELEN (SOLid PAGE LENgth). Certain commands, such as SOLLIST, SOLMASSP and SOLMAT, flip you to the text screen (on single screen systems) and display several lines of information. The SOLPAGELEN variable sets the number of lines these commands display before pausing. For continuous scrolling, set SOLPAGELEN to 0.

- SOLSERVMSG (SOLid SERVer MeSsaGes). While AutoCAD is converting the display of solids to wireframe or mesh representation, or performing Boolean operations or mass properties calculations, it displays progress messages. Also, various error messages are displayed. SOLSERVMSG specifies how many messages will be displayed.

If SOLSERVMSG = 0, no messages.

If SOLSERVMSG = 1, error messages only.

If SOLSERVMSG = 2, error messages and beginning/end of progress messages.

If SOLSERVMSG = 3, error messages and full progress messages.

- SOLAMECOMP (SOLid AME COMPatibility). The command syntax (prompt sequence) for some AME commands has changed between AME R1 and AME R2. This variable controls which syntax AutoCAD expects, and is especially relevant if you have scripts or AutoLISP programs written for AME R1 but are currently running AME R2. Rather than changing the variable at the command prompt, add the line

    SOLAMECOMP AME1

to the beginning of AME R1 scripts and add the line

    SOLAMECOMP AME2

to the end of the script. You can make similar changes in your AutoLISP programs.

- SOLUPGRADE (SOLid UPGRADE). AME R1 uses single precision and AME R2 uses double precision. When a solid created with AME R1 is loaded into AME R2, it is possible to upgrade to double precision if SOLUPGRADE = 1, but if SOLUPGRADE = 0 single precision is retained. Upgraded solids may undergo slight changes that are discussed in the Introduction under "Advanced Modeling Extension Release 2."

Moving On

In this chapter we've shown you a variety of ways to move and modify solids. After carefully fashioning the model, you end up with a model packed with geometric and surface information. And since a material is assigned to the object, mass properties analysis can be performed on it.

The next chapter explores the various types of information that can be generated quickly for any solid model, explaining both the concepts and the commands AutoCAD uses for mass properties analysis.

ANALYZING THE SOLID: MATERIAL PROPERTIES

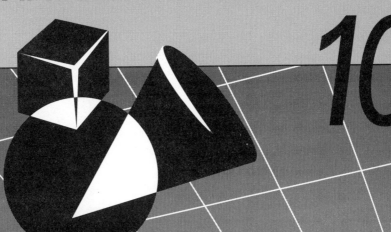

10

Analyzing the Solid: Material Properties

This chapter presents three commands that relate to the analysis of the solid as well as the ACAD.MAT file. The three commands are SOLAREA, SOLMASSP and SOLMAT.

The SOLAREA Command (Alias: SAREA)

The SOLAREA command calculates the surface area of one or more solids or regions. If you select several solids or regions, their total surface area is displayed. (The total for solids will be displayed separately from the total for regions.)

If the solid has not already been meshed, it is meshed for the purpose of calculating the surface area (although the display remains wireframe representation). The surface area is based on the sum of the areas of all the elements in the mesh. This means that the calculated surface area is only approximate. In general, the higher the setting of variable SOLWDENS (higher than 3), the more accurate the mesh and the more accurate the calculation.

For example, a cylinder that has a radius of 1 and a height of 2 has an actual surface area of 18.850. However, the SOLAREA command reports an area of

18.423	(2.27% low)	when SOLWDENS = 1
18.423	(2.27% low)	when SOLWDENS = 2
18.423	(2.27% low)	when SOLWDENS = 3
18.609	(1.28% low)	when SOLWDENS = 4
18.695	(0.82% low)	when SOLWDENS = 5
18.742	(0.57% low)	when SOLWDENS = 6
18.771	(0.42% low)	when SOLWDENS = 7
18.789	(0.32% low)	when SOLWDENS = 8
18.802	(0.25% low)	when SOLWDENS = 9
18.811	(0.21% low)	when SOLWDENS = 10
18.818	(0.17% low)	when SOLWDENS = 11
18.823	(0.14% low)	when SOLWDENS = 12

Notice that when SOLWDENS is set at 1 or 2, it produces the same area as when it is set at 3. Even though the wireframe representation of these meshes has only one and two tessellation lines per quadrant, respectively, their mesh representations both have three elements per quadrant (same as when SOLWDENS = 3). A mesh with only one or two elements per quadrant would be much too crude, so a mesh with three elements per quadrant is used even when SOLWDENS is set at 1 or 2.

The SOLMASSP Command (Alias: MP or MASSP)

The SOLMASSP command calculates certain mass properties of one or more solids or regions. If you select several solids, they are considered a unit and one report is given. For example, the reported volume in such a case is the sum of the volumes of the individual solids.

After the report, you are given an opportunity to place the report in a file. If you respond with Y, you're asked for a file name. The file will automatically be given the extension .MPR.

Sample Report

As you can see from the sample listing below, several different aspects of the object are analyzed. The ray projection and level of subdivision relate to the technique used to analyze the object. The mass, volume, bounding box and centroid provide a dimensional and translational analysis of the object. The moment of inertia, products of inertia, radii of gyration and principal moments provide an analysis of the rotational dynamics of the object around the UCS axes and around the object's centroid. Each of the various report sections is explained below.

If the selected object is a region, then area and perimeter are displayed in place of mass and volume, and the following items are displayed only if the region lies in the XY construction plane of the current UCS: moments of inertia, products of inertia, radii of gyration and principal moments.

The following is a report from a solid created by subtracting a cylinder from a box. The box was 4 units long, 4 wide and 1 high. The cylinder extended vertically through the center of the box and had a radius of 1 unit. Notice that the report below gives SI units (centimeters, grams, etc.). The units used in this report can be controlled by setting SOLLENGTH, SOLAREAU, SOLVOLUME and SOLMASS variables.

Mass Property Listing From the SOLMASSP Command

Ray projection along X axis, level of subdivision: 3.

Mass: 101.4 gm
Volume: 12.9 cu cm (Err: 0.4241)
Bounding box: X: 8 -- 12 cm
                     Y: 2 -- 6 cm
                     Z: 0 -- 1 cm
Centroid: X: 10 cm (Err: 0.3289)
                     Y: 4.006 cm (Err: 0.2193)
                     Z: 0.5023 cm (Err: 0.04013)
Moments of inertia: X: 1822 gm sq cm (Err: 158.5)
                    Y: 10332 gm sq cm (Err: 335.5)
                    Z: 12086 gm sq cm (Err: 429.7)
Products of inertia: XY: 4061 gm sq cm (Err: 222.3)
                     YZ: 203.9 gm sq cm (Err: 19.2)
                     ZX: 509.2 gm sq cm (Err: 40.68)
Radii of gyration: X: 4.239 cm
                     Y: 10.1 cm
                     Z: 10.92 cm

Principal moments (gm sq cm) and X-Y-Z directions about centroid:

I: 169 along [1 8.496e-13 -3.231e-16]
J: 322.6 along [2.407e-17 0.000352 1]
K: 169.4 along [8.496e-13 -1 0.000352]

Ray Projection Axis   In order to calculate the volume, rays are projected in the direction of the X, Y or Z axis of the current UCS. The axis is selected with the SOLDECOMP variable.

Level of Subdivision   The level of subdivision governs the accuracy of the volume calculation. It is set with the SOLSUBDIV variable.

Mass   Mass is sometimes equated with weight. However, an object's mass does not depend on the strength of the gravitational force. Rather, the mass of an object depends on its volume and the density of the material assigned to it: Mass = Density x Volume. An object's mass and weight are the same only under certain circumstances.

Technically, mass is a measure of an object's inertia or its resistance to linear acceleration. If an object is located at the earth's surface and is stationary, its weight is the same as its mass (because the acceleration tending to act on it is the acceleration of gravity). In this case, the object's mass can be determined simply by weighing it. But if the object is located above or below the earth's surface, its weight is less than its mass. While an object's weight changes as its distance from the earth's surface changes, its mass is constant.

Volume   The volume of an object is the amount of space it occupies, regardless of the object's material.

Volume is an approximation, the accuracy of which is governed by the setting of the variables SOLSUBDIV and SOLDECOMP. The volume is not affected by the setting of SOLWDENS when the solid was created.

Bounding Box   The bounding box of a solid is the smallest box that could contain the entire solid. The sides of this box are always parallel to the three principal planes of the current UCS. For many solids, rotating the solid or the UCS even a small amount can make a significant change in the size of the solid's bounding box.

Centroid   The centroid (or centroid of volume) of a solid is considered the same as its center of mass or center of gravity, assuming the material of the solid is homogeneous. The centroid is the point where half the volume is on one side of the point and the other half is on the other side of the point, no matter how the sides are divided. In other words, the centroid is the point from which the object could be suspended and all gravitational forces would cancel each other.

The report gives the X-Y-Z location of this center point, and the SOLMASSP command places a point at this location. The point can be seen more easily if you set the system variable PDMODE to something other than 0 or 1.

Moment of Inertia   The report gives the moment of inertia in relation to the three axes of the current UCS.

In very simple terms, the moment of inertia of any solid object tells how hard it is to start spinning that object around a certain axis. While inertia applies to linear acceleration, moment of inertia applies to angular or rotational acceleration. An object's moment of inertia is a measure of the turning force (torque) required to accelerate it around a given axis. (This is mass moment of inertia as opposed to area moment of inertia.)

Both location and orientation of the axis are very important. Using an axis that runs through the centroid of an object will give the object a smaller moment of inertia than a parallel axis located a certain distance away from the centroid. Also, an axis that runs through the centroid and runs parallel to the length of a long, skinny object will give the object a smaller moment of inertia than an axis running perpendicular to that object's length. As mass is increased near the perimeter of an object and decreased near its centroid, moment of inertia increases. Thus, the spinning skater has a greater moment of inertia when the arms are extended than when they are held close to the body.

Products of Inertia   Product of inertia applies to dynamic balance rather than static balance. When an axis of rotation runs through an object's centroid, the object is statically balanced. In this case, gravitational forces and translational forces applied to the centroid will not apply any torque to the object. However, when an object that is statically balanced wobbles when it's rotated, the forces that cause it to wobble are product-of-inertia forces. When its products of inertia are 0, it is dynamically balanced.

Radius of Gyration   An object's radius of gyration is the distance from the rotational axis to the point where its mass could be concentrated without changing its moment of inertia.

Principal Moment   An object's principal moment is the maximum moment of inertia around a centroidal axis oriented in such a fashion that it produces a zero product of inertia.

The SOLMAT Command (Alias: MATERIAL or MAT)

The SOLMAT command is used to assign a particular material to a given solid or region. It's also used to keep a record of the property definitions of each material.

Material properties are important for some of the calculations that need to be done on solids. For example, the weight of an object is dependent on both the volume of the solid and the density of the material assigned to the object.

To see the material assigned to any particular solid, use the SOLLIST command.

AutoCAD keeps a list of materials and their properties in the drawing. It also keeps a separate list of materials and their properties in a file called ACAD.MAT, and can keep lists in material files with other names as well. (ACAD.MAT is the default material file.) A copy of the ACAD.MAT material file, which is supplied with AutoCAD AME, is included at the end of this section.

Material definitions can be imported into a drawing from a file, or exported from the drawing to a file. Material definitions, both in the drawing and on file, can be changed from within the drawing at any time.

The SOLMAT prompt contains several options, which are explained below. Each time you complete one of these options, the main prompt reappears. Press `Enter` or use `Ctrl-C` to exit the SOLMAT command.

Enter

 C (Change) To assign a new material to one or more existing solids. You will be prompted to select the solids. Then you will be asked for the new material. The default material is determined by the SEt option explained below. The name of the material you enter must match exactly one of the names in the material list. Enter `?` to get a list of these names, then enter the file name.

 E (Edit) To revise the property definitions of the materials already recorded in this drawing. You'll be prompted for the name of the material. A list of properties will be displayed, each with a number in front of it. You can enter the number of any property in order to revise that property, then enter the new value. When you're done revising the values, enter `0` to record your revisions in the drawing. When prompted, enter `Y` if you want these same revisions stored in the external material file.

X (eXit) To exit SOLMAT and return to the command prompt.

LI (LIst) To display the properties of any material. When prompted, enter the name of the material. If the material is defined within the current drawing, the current drawing is the source of the listing. If it is not defined internally, the listing comes from the default material file.

LO (LOad) To load a material definition from one of the material files into the current drawing. AutoCAD AME will search ACAD.MAT first, and load the material definition if it finds the material in that file. If it does not find it in ACAD.MAT, you'll be prompted for the name of a different material file.

N (New) To add a new material definition within your drawing and, optionally, in an external file. You'll be prompted for the name of the new material and for a description of it. Then a list of properties will be displayed, with all the values blank. You can edit it the same way you would in the Edit option. Then you're asked if you want to save this new definition in a file. If you enter Y, you're prompted for the file name.

R (Remove) To remove the name of a material from within your drawing. When prompted, enter its name.

SA (SAve) To save on file a material definition that currently exists in your drawing. Then you're prompted for the name of the material, then the name of the file.

SE (SEt) To set the default material that will be assigned to subsequently created solids.

? For a list of material definitions currently recorded in your drawing and saved on file. Then you're prompted for the name of the file. A listing displays in two parts: materials presently defined in the drawing, and materials defined in the file.

The ACAD.MAT File

Following is the ACAD.MAT file that is included with AutoCAD. Notice the file's format, such as the asterisk (*) before the material name and the semicolon (;) in front of comments. If you create a new material file from within AutoCAD, using SOLMAT New, this format is used automatically. If you use your text editor to edit either the ACAD.MAT file or one of your own material files, be sure to maintain this exact format. Currently, AME uses only the property of density. If your calculations do not require a particular property, you can place any number at that location in the file.

Notice also the listing of the various properties. This listing pertains to the format of the file. The meaning and use of each property is explained after the file listing and in Chapter 5 of the *Advanced Modeling Extension Reference Manual*.

System standard materials

; The format of this file is, in the following order:

; *<Material_name>, <Description>

; Density	- in kilograms per cubic meters.
; Young's_modulus ;	- Young's modulus of linear elasticity in giga-newtons per square meter.
; Poisson's_ratio ; ;	-Dimensionless ratio of lateral-compressive strength to longitudinal extensional strain.
; Yield_strength ;	-Point at which linear elasticity breaks down, in mega-newtons per square meter.
; Ultimate_tensile_strength ; ;	- Tensile strength limit; beyond this the material will break, in mega-newtons per square meter.
; Thermal_conductivity ;	- Conduction of heat, in watts per meter degree Kelvin.
; Coefficient_of_ ; linear_expansion	- Linear expansion/10^6 per degree Kelvin.
; Specific_heat ; ;	- Energy input required to raise one gram of the material by one degree Kelvin, in kilojoules per kilogram degree Kelvin.

; All values are given at approx. 25 degrees centigrade.

; The parameters are all real numbers and may continue onto as
; many lines as are required.

*Aluminum

2710 73 0.33 20 70 204 22 0.896

*Brass, Soft Yellow Brass

8470 109.6 .331 103.4 275 116 20.5 .369

*Bronze, Soft Tin Bronze

8874 109.6 .335 128 275 62 18.3 .436

*Copper

8940 117.5 0.345 330 380 386 16.7 0.383

*Glass

2600 65 0.23 1 70 0.9 8 0.84

*HSLA_Stl, High Strength Low Alloy Steel

7840 200 .287 275.8 448 47 12 .42

*Lead

11370 14 .43 8.96 18 37 53.2 .130

*Mild_Steel

7860 220 0.275 207 345 56 12 0.46

*NICU, Monel 400

8830 179.3 .315 220 558 21.8 10.9 .428

*Stainless_Stl, Austenic Stainless Steel

8030 190.3 .305 228 545 14 17.4 .456

All values are given at approximately 25 degrees centigrade (77 degrees Fahrenheit).

AutoCAD AME currently uses only the property of density. Other properties can be accessed by AutoLISP programs and other external programs for special calculations.

Density Density tells how much mass is contained in one cubic unit of the material. In other words, density is mass per volume.

Density = Total mass / Volume

Density may be given in pounds per cubic inch or kilograms per cubic meter, etc.

Density can be used in calculating the total mass of a solid.

Total mass = Volume X Density

For example, a solid made of aluminum (density = 2710 kilograms per cubic meter) that has a volume of .045 cubic meter would have a total mass of 121.95 kilograms.

Young's Modulus, or Modulus of Elasticity

Young's modulus compares stress versus strain (elongation). In simple terms, it tells how stiff the material is—that is, how hard it is to stretch the material.

Many materials will stretch a certain amount when a tensile (pulling) force is applied; and when twice the force is applied, they will stretch twice as much. When the force is removed, the material (still in its elastic state) returns to its original length. Up to a certain limit, known as the *proportional limit* (which for practical purposes is at or just below the elastic limit), this ratio between the force and the amount of elongation remains constant. In other words, the elongation is proportional to the force.

The modulus of elasticity is the ratio between stress (the force per area) and the elongation (the amount of elongation per original length). That is, it is stress divided by elongation. Since elongation is a simple ratio, say inches per inches, it is actually a unitless number. So the modulus of elasticity has the same units as the stress (force per area). For example, if the stress is measured in pounds per square inch and the elongation is measured in inch per inch, the modulus of elasticity would be stated in pounds per square inch (psi). Another typical unit for the modulus of elasticity is giga-newtons per square meter.

Modulus of elasticity is determined experimentally, and various sources list different values. Nevertheless, some typical values are given below. The higher the modulus of elasticity, the harder it is to stretch the material.

Aluminum - 10,000,000 psi
Brass - 11,000,000 psi
Copper - 15,000,000 psi
Steel (A572-50) - 29,000,000 psi

The modulus of elasticity can be used to determine the amount of elongation according to the following formula.

$$\text{Elongation} = \frac{\text{Force x Length}}{\text{Area x Modulus-of-Elasticity}}$$

For example, if a weight of 8,000 pounds is hung from a 36-inch straight steel member measuring .5 x .5 inch (.25 inch cross-sectional area), the elongation would be .040 inch.

$$\text{Elongation} = \frac{8,000 \ \text{x} \ 36}{.25 \ \text{x} \ 29,000,000} = .040 \ \text{inch}$$

Poisson's Ratio

When a member is stretched, its cross-sectional dimension decreases. When it's compressed, its cross-sectional dimension increases. Poisson's ratio is the ratio of this cross-sectional increase or decrease to the amount of stretching or compression. It is a strict ratio with no units.

Typical Poisson's ratios range from roughly one-quarter to one-third. For example, the ratio for Mild steel is .275, and for Aluminum is .33.

Yield Strength

When material is stressed past its elastic limit, it is said to yield. The yield strength of the material is the amount of stress required to reach this yield point. When the material experiences stress beyond its yield strength, "permanent set" takes place and the material does not return to its original shape when the force is removed. At this point, the material has not failed (broken) but is permanently deformed. Yield strength is also called bending point.

Yield strength is measured in such units as pounds per square inch (psi) and mega-newtons per square meter.

Ultimate Tensile Strength

When stresses are introduced greater than the yield strength of the material, finally the material fails (breaks). The amount of stress the material can take just before failure is its ultimate strength. Ultimate strength is measured in such units as pounds per square inch (psi) and in mega-newtons per square meter.

Thermal Conductivity

A material's thermal conductivity is its ability to transmit heat. Thermal conductivity is measured in watts per meter degree Kelvin.

Coefficient of Linear Expansion

The coefficient of linear expansion tells how much a material expands as it is heated up. It is the ratio of the linear expansion per unit length per amount of temperature increase.

$$\text{Coefficient} = \frac{\text{Linear expansion / Length}}{\text{Degrees}}$$

The coefficient of linear expansion is measured in such units as inches per inch per degree Fahrenheit and in millimeters per millimeter per degree centigrade, etc. This coefficient can be used to calculate amount of expansion.

$$\text{Linear expansion} = \text{Coefficient} \ \text{X} \ \text{Degrees} \ \text{X} \ \text{Length}$$

For example, if a 40-inch-long piece of aluminum (coefficient = .0000128 inches per inch per degree Fahrenheit) is heated from 70 degrees to 120 degrees, it will be .026 inch longer.

$$\text{Linear expansion} = .0000128 \ \text{X} \ 50 \ \text{X} \ 40 \ = \ .026$$

Specific Heat

Specific heat is the amount of heat required to raise the temperature of a certain amount of a given material by one degree—heat per mass per degree.

$$\text{Specific heat} = \frac{\text{Heat/Mass}}{\text{Degree}}$$

Some of the units that can be used are as follows: heat can be measured in Joules; mass of the material in grams or kilograms; temperature difference in degrees centigrade (Kelvin) or Fahrenheit.

Moving On

Now it's time to try out what we've been describing in these last two chapters: modification and analysis of the model. The following chapter devotes one project to each of these topics.

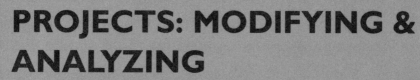

PROJECTS: MODIFYING & ANALYZING

11

• •

Projects: Modifying & Analyzing

T his chapter features two projects: Project 11A creates a Pivot Block
and illustrates the SOLMOVE and SOLCHP commands; Project 11B
creates a Stop Block and illustrates the SOLAREA, SOLMASSP and
SOLMAT commands.

Project IIA: Pivot Block, Modification

To create a Pivot Block, our approach will be to stay in the WCS at all
times, create most of the primitives at 0,0, then move and rotate them into
position with the SOLMOVE command. We'll then modify the design of
the block with the SOLCHP command.

Figure 11-1:
Original Pivot
Block.

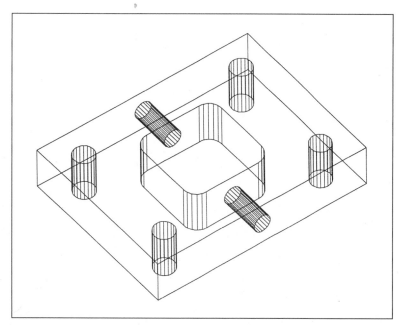

1. Start AutoCAD and create a drawing called PIVOT, using the SMB prototype drawing you created in Chapter 7, "Projects: Boolean Operations." If you didn't complete that project, you may want to do that now (it's a very short project). Or you could use the SMB prototype drawing on the *Solid Modeling With AutoCAD* companion diskette available with this book.

2. Load AME (Release 11 only). Make sure you're in Model Space on layer SM.

   First, create the basic box from which everything else will be subtracted.

3. Create a box at 0,0 that is 3 x 4 x .75.

4. Use the Center option of the ZOOM command to center each view around the point 1.5,2,.5 with a scale of 1xp.

5. Set SOLWDENS to 5.

   ```
   SOLWDENS [Enter]
   5 [Enter]
   ```

   Next create the four fastening holes in the corners.

6. Create a cylinder at 0,0 with .375 diameter and .75 height.

7. Use SOLMOVE to move the fastening hole to .5,.5.

   ```
   SOLMOVE [Enter]
   L [Enter][Enter]
   tx.5,ty.5 [Enter][Enter]
   REDRAWALL [Enter]
   ```

8. Make a rectangular array of the fastening hole, 2 rows, 2 columns, 3.00 row spacing, 2.00 column spacing.

Next, create the horizontal pivot hole. Create it vertically and reposition it with SOLMOVE.

9. Create a cylinder at 0,0 that is .3125 diameter and 3.00 high.

10. Move this cylinder into position with the SOLMOVE command. Remember to attach the icon to the cylinder before the first move.

```
SOLMOVE [Enter]

L [Enter][Enter]

e [Enter]
```

Pick bottom edge of cylinder.

```
af [Enter]
```

Pick the left face on the far side of the box (if needed, enter N until left face is highlighted). [Enter]

```
tx.375,ty2,ry180  [Enter][Enter]

REDRAWALL [Enter]
```

Next, create the extrusion that will become the large center opening.

11. Use PLINE to create a square, starting at 0,0, that is 1.5 on all sides. Fillet all four corners of this polyline with a .25 radius.

12. Use SOLEXT to extrude the polyline to a height of .75 (no taper).

13. Use SOLMOVE to center the extrusion in the box.

```
SOLMOVE [Enter]

L [Enter][Enter]

tx.75,ty1.25  [Enter][Enter]

REDRAWALL [Enter]
```

14. Subtract the four fastening holes, horizontal pivot hole and extrusion from the box.

15. Save your drawing.

16. In Paper Space, zoom up on the upper right viewport, then return to Model Space to mesh and hide/shade the block to check its appearance.

17. Return the block to wireframe representation. In Paper Space, ZOOM Previous, then return to Model Space.

Figure 11-2:
Modified Pivot
Block.

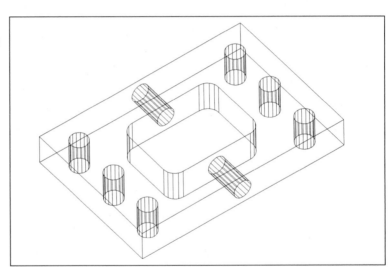

Now we'll modify the Pivot Block so it's .125 thinner and .5 longer. Also, the horizontal pivot hole will become .375 diameter. We will add one more fastening hole on each end, and enlarge the center opening.

18. Make the box .625 thick and 4.5 long.

```
SOLCHP [Enter]
```

Pick the block.

Pick the box.

```
S [Enter]
```

```
3 [Enter]

4.5 [Enter]

.625 [Enter]

E [Enter]  (Do not exit SOLCHP.)
```

19. Move the two back fastening holes .5 in the Y direction.

Press Enter until one of the back fastening holes is highlighted.

```
M [Enter]

0,.5 [Enter][Enter]
```

(Do the same with the other back fastening hole.)

```
E [Enter]  (Do not exit SOLCHP.)
```

20. Make the horizontal hole .375 diameter; move it .0625 in the negative Z direction and .25 in the Y direction.

Press Enter until the horizontal hole is highlighted.

```
S [Enter]

.1875 [Enter][Enter]

3 [Enter]

M [Enter]

0,.25,-.0625 [Enter][Enter]

E [Enter]  (Do not exit SOLCHP.)
```

21. Create another copy (instance) of one of the fastening holes.

Press Enter until one of the fastening holes is highlighted.

```
I [Enter]

X [Enter]
```

The copied cylinder will be placed at the same locations as the original.

22. Move the copied hole one inch so it's midway between the two corner fastening holes. Then copy it to the other end of the Pivot Block. Redraw the screen. Remember that these two holes, although they are placed within the block, are not yet part of the composite.

23. Subtract the two new holes from the composite.

24. Re-form the center opening. This requires that you recover the polyline from which the center opening was extruded, enlarge it, extrude it, then replace the old opening with the new one.

    SOLCHP [Enter]

Pick the Pivot Block.

Pick the center opening (or press Enter until it is highlighted).

    S [Enter]

    Y [Enter]

    X [Enter]

25. The polyline will be located immediately under the extrusion. In the upper left viewport, move it 3 inches to the right and stretch it .5 in the Y direction. Then extrude it .75 (no taper).

26. Use SOLCHP to replace the old extrusion with this new one.

    SOLCHP [Enter]

Pick the Pivot Block.

Pick the center opening (or press Enter until it is highlighted).

    R [Enter]

Pick the enlarged extrusion.

    N [Enter] (Do not exit SOLCHP.)

27. Move the new extrusion into position.

28. Change the color of the seven holes to red (1). Exit SOLCHP.

29. Save the drawing.

This completes the modification of the Pivot Block. If it seems to you that it would have been almost as easy to re-create the block from scratch, you are correct. But that's only because the block was quite easy to model in the first place, and because we made so many changes. In most situations, modifying an existing block with SOLCHP is the best way to proceed.

Project 11B: Stop Block, Analysis

This project creates a simple Stop Block for analysis purposes.

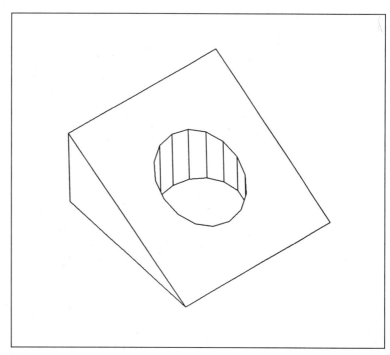

Figure 11-3: Stop Block for analysis.

I. Start AutoCAD and create a drawing called STOP that uses the SMB prototype drawing you created in Chapter 7. If you did not complete that project, you may want to do that now (it's a very short project). Or you could use the SMB prototype drawing on the *Solid Modeling With AutoCAD* companion diskette.

2. Use the Center option of the ZOOM command to center the views in each viewport around 5,2,.5 with a scale factor of 1xp.

3. Make sure you are in Model Space on layer SM.

4. Load AME (Release 11 only).

We will create a very simple composite made up of two primitives.

5. Create a wedge at 4,1 that is 2 x 2 x 1.

6. Create a cylinder at 5,2 that is 1 diameter and 1 high.

7. Subtract the cylinder from the wedge.

Calculated by hand, the actual surface area of this Stop Block is 12.379432, and its actual volume is 1.607301. You can use these numbers for comparison with the reports generated by SOLAREA and SOLMASSP.

8. Use SOLAREA to find the surface area of the Stop Block. The SOLAREA command generates a mesh from which it calculates the area. To see the area out to six decimal places, use SOLLIST.

When we use SOLMASSP to analyze the mass properties of the Stop Block, we will change the material assigned to the block and the location of the block in order to see the differences these changes make in the report. We will also change variables SOLDECOMP and SOLSUBDIV in order to see the difference they make in the accuracy of the report.

9. Use SOLLIST to check the material assigned to the Stop Block. It should be MILD_STEEL. (If it isn't, use SOLMAT to assign MILD_STEEL to the Stop Block.)

   SOLMAT [Enter]

   C [Enter]

   Pick block. [Enter]

   MILD_STEEL [Enter][Enter]

10. Make sure variable SOLDECOMP is set to X and SOLSUBDIV is set to 3.

    SOLDECOMP [Enter]

    X [Enter]

    SOLSUBDIV [Enter]

    3 [Enter]

11. Use SOLMASSP to calculate the mass properties of the Stop Block. Save the report in a file called STOP1. (AutoCAD will automatically give this file the extension .MPR.)

    SOLMASSP [Enter]

    Pick block.

    [Enter]

    Y [Enter]

    STOP1 [Enter]

    (To preserve this report, you could also do a "print-screen.")

12. Use SOLMAT to assign ALUMINUM to the Stop Block. Recalculate mass properties. Save the report in a file called STOP2. (You must use a different file name, because AutoCAD overwrites an existing file with the same name rather than concatenating reports.) Use the TYPE command. Compare the two reports. Notice that the change in material has changed mass, moments of inertia, products of inertia and principal moments.

13. Move the Stop Block 4.00 to the left (negative X direction). Recalculate mass properties. Save the report in a file called STOP3. Compare this report with the previous report. Notice that the change in location has changed centroid (X), moments of inertia (Y and Z), products of inertia (XY and ZX) and radii of gyration (Y and Z).

14. Change SOLDECOMP to Y. Then use SOLMASSP to analyze the Stop Block and notice the effect this change has on the report.

15. Change SOLSUBDIV to 6. Then use SOLMASSP to analyze the Stop Block and notice the effect this change has on the accuracy of the report.

16. Set SOLWDENS to 7. Then reconstruct the Stop Block, or replace the cylinder with a new cylinder. Use SOLAREA to find the surface area of the Stop Block and notice the effect this change has on the accuracy of the surface calculation.

Remember that the area calculation done by SOLAREA is affected by the setting of SOLWDENS at the time the primitives were created, inasmuch as SOLWDENS affects the fineness of the mesh used to calculate area (especially curved surfaces).

Also recall that mass properties calculations done with SOLMASSP are not affected by SOLWDENS. But they are affected by SOLDECOMP and SOLSUBDIV. In addition, of course, the material assigned to the object and the location and orientation of the object affect certain portions of the analysis.

Moving On

So your model is more than just a static shape. You can change it and, in effect, try out different designs before settling on the final version. The ability to quickly analyze the model, then modify the model based on that analysis is a significant contribution of solid modeling.

But in many situations the process will not stop there. The model will serve an additional purpose—producing traditional 2D engineering drawings. In other situations the model may be part of a larger assembly. The next chapter discusses the various views, procedures and commands needed to accomplish both extracting 2D views and building assemblies.

DETAIL DRAWINGS & ASSEMBLIES

12

DETAIL DRAWINGS & ASSEMBLIES

S olid models have many purposes. In some situations a model will be created primarily for analysis by AutoCAD's built-in solid inquiry commands, SOLAREA and SOLMASSP; in other cases, mainly for use by Finite Element Analysis (FEA) or Computer-Aided Manufacturing (CAM) software, or to produce 2D engineering drawings of an object. (And, often a solid model is used for a combination of purposes.)

Later in this chapter, you'll find several AutoCAD AME commands designed to help you create 2D drawings from a 3D solid model.

Solid Model Views

One of the reasons 3D modeling can save time is that once the model is constructed, it can be viewed from any direction and in several different ways without any further line construction. The types of views that can be generated directly from any 3D model (wireframe, surface or solid) are listed below. In these views, hidden lines can be removed from a surface or solid model.

- Standard orthographic views of the model itself (the traditional top, front and side views).

- Auxiliary views of the model itself (primary, secondary, etc.).

- Perspective views (full 3-point perspective).

- Clipped views.

Since the above aspects of viewing a 3D model are common to wireframe, surface and solid modeling, they have already been discussed in Chapter 3, "General 3D Commands: UCSs, Space & Viewing." In particular, see the sections on the VPOINT, PLAN and DVIEW commands.

2D View Features

In addition to the types of views just mentioned, other types of views can be extracted from a solid model, including

- Feature isolation—SOLFEAT command.

- Section views (single cutting plane, any orientation, including automatic cross-hatching)—SOLSECT command.

- Profile view with hidden lines (not to be confused with the hidden line removal mentioned above)—SOLPROF command.

Features With the **SOLFEAT** Command

The SOLFEAT command replicates a single feature of the solid—either a face or an edge. This command produces 2D entities, but not regions. This unique capability of solid models, which allows a given feature to be easily isolated from the rest of the model, is helpful in very complex or feature-rich models.

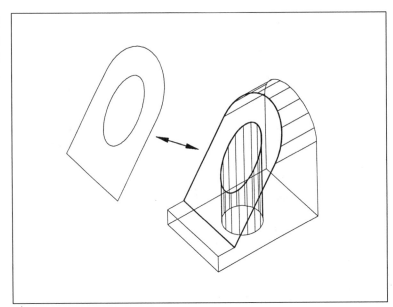

Figure 12-1: Feature (face) produced with SOLFEAT.

Your model must be shown in wireframe representation for SOLFEAT to work. If you do not change it to wireframe (with the SOLWIRE command) before you use SOLFEAT, you will be given an opportunity within the SOLFEAT command.

SOLFEAT isolates a feature by creating an unnamed block at the location of the feature it is replicating. The block will be either a flat 2D block or a 3D block, depending on the selected feature. It may contain lines, circles, arcs and/or polylines. (See "Note on Anonymous Blocks" later in this section.)

First you're prompted for an edge or a face. If you want to select an edge, enter E, then select the edge.

```
SOLFEAT [Enter]
Edge/<Face>:
```

If you want to select a face (the default response), press Enter (or enter F), then select one of the face's edges. The face can be a curved surface. Of course, each edge can belong to two faces, so AutoCAD will highlight one of the faces having that edge. If that's the desired face, press Enter. Otherwise, enter N so the next face will be highlighted, then press Enter. This process is repeated allowing you to select as many faces (or edges) as you want. If you enter All instead of selecting individual faces (or edges), then all faces (or edges) will be replicated, each on a separate block.

After the feature block is created, you may want to move it to a different location or write it to disk. Since the block will be created at the same location as the feature it's replicating, the block may not appear on screen (it will be highlighted, but it will appear no different than the highlighted feature). But if you switch to a layer that has a color different from the color the solid had before you used SOLFEAT, you'll be able to see the block appear as it is created. (See also "Viewport-Specific Layers" in Chapter 2, "Projects: Setup & Overview.") Since you usually want your profile to show up only in the current viewport, a good layer to use is the one that was set up for solid-line profiles in the current viewport (layer PV-...). These layers already exist in the prototype drawing created in Project 2A.

Regardless of whether you switch to a layer with a different color, you can still select the block either by using the "Last" option or with the pickbox. The feature can then be used as the basis for constructing a more complete view of that portion of the object. Of course, the block can be exploded and then modified.

SOLFEAT can also be used on regions.

Sections With the SOLSECT Command

The SOLSECT command creates a cross section of one or more solids. First you are prompted to select objects. You can select a single solid or several.

Then you are prompted to position the sectioning plane using the same procedure used for Baseplanes. If you have set up an appropriate UCS before starting SOLSECT, you can use the XY option when prompted to

position the sectioning plane. Setting up an appropriate UCS before starting SOLSECT also allows you to save the name of the UCS, which could
help you recall it later.

SOLSECT will produce one or two blocks. If no cross hatching is requested, only the block for the outline of the section will be produced. If
cross hatching is requested (see the end of this section for details), it is
placed in a separate block.

The block(s) that are created are flat, 2D blocks. They represent only the
part of the solid that is actually in contact with the sectioning plane. Thus,
it is only a partial section view because the part of the object behind the
sectioning plane is not included as it is in standard engineering drawings.
In many situations you will want to complete the section view. This might
involve adding lines, etc., manually, or using SOLPROF to produce a
profile from which you can steal features to complete the section view.

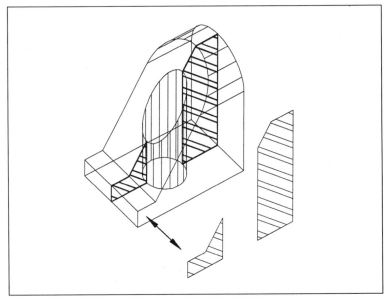

Figure 12-2:
Hatched section
produced with
SOLSECT.

SOLSECT will produce three different types of entities within the
section view. If variable SOLSECTYPE is set to 1, the outline of the section
block is composed of lines, arcs, etc. If SOLSECTYPE is set to 2, it is composed of polylines. If SOLSECTYPE is set to 3, the outline is composed of
one or more regions.

The section block (an anonymous block) is placed "within" the solid. You'll probably want to select the section block in order to move it or write it to disk. Even though it's created within the solid, you can select it with the usual pickbox or with "L" (last) since it was created after the solid. (See "Note on Anonymous Blocks" later in this section.)

If you want the section to be cross-hatched automatically, set the variable SOLHPAT to the name of the desired hatch pattern. Set the variable SOLHSIZE to control the size of the hatch pattern, and set SOLHANGLE to control its angle. If you do not want the section cross-hatched automatically, set SOLHPAT to "none."

Profiles With the SOLPROF Command

The SOLPROF command creates a profile of a solid, including all its edges, according to the view in the current viewport. (SOLPROF does not work with regions.) The profile will have no tessellation lines; it can use hidden lines for hidden edges at your request. The profile is either a 3D or 2D block created from lines, circles, arcs and/or polylines. It is generated according to the current viewing direction, so it does not necessarily make sense when viewed from another direction (particularly if hidden lines are shown with a hidden linetype).

Figure 12-3: Profile produced with SOLPROF.

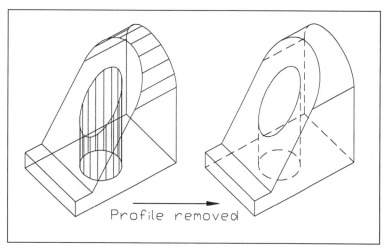

Profile removed

TILEMODE must be set to 0, and you must be in Model Space for this command to work. This may involve as many as three steps.

1. Set TILEMODE to 0.

2. Create one or more viewports with the MVIEW command.

3. Switch to Model Space with the MSPACE command.

Some of these operations may already have been accomplished, either by you previously in the drawing or by your prototype drawing. (You'll recall that in all our projects, we keep TILEMODE at 0 and set up all our viewports in Paper Space, thereby accomplishing the three steps mentioned above.)

After you enter SOLPROF, you're prompted to select one or more solids you want profiled. After selecting the solid(s), you're asked if you want hidden lines displayed on a separate layer (so they can be easily assigned a hidden linetype). If you respond N, only one block is created, with all lines using a continuous linetype. If you respond Y, visible lines are profiled in one block, using a continuous linetype, and hidden lines are profiled in a separate block on a separate layer.

Each profile block is placed on a layer whose name has two parts separated by a dash. The first part is either PV or PH (for Profile Visible and Profile Hidden), and the second part is the handle of the current viewport. For example, if you're in the viewport with handle 3, the continuous (solid, visible) lines would be placed on layer PV-3 and the hidden lines on layer PH-3. If they're needed, AutoCAD creates these layers automatically. You can alter the color and linetype settings on these newly created layers after using SOLPROF—or even better, set up the appropriate layers ahead of time as we did in the prototype drawing created in Chapter 2. See Project 2A for additional information on setting up layers for extracting profiles. See also "Note on Anonymous Blocks" below.

SOLPROF also asks if you want the profile projected onto a plane, that is, flattened onto a plane perpendicular to your viewing direction. Both 2D (flattened) profiles and 3D (unflattened) profiles have their advantages. In flattened profiles, lines appearing as points are eliminated, edge views of circles and arcs are replaced with lines, and there are not as many redundant hidden lines, so cleanup is a little easier. But in unflattened profiles, you are able to access centers of oblique circles (assuming the appropriate UCS is established) and other features that may be lost in the flattening process. Also, hidden lines may display more realistically on oblique curves (which are still circles and arcs in the unflattened profile rather than polylines in a flattened profile). Remember that it is not necessary to flatten the profile for dimensioning since all dimensions are projected onto the current XY construction plane. After a little experience with both flattened and unflattened profiles, you will be able to decide which type best serves your purposes for different views.

Finally, SOLPROF asks if you want tangential edges removed. In the profile of the Skully above, (Figure 12-3), tangential edges show where the top curved surface meets the flat sides. Normally you want these edges deleted.

After you create the profile block(s), you may want to select them—perhaps to move them or write them to disk. Even though the block is created at the same location as the edges they represent, you can still select them with the usual pickbox, since they were created after the solid.

In other situations when you don't want to move the profile or write it to disk, all you need to do is freeze the layer the model resides on, so that only the profile block or blocks are visible.

Note on Anonymous Blocks

Each of the preceding commands places geometry into a block with no name. Having the geometry in a block makes it convenient to manipulate it as a unit. However, if you want to manipulate the geometry by name, you can use the BLOCK command to place it in another block that you name, exploding it first if desired.

Manipulating Viewports in Paper Space

As you read the next few sections, keep in mind the important distinction between the viewport itself and the view within the viewport. The *viewport* is the rectangular border that's treated as an object in Paper Space. (The terms "viewport" and "viewport border" refer to the same thing.) However, the *view* is the picture of the model that appears in the viewport.

In Paper Space, viewports are just like other objects in many respects. They can be edited with the commands ERASE, MOVE, COPY, ARRAY, SCALE, STRETCH, MIRROR, ROTATE and CHPROP. You can osnap to the endpoint, midpoint, etc., of a viewport. Also, dragging will work with viewports, but the views in the viewports do not drag. We need to look a little more closely at the effects of each of these editing commands on both the viewport and the view within the viewport. Keep in mind that the following discussion assumes you're using these commands in Paper Space.

The ERASE command erases a viewport just as it would any other object. Viewports can be selected individually with the pickbox or selected with either a regular or crossing window. When the viewport is erased, the view that was in the viewport disappears. If you want to get rid of a viewport (border) and keep the view, use CHPROP to change the border to a layer you can freeze. In the prototype drawing created in Chapter 2, viewports were created on layer VPBORDER for this reason.

The MOVE command moves a viewport and the view within it. You can use any of the usual procedures to indicate the endpoints of the displacement vector. When you move a viewport, the view follows. The view keeps its same center point and magnification within the viewport.

The COPY command copies the viewport and the view within it. You can use any of the usual procedures to indicate the endpoints of the displacement vector.

The ARRAY command can produce both rectangular and polar arrays of viewports and their views. In polar arrays, the viewports are never rotated.

When you produce extra viewports, whether you use the MVIEW, COPY or ARRAY command, remember that the maximum number of viewports that can be "on" at any one time is governed by the variable MAXACTVP, and that the on/off status of individual viewports is governed by the MVIEW command.

The SCALE command scales a viewport but does not scale the view within the viewport. If you reduce the size of a viewport too much, you may lose all or part of your view, in which case you'll have to pan or zoom it back into position in Model Space. Often it's handy to anchor the base point for the scaling operation at a corner of the viewport or at the midpoint of one of its sides.

The STRETCH command (always with a crossing window) is the most flexible command for manipulating viewports. It can be used to move one, two, three or four edges of a viewport at once.

Suppose you enter STRETCH and window a viewport's right edge. If ortho is on, only the right edge will move. If ortho is off, then the top and bottom edges of the viewport will also slide up or down as you move the right edge.

Now suppose that instead of windowing one whole edge, you window just one corner of the viewport. Then you can stretch either side by itself if ortho is on or stretch the two adjoining sides simultaneously if ortho is off.

When you stretch a viewport, the view within the viewport is not moved or stretched. If you stretch the viewport too small, you may lose part or all of your view, in which case you'll have to pan or zoom it back into position in Model Space. However, if you enclose an entire viewport in your crossing window, then the viewport will be moved as if you had selected it for the MOVE command, and the view will move with the viewport.

The MIRROR command allows you to mirror a viewport, either retaining or deleting the original viewport. The view within the viewport is copied to the new viewport but is not mirrored.

The ROTATE command can be used to rotate a viewport, but the behavior of the viewport will not be like other rotated objects. The viewport will change positions (its center will rotate to the new position, assuming its center does not coincide with the center of the rotation), but the sides of the viewport will not rotate. The viewport will retain its original size, shape and orientation. The view within the viewport will move with the viewport.

The CHPROP command can change a viewport's color or layer, but a viewport's linetype will always be continuous.

Lining Up Orthographic Views & Auxiliary Views

In traditional drafting, the view's placement and alignment are important.

Drafting Standards

In the United States we use third-angle projection. Third-angle projection requires that the view of the top of the object be placed above the view of the front of the object, and the view of the right side of the object be placed to the right of the front view. First-angle projection, more common in Europe, places the top view below the front and the right-side view to the left of the front. AutoCAD allows you to line up the views any way you want, so both third-angle and first-angle projection are easy to set up. (All the drawings in this book use third-angle projection.)

No matter which projection system is used, the main orthographic views and auxiliary views must be lined up precisely. They must be the same scale (magnification), and corresponding features between views must line up along the same horizontal or vertical line for orthographic views or along the same angular line for auxiliary views. In contrast, there is more flexibility in locating both enlarged views and "removed" section views based on cutting plane indicators (typically labeled as "SECTION A-A," etc.).

Considering both viewports and views, there are four possibilities.

Viewports lined up	Views lined up
1. YES	YES
2. NO	YES
3. YES	NO
4. NO	NO

Since standard drafting practice calls for main orthographic views and auxiliary views to be lined up, we are concerned with creating situations 1 and 2 above. We must have views lined up.

Two Methods for Lining Up Views

The two basic methods for lining up views in different Paper Space viewports are (1) using the ZOOM command's Center option and XP feature while you're in Model Space, and (2) using osnap on the model while you're in Paper Space. As we explore both of these approaches, we'll consider only two viewports.

Assume you're in Paper Space, with two different viewports, each with its own unique view of the model. The procedures involved in lining up these two viewports can easily be applied to lining up the third and following viewports with the first two viewports.

The two methods described in the following sections are important to know. There are times when you need to line up viewports manually and no other methods are appropriate. However, AME supplies two other programs that assist you in creating and lining up viewports. The most useful is the Solview program, which contains two commands, SOLVIEW and SOLDRAW. The SOLVIEW command is very flexible, allowing you to create orthographic, auxiliary and section views. The AutoLISP program MVSETUP has a more limited use. Each of these programs is discussed later in this chapter.

Lining Up Views—Method 1

Using ZOOM Center and XP in Model Space   This is the method we've used in all the previous projects. The principle behind Method 1 is simple: if two viewports are the same size and are lined up, then the centers of these viewports are lined up. Further, in Model Space, if the two different views in those viewports are centered around the same point and are the same scale in relation to Paper Space, then those views are lined up.

You can use the ZOOM command, Center option, to place the same point at the center of the view in both viewports. You can also use the XP feature of the ZOOM command to make sure the magnification of the view maintains the same ratio to Paper Space in both viewports.

Therefore, if the same point is placed at the center of both viewports, and the magnification in both viewports is the same, the views will be lined up properly as long as the viewports themselves are lined up. You can see an example of this approach in Project 2B, step 4.

This approach works easily when the two viewports are the same size and are lined up with each other. It also works if the two viewports are not the same size but their centers are lined up. You can easily line up the centers of two viewports (even though they're not the same size) by using point filters and osnap to place the midpoint on the edge of one viewport in line with the midpoint on the edge of the other viewport.

Method 1 can also be used for lining up an auxiliary view. Let's assume that in viewport 1 you have a front view of an object; you want to place in viewport 2 an auxiliary view that will be above and to the right of this front view, 30 degrees above horizontal. You'll need to do four things.

First, make sure you have a plan view of the angular feature that requires the auxiliary view.

Second, the auxiliary view must be rotated 30 degrees. This can be done easily with the TWist option of the DVIEW command.

Third, you need to center the views in both viewports around a common point in or near the model, and scale the view in both viewports the same in relation to Paper Space. This is easily done with the Center option and the XP feature of the ZOOM command.

Fourth, you need to place viewport 2 so that its center is 30 degrees above and to the right of the viewport 1 center. This can be done in several ways.

One approach involves using a construction line. In Model Space, you could place a 30 degree construction line where needed, then move each viewport from its own center to the appropriate endpoint or other point on the 30 degree line. (You can address the center of the viewport by using point filters and immediate osnap modes to filter in the X coordinate of the midpoint of a horizontal edge, then the YZ coordinates of the midpoint of a vertical edge.) This method gives you a tangible line to "slide" the auxiliary view along. However, it involves three separate steps—creating the construction line, moving the views and erasing or freezing the construction line.

Another approach requires only two steps: move viewport 2 to the center of viewport 1 by using point filters and the midpoints of the edges of the viewports. Then use polar coordinates to move viewport 2 to its desired location.

Method 1 allows you to line up your views before you have any model in Model Space.

Lining Up Views—Method 2

Using Osnap on Model Space While in Paper Space   This method requires a model already in Model Space that's visible within each of the viewports to be lined up.

While in Paper Space, you cannot pick any entities in Model Space. However, you can osnap to them. This makes it easy to line up the corresponding features in two views.

For example, suppose you have a viewport on the left and another viewport on the right. These two viewports are not necessarily the same size, but their views are scaled the same in relation to Paper Space. You want to line up their views horizontally by moving the right viewport so its view lines up with the view in the left viewport.

Enter the MOVE command and pick the right viewport. For the base point, enter the appropriate osnap mode and pick a feature of the object in the right viewport. For the second point, filter in the Y value (enter . Y), enter the appropriate osnap mode and pick the corresponding feature of the object in the left viewport. When you're prompted "(need XZ):" then pick any point to the right of the left viewport.

This method also works for lining up auxiliary views. Again, assume you want viewport 2 placed 30 degrees to the right and above viewport 1. First, place viewport 2 on top of viewport 1, lining up a feature in viewport

2 with the corresponding feature in viewport 1. (Use the MOVE command and immediate osnap modes to move viewport 2 from a particular feature on the view in viewport 2 to the same feature on the view in viewport 1.) Then use polar coordinates to move viewport 2 to its desired location.

Method 2 is illustrated in the next chapter, Projects 13A (steps 36 and 37) and 13B (steps 22 and 23).

After you line up one viewport with another, you can move the edges of that viewport without changing either the location or the magnification of the view. Perhaps the best way to accomplish this is to use the STRETCH command with a crossing window to slide one or two sides of the viewport at a time, as explained earlier in this chapter (see "Manipulating Viewports in Paper Space"). Remember that moving the viewports will usually misalign the views, but stretching one or two edges will not move the views at all.

When your view alignment is completed, you should use the VIEW command to save a view in each viewport, perhaps using the viewport's handle as the name of the view. As you work with your model in the different viewports, zooming and panning around, you can easily end up with views that are not lined up. Having a saved view makes it easy to restore the alignment (assuming the viewport stays the same size and in the same location).

SOLVIEW & SOLDRAW

The SOLVIEW and SOLDRAW commands are part of an ADS application that must be loaded by entering

```
(xload "solview")
```

These commands are classified (in AME R2) as a "bonus feature." This means that they are still under development and not fully tested or supported by Autodesk.

The SOLVIEW command creates Paper Space viewports that can be aligned (1) according to a UCS (WCS, Current UCS or a named UCS), or (2) orthogonally from an existing viewport, or (3) perpendicular to an angled feature of the model in an existing viewport as an auxiliary view. The viewport border lines are placed on layer VPORTS.

Keep in mind that it is good practice to use several viewports *as you create* your model; don't wait until your model is finished and you want to produce a multi-view drawing. We have followed this practice using the

SMA and SMB prototype drawings. For this reason your basic views should already exist and you may not need to use the SOLVIEW command. However, SOLVIEW can be handy for creating auxiliary views. (You might also want to consider the ADDVP.LSP program described in Appendix A.)

SOLVIEW asks you to name each view. Layers are created using the name you supply. Later SOLDRAW places profiles and sections on those layers.

For example, if you name a view TOP, the layers that are created for that viewport are:

TOP-VIS—for visible lines

TOP-HID—for hidden lines

TOP-DIM—for dimensions

TOP-HAT—for cross-hatching (created for section views only)

You can set up these layers ahead of time and assign the colors and linetypes of your choice.

A typical sequence for the use of SOLVIEW and SOLDRAW follows. This sequence assumes your model is oriented so that you have a top view of it when you obtain a plan view in the WCS.

1. Set TILEMODE to 0 and set up your Paper Space limits before using SOLVIEW.

2. Use SOLVIEW, then the UCS option, then the World option to create a viewport for a top view. Place the view in the upper portion of Paper Space and name the view TOP.

3. Use the Orthogonal option to create a viewport for a front view, select the bottom edge of the top viewport, and place the front view an appropriate distance below the top view. Name the view FRONT.

4. Use the Orthogonal option to create a viewport for a side view using a procedure similar to the one above.

5. If needed, use the Auxiliary option to create an auxiliary view or the Section option to create a section view.

6. Use the LAYER command to place the desired colors and linetypes on the layers created by SOLVIEW.

WARNING: do not place any objects on these layers, since the SOLDRAW command, run on a given viewport, deletes objects on the -VIS, -HID and -HAT layers associated with that viewport.

7. Use SOLDRAW to extract the views in each of the viewports.

When you create an orthogonal view, you are asked to pick the side of an existing viewport, then the new viewport is aligned perpendicular to that side. When you create a section view or auxiliary view, you are asked to indicate two points on an edge view of an inclined plane in the adjacent view, then the new viewport is aligned perpendicular to that plane. A temporary viewport is opened up that covers the entire graphics area. You can move the object within this viewport closer to or farther from the existing view, until you are satisfied with its position. Then you are asked to clip the corners of the new viewport and give it a name.

The SOLDRAW command is dependent on the SOLVIEW command in that it completes the process by extracting the profiles and sections within these viewports as determined by the SOLVIEW command. SOLDRAW creates the profiles and sections based on the choices you make when you establish the viewports with the SOLVIEW command. For example, if you ask for a UCS-, Ortho- or Auxiliary-view, a regular profile is produced within that viewport. However, if you ask for a Section view, a duplicate solid is cut along the cutting plane for the creation of a partial profile (this duplicate solid is later discarded) and a section is also produced. You end up with a complete section view showing the portion of the solid in contact with the cutting plane as well as the part of the solid behind the cutting plane.

Watch out for layer confusion. SOLDRAW uses layers based on names you supply as you create viewports with SOLVIEW. In contrast, the SOLPROF command uses layers beginning with PV- and PH- and the viewport handles. This requires some diligence if you have already set up viewports with layers based on viewport handles (as we did in our prototype drawings) and if you plan to use SOLVIEW and SOLDRAW in such a drawing. Whether you plan to add a viewport using SOLVIEW or use SOLPROF to re-extract a profile in a viewport created by SOLVIEW, you need to remember that you have two sets of layers for similar purposes. You must give attention to which layers are being used in each viewport.

If you like the SOLVIEW and SOLDRAW commands, you may want to set up your prototype drawing so it includes the appropriate layers with their colors and linetypes. Remember, however, not to place permanent information on any -VIS, -HID or -HAT layers, because this information will be erased if you decide to re-extract a view with SOLDRAW. Also remember that the SOLPROF command still creates and uses layers based on the viewport handles.

The MVSETUP Program

If the MVSETUP program file has been loaded onto your system, you can load the MVSETUP program into the drawing editor by entering

```
(load "mvsetup")
```

Then run the program by entering MVSETUP at the Command prompt. If TILEMODE is 1 (the "on" setting), this program operates just like the old Setup option that was available on the root screen menu of Release 10. It still creates certain scaled formats incorrectly, so you'll want to use this part of the program with caution.

If TILEMODE is 0 (the "off" setting), you can insert standard title and border formats, create or scale viewports, or align viewports. It is this last option that's of interest at this point. If you request "Align viewports," you're given the options: Angled, Horizontal or Vertical alignment, Rotate view or Undo.

The Horizontal and Vertical options require that you pick a point within the base viewport and then a corresponding point within the viewport to be aligned. The program does not automatically scale the view in the aligned viewport to match the scale of the view in the base viewport. Method 2, explained above, accomplishes the same thing with about the same amount of effort. One difference between MVSETUP and Method 2 is that in Method 2 the viewport is moved, while MVSETUP pans the view within the viewport.

The Rotate view option does the same thing that DVIEW TWist does. The Angled option works properly only when viewport scaling is 1xp and when the base viewport is in plan view, which is seldom the case.

The PROJECT Program

If the PROJECT program file has been loaded onto your system, you can load it into the drawing editor by entering

```
(load "project")
```

Then run the program by entering PROJECT at the Command prompt.

You can use this program to project the output blocks of the SOLFEAT, SOLSECT and SOLPROF commands onto either the X-Y construction plane of the current UCS or a different UCS. The blocks must be exploded before using PROJECT.

Level of Interaction Between Model & Drawing

AutoCAD AME currently has capabilities that would be classified as (1) one-way and (2) manual.

I. The interaction is one-way because the model can influence the 2D drawing, but not vice versa. And this is probably the way it should be. Since several views are dependent on one model, it makes sense that the thing to change is the model. Also, when you make a change to one view of a drawing, that change in itself doesn't necessarily determine all other views. Therefore, an approach in which the user attempts to change the model or other views automatically by changing one of the 2D views would not be feasible.

2. The interaction is manual because changes made to the model do not automatically affect the 2D drawing. When you change the model, you must either manually change the 2D views you extracted from the model or erase them and re-extract them from the newly revised model. In more expensive solid modeling systems, changes made to the model appear automatically in the 2D drawing. This is a significant limitation in AutoCAD's current approach to solid modeling.

In general, you should not attempt to modify your design by modifying any 2D extractions, whether features, sections or profiles. These modifications will not affect the model from which they were originally extracted. Further, any modifications you attempt to make to a profile in one view will not show up in other views, because profiles are placed on layers that are unique to the viewport in which the profile was made. In most cases, the layer that a profile resides on in one viewport should be frozen in all other viewports. So, even though it may look like you just moved a hole or stretched an edge in one view, corresponding changes will not appear in the other viewports.

Your best rule of thumb is to delay extracting 2D views until as late in the process as possible. When you do need to revise the object after extracting 2D views, revise the model and re-extract those views that are affected.

Assemblies

You can create an assembly out of several solid models by importing each model into an assembly drawing. You can import models as xrefs by using the Attach option of the XREF command. It is advisable to turn HANDLES on in your assembly drawing before importing the solids. For more information on xrefs, see *AutoCAD: A Concise Guide to Commands and Features*, Second Edition.

Do not use the INSERT command; bad HANDLES or corrupted composites may result. Also, do not attempt to save solids to disk with the WBLOCK command. Instead, use the WBLKSOL program supplied with AME (see Chapter 15, "AutoLISP & API Programs Supplied With AME").

When you import a part as an xref, its location and orientation in the assembly are determined by its location and orientation *in relation to the WCS in its own drawing*. You may have saved the part drawing while a different UCS was current, but that UCS will not affect its location or orientation when it's imported.

You'll find it easy to properly orient the individual parts (imported solids) in relation to each other if you create them in their assembled orientation to begin with. Select a main origin point in the assembly, then as you create each individual model, locate and orient it so it can be imported directly into the assembly without requiring complicated moves. The simplest situation is when each part can be imported into the assembly and placed at 0,0,0 without any rotation, or merely translated along one or two axes.

When you import a model into an assembly drawing, you cannot treat it as a true solid until it's exploded. In the case of an xref, this means it must be bound (using the Bind option of the XREF command) before it can be exploded. You won't be able to use any of the Boolean operations or commands such as SOLLIST or SOLMOVE until the block is exploded.

The HIDE and SHADE commands will work in an assembly if the parts were imported as xrefs, then bound and meshed in the assembly drawing. An xref that remains unbound in an assembly will not hide or shade unless it was meshed in its original drawing.

You'll find that AutoCAD has to work hard to handle assemblies with many components. Where complex assemblies are the norm, AutoCAD would serve best as the modeler for individual parts, while a more expensive solid modeler would handle the assemblies.

Checking for Interference

When you bring several parts together into an assembly, it is helpful to check for interference (overlap) between any of the parts. The SOLINTERF command lets you check for interference between two solids (primitives or composites), between several solids or between two groups of solids.

Interference is the condition that exists when one solid overlaps (contains volume in common with) another solid. Solids that merely touch each other, even if they have one or more surfaces in common, are not examples of interference.

The SOLINTERF command allows you to select one set of solids, or two sets. If you select just one set, each solid in that set will be tested against every other solid in the set to see which pairs of solids produce interference. If you select two sets, each solid in the first set is tested against every solid in the second set. When you want to check just one solid against another, you can place both solids in the first set (with no solids in the second set) or place one solid in each set.

When you select two sets, either set can contain just one solid. This is an efficient way to check for interference between a new part that you just added to an assembly and the other parts that have already been checked.

If there is no interference, AutoCAD reports that fact. If there is interference, AutoCAD reports the number of solids and number of pairs of solids that interfere with other solids. You are then given two other options that can show more precisely where the interference is.

First, you are asked if you want common volume calculated. This is not an offer to calculate the amount of common volume, but to create a separate solid (an intersection) for each interfering pair. You may find it helpful to use the COLOR command to establish a contrasting color so the new solids will show up clearly. If there are a large number of interfering pairs, this can be time-consuming and can add a large number of new solid composites to your drawing. These new solids are usually of no value other than to show you exactly where the interference occurs. In most cases you want to erase them when you are done with the SOLINTERF command (or undo the command).

Second, you are asked if you want to see each interfering pair highlighted. If you answer Yes, AutoCAD lets you walk through all interfering pairs in turn.

The SOLIN & SOLOUT Commands

The purpose of these commands is for transferring solids to and from AutoSOLID Version 3.1. The SOLIN and SOLOUT commands are not intended for use in creating assemblies of parts created with AutoCAD AME. In fact, if you attempt to use SOLIN and SOLOUT to create assemblies, you'll find that some information will be lost—namely tapered extrusions, elliptical cylinders and cones, and certain chamfers and fillets (the file format used by these commands does not support these entities).

Moving On

Although many of these procedures and commands may seem new and complicated, they'll make much better sense with a little practice. The following chapter provides some of that practice by making use of standard orthographic views, auxiliary views and assembly procedures.

PROJECTS: DETAIL
DRAWINGS & ASSEMBLIES

13

Projects: Detail Drawings & Assemblies

This chapter features four projects: Project 13A creates a Paper Caddy and illustrates the use of one auxiliary view and all 2D-extraction commands—SOLFEAT, SOLSECT and SOLPROF. Project 13B creates a Positioning Clip and illustrates use of both primary and secondary auxiliary views. Project 13B-Alternate illustrates the use of SOLVIEW and SOLDRAW. Project 13C puts a simple assembly together, illustrating the use of xrefs in creating solid assemblies.

Project 13A: Paper Caddy

This project creates the Paper Caddy shown in figure 13-1. The lower left view includes a section extracted with the SOLSECT command. The lower right view is a standard view with hidden lines created with the SOLPROF command. The auxiliary view was created with the SOLFEAT command and lined up with the lower left view, using Method 2 described in the previous chapter. (See color illustration C-9 on page 171.)

I. Start AutoCAD and create a drawing called CADDY, using the SMB prototype drawing you created in Chapter 7, "Projects: Boolean Operations." If you did not complete that project, you may want to do that now (it's short), or you could use the SMB prototype drawing on the companion diskette available with this book.

2. Go to Paper Space, switch to layer BORDER, and place the text "PAPER CADDY" in the title line (height .25).

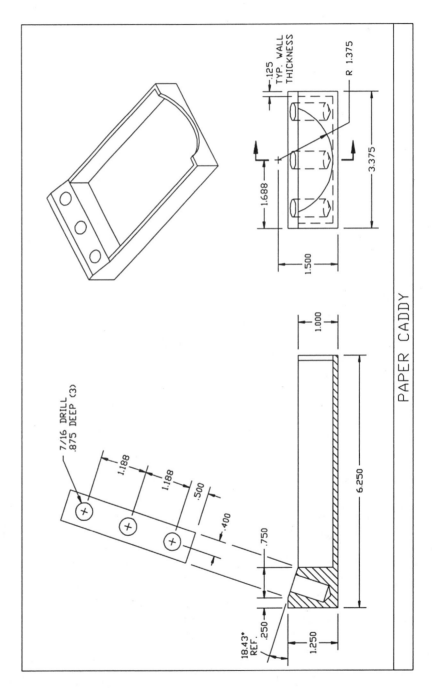

Figure 13-1: Paper Caddy, dimensioned.

We will maintain the three standard orthographic views throughout the modeling phase, then for dimensioning purposes we'll change the upper left view to an auxiliary view of the caddy's sloped feature.

3. While still in Paper Space, use the STRETCH command to adjust all four viewports at once. (Use a crossing window to enclose just the center point [where the four viewports meet]. Then enter a base point of 0,0 and a 1,-1 displacement.)

4. Return to Model Space and switch to layer SM. Use the UCSICON command to make sure the UCS icon is on in all viewports, and place the icon at the origin in all viewports (use the All option).

5. Use UNITS to set angular units to four-place accuracy.

6. Use ZOOM Center to center the view in all four viewports around 3,1.5,.5 at full scale (1xp). Use VIEW to save the views in each viewport using the handle of the viewports as their names.

7. Load AME (Release 11 only).

8. Restore the Front UCS. Set snap at .25.

9. In the lower left viewport (handle 4), create a polyline that outlines the shape of the left edge of the caddy, then extrude the polyline 3.375 in the negative Z direction (no taper).

10. Restore WCS. In the upper right viewport (handle 2), create a box at 1,.125,.125 that is 5.125 x 3.125 x 1.

11. Restore the Right UCS. In the lower right viewport (handle 5), create a cylinder at 1.688,1.5, 6.25, radius 1.375, height -.25.

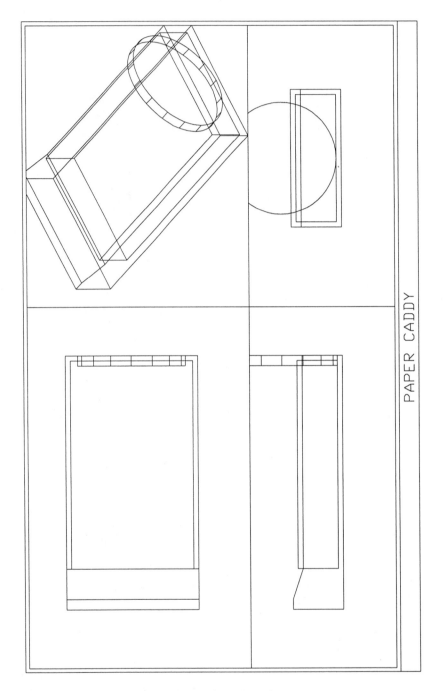

Figure 13-2: Extrusion, box and cylinder before subtraction.

12. Subtract the box and cylinder from the extrusion.

13. Save your drawing. Mesh the composite and check its appearance with HIDE or SHADE. Then return the model to wireframe representation.

14. In the upper right viewport (handle 2), zoom up on the slope.

15. Use the 3point option of the UCS command to place a UCS on the slope. (The origin should be at the lower left corner of the slope, the X axis should run through the lower right corner, and the Y axis should run through the upper left corner.) Save this UCS under the name Slope.

16. Place a cylinder at .5,.4, diameter .4375, height -.875. Place a cone that is the same diameter, height -.126 on the bottom end of this cylinder.

17. Union the cylinder and cone, then copy this hole composite to the two other locations, 1.188 apart.

18. Subtract the three holes from the main composite.

19. Restore View 2 in viewport 2, then save the drawing.

This completes the modeling phase. Now we'll set up the auxiliary view in the upper left viewport and extract the slanted feature.

20. Make the upper left viewport current. While the Slope UCS is still current, use PLAN to produce a plan view of the slope. Pan the view to the center of the viewport.

21. Rotate the view 71.57° with the TWist option of the DVIEW command. (The amount of twist needed can be determined by using DIST in the appropriate UCS in viewport 4 to measure the slope.)

22. Return to WCS. Center the view using the same procedure you used earlier in step 6. Save this view under the name SLOPE.

23. In viewport 3, make layer PV-3 current. (This is the layer set up for profiles in the upper left viewport, but we'll use it for the SOLFEAT command, so the extracted slope feature does not appear in the other viewports.)

24. Extract the slope. It should appear in yellow.

    ```
    SOLFEAT  [Enter][Enter][Enter]
    ```

    Pick the bottom edge of the slope. (If needed, enter N until the slope is highlighted, then press Enter.) [Enter]

    ```
    REDRAWALL  [Enter]
    ```

    Next, set up a UCS as a cutting plane, select a hatch pattern and create the section in the lower left viewport.

25. Restore the Front UCS, then move the origin of the UCS 1.688 in the negative Z direction. Save this UCS under the name SECTION.

26. In viewport 4 make layer PV-4 current (so the extracted section shows up only in this viewport).

27. Set up a standard cross-hatch pattern, then use SOLSECT to extract the section view.

    ```
    SOLHPAT  [Enter]
    ANSI31  [Enter]
    SOLHSIZE  [Enter]
    1  [Enter]
    SOLHANGLE  [Enter]
    0  [Enter]
    SOLSECT  [Enter]
    ```

Pick the model.

```
[Enter]
XY [Enter]
0,0,0 [Enter]
```

- Next, create profile views in the lower right and upper right viewports.

28. In the upper right viewport reduce the view scale to .75. Use SOLPROF to extract a profile view. Notice that we do not need to change layers, since the SOLPROF command always places its profile block(s) on certain layers determined by the current viewport handle.

Pick the upper right viewport (handle 2).

```
ZOOM [Enter]
.75xp [Enter]
SOLPROF [Enter]
```

Pick the model.

```
[Enter]
Y [Enter]
Y [Enter]
Y [Enter]
```

29. Do the same in the lower right viewport, but keep the view at 1xp.

30. Return to WCS and save the drawing.

31. Freeze layer SM.

A certain amount of "cleanup" of the extracted views is required.

32. In the upper right viewport, erase the block with the hidden lines.

33. In the lower right viewport (handle 5), restore the RIGHT UCS. Make layer PH-5 current and freeze layer PV-5. Explode the block with the hidden lines. Use CHPROP to return the color of the lines to Bylayer. Erase all unneeded hidden lines.

34. Thaw layer PV-5, explode the solid-line block and use CHPROP to return the color of the lines to Bylayer (you can window the whole view since all lines should be Bylayer).

35. In the lower left viewport (handle 4), restore UCS SECTION and layer PV-4, then add the five lines needed to complete the section view.

    Line up the auxiliary view with the view in the lower left viewport.

36. In Paper Space, use immediate osnap modes to move the upper left viewport (handle 3) on top of the lower left viewport (handle 4) so that any point in one viewport coincides with its corresponding point in the other.

    ```
    PSPACE [Enter]
    MOVE [Enter]
    ```
    Pick viewport 3.
    ```
    [Enter]
    ```
    Osnap to one of the endpoints on the slope in viewport 3.

    Osnap to the corresponding endpoint on the slope in viewport 4.

37. Use polar coordinates to move the upper left viewport a distance of 2.5 at an angle of 71.57°.

38. Stretch the lower right corner of viewport 3 so it no longer overlaps the other viewports.

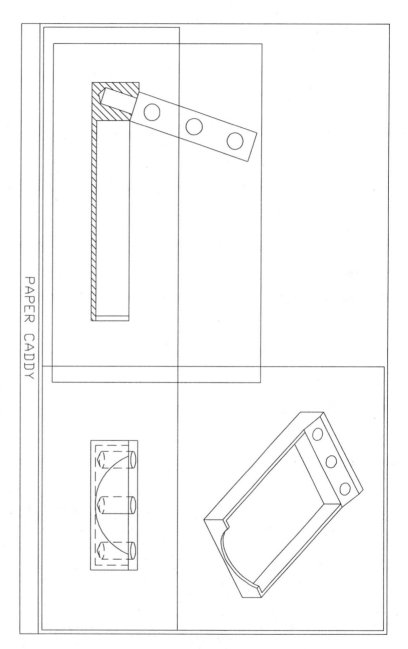

Figure 13-3: Preparation for positioning auxiliary view.

Dimension the drawing.

39. In Model Space, in viewport 4, with UCS SECTION current and layer DIM4 current, dimension the section view. You may want to set the units to 3-place accuracy before dimensioning.

40. Do the same in the upper left and lower right viewports. Remember to set up the appropriate UCS and layer for each viewport. In the upper left viewport, you'll probably want to rotate the Slope UCS around Z by -90° in order to handle the horizontal and vertical dimensions and the text alignment more easily.

41. Turn the grid off in all viewports. Restore WCS.

42. In Paper Space, freeze layer VPBORDER.

43. SAVE the drawing. Plot your masterpiece.

Project 13B: Positioning Clip

This project creates the Positioning Clip shown in Figure 13-4. Besides the same four views we've used in most of the previous projects (three orthographic views and one oblique view in the upper right corner), there's also a primary auxiliary view needed to dimension the 55 degree dihedral angle and the .25 radius, and a secondary auxiliary view needed to dimension the placement of the holes in the top part of the clip. This project also demonstrates the process of creating additional viewports with their associated layers when there aren't enough viewports already included in the prototype drawing. (See color illustrations C-10 and C-11 on pages 171-172.)

1. Start AutoCAD and create a drawing called PCLIP, using the SMA prototype drawing you created in Chapter 2, "Projects: Setup & Overview." Or, use the SMA prototype drawing on the companion diskette available with this book.

2. Go to Paper Space, switch to layer BORDER, and place the text "POSI-TIONING CLIP" in the title line (height .25). Return to Model Space and to layer SM.

We will maintain the viewports for the three standard orthographic views and the oblique view in the upper right corner throughout the modeling phase, then add two new viewports when we need to extract views. As you create the model, you may want to use the upper right viewport for temporary views of the angular features.

For the modeling portion of this project, I'll make a few suggestions and leave most of the work up to you. If you have completed the earlier projects, this will be a welcome challenge. You'll need to study the dimensions on the Positioning Clip drawing on page 284.

The Positioning Clip is the union of five extrusions/revolutions and one box, minus five cylinders. Color illustration C-10 (page 171) shows these six primitives. Begin at the bottom of the clip and work your way up, one primitive at a time, creating all six primitives before unioning them.

3. In Model Space, in WCS, center the four views around .75,-.75,1 scaled at 1xp. Use the VIEW command to save these centered views, using each viewport's handle as the view name. This will allow you to zoom and pan around while you are working in the viewports and then easily return to the centered view.

You will often need to zoom up to work on the model. Remember that you can do this in Model Space within any viewport, but then your view is still only a small portion of the screen. Therefore, you may often want to switch to Paper Space, zoom in on the desired viewport, then return to Model Space where you can zoom in further if needed.

4. Restore the Front UCS, and make the lower left viewport (handle 4) current. Load AME (Release 11 only).

5. Create the first primitive (beginning at the bottom). 0,0,0 is at the lower left corner of this front view of the clip. Create the first primitive by extruding a polyline. Based on the three dimensions in the right view, the polyline should extend only .75 up in the Y direction.

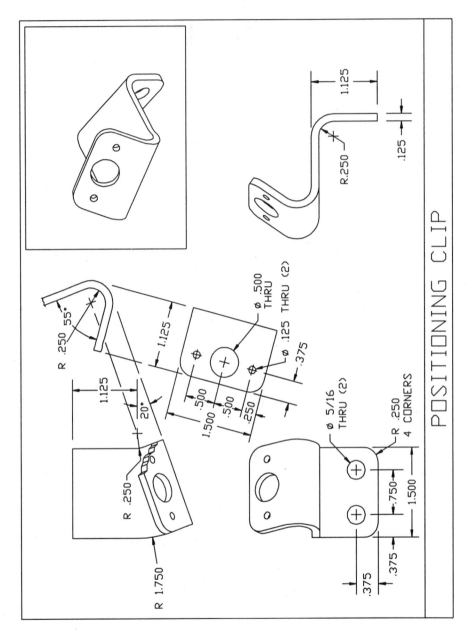

Figure 13-4: Positioning Clip, dimensioned.

6. Create the second primitive (just the .25 radius bend). Restore the Right UCS, use the lower right viewport (handle 5) and draw a polyline containing two 90° arcs and two lines, then extrude the polyline. Setting snap at .125 makes this easier. (This segment could also be created by revolving a .125 x 1.5 rectangular polyline.)

   NOTE: A single extrusion could create the second and third primitives .

7. The third primitive is a box 1.5 x -.75 x .125 in the WCS.

8. The fourth primitive is a fan shape that can be created either from two 20° arcs and two lines extruded .125 or (more easily) one 1.5 x .125 rectangle revolved through 20° around the center of the .25 radius in the top view.

   For the remaining two primitives, you'll find it helpful to set up and save a UCS for each primitive. After creating each new UCS, you may want to use the upper right viewport to obtain a plan view in that UCS for the purpose of constructing the geometry.

9. The fifth primitive is similar to the second. However it does not run parallel to the principal axes. You'll need to set up an X-Y construction plane to create the polyline for this extrusion (or revolution). For example, if you plan to create a polyline containing two 125° arcs, you could start with the Right UCS, move its origin to an appropriate point, then rotate it around its Y axis 20°. Or, you may find it easier to revolve a rectangle, in which case you could create the needed UCS using the 3point option. Whichever method you use, make sure you save a UCS that has its Z axis parallel to the centerline of the primitive, called AUX1, which you will need later.

   NOTE: There is a SOLUCS command we haven't mentioned before. Its purpose is to provide an easy way to attach a UCS to the face or edge of a solid. However, when you choose a solid's face or edge, you have no control over the orientation of the axes. On a rectangular face, for example, the origin of the UCS will be placed at one of the corners, but you cannot select that corner by picking a point near the corner when you select an edge. The 3point option of the UCS command provides a more direct way of controlling the placement of a UCS.

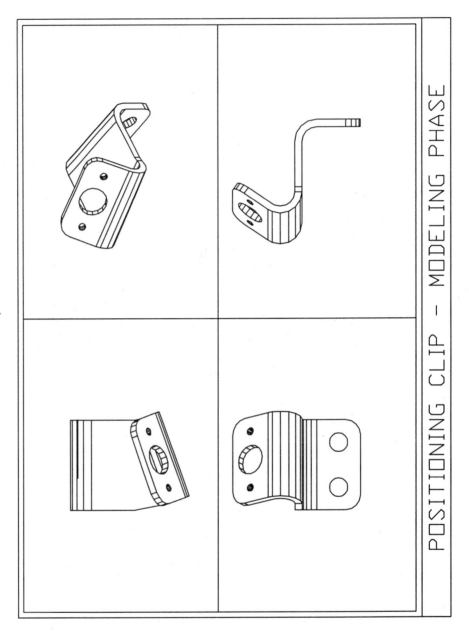

Figure 13-5: Positioning Clip, modeling phase.

10. The sixth primitive is similar to the first. One easy way to position an X-Y construction plane for creating the polyline is to use the 3point option of the UCS command to place a UCS on the top edge of the fifth primitive, then rotate it around its X axis 90°. Save this UCS under an appropriate name such as AUX2. (Also remember to save your drawing occasionally.)

11. Union all six primitives.

12. While you're in the AUX2 UCS, create the cylinders for the three holes in the top of the clip. Then restore the front UCS, create the two cylinders in the bottom of the clip, and subtract all five cylinders from the clip.

Now we need to create two extra viewports to hold the primary and secondary auxiliary views.

13. In Paper Space, use the MOVE and STRETCH commands to re-position the four original viewports as shown in Figure 13-6. Then, on layer VPBORDER, use MVIEW to create the two new smaller viewports.

Your original four viewports had handles 2, 3, 4 and 5 because they were created as the first four entities in the prototype drawing. In contrast, these two new viewports will have handles perhaps three digits long. If you list these new viewports while you're in Paper Space, their handles will be displayed. You should write down these handles because you'll need to know them in order to set up the appropriate profile layers later. Since we don't know what the actual handles are in your drawing, we'll refer to them as JJJ (top-center) and KKK (middle).

14. In Model Space, make viewport JJJ current and restore UCS AUX1. Obtain a PLAN view. To orient the model in this view, use the TWist option of the DVIEW command and rotate the view 110°. Use ZOOM 1xp to make sure the scale of the view is correct. (Don't worry about lining up the view yet; we'll do that after we extract the 2D views.)

15. Do the same in viewport KKK (rotating the view 75° after obtaining a plan view).

16. Set up layers to be used for extracting 2D profiles. Use VPLAYER's New-frz option to create layers DIMJJJ, PV-JJJ, PH-JJJ, DIMKKK, PV-KKK and PH-KKK (replace JJJ and KKK with the actual handles of these two viewports). Then use VPLAYER to thaw the appropriate layers in each of the new viewports. Finally, use the LAYER command to assign magenta (6) to the new dimensioning layers (DIM*), yellow (2) to the new visible layers (PV*) and red (1) to the new hidden line layers (PH*). Assign hidden lines to the hidden line layers.

17. In viewport KKK, use SOLFEAT to extract a face feature; in all the other viewports, use SOLPROF to extract a profile, remembering to place hidden lines on a separate layer and delete tangential edges. Make sure layer PV-KKK is current when you extract the feature. It doesn't matter what layer is current when you extract the profiles.

18. Freeze layer SM so you can work just with the extracted views.

19. Since this clip has uniform thickness and all holes are thru-holes, hidden lines are not needed. They would create more clutter than clarity. So erase the hidden-line block in each viewport.

20. Also in each viewport, explode the solid-line block, then use CHPROP to restore the color of the entities to Bylayer. If you explode the feature block in viewport KKK, you'll have to return the entities to the appropriate layer (PV-KKK) as well as restore their color to Bylayer.

21. In viewport JJJ, erase the unneeded portion of the profile. Have you saved your drawing lately?

We will illustrate first lining up one of the orthographic views, then lining up an auxiliary view. Both operations are done in Paper Space. Before lining up the views, make sure the views are at 1xp scale.

Figure 13-6: Positioning Clip, view extraction phase.

22. Suppose viewport 3 (upper left) is no longer lined up with viewport 4 (lower left). To line up viewport 3 with 4:

    PSPACE [Enter]

    MOVE [Enter]

    Pick viewport 3. [Enter]

    ENDPOINT [Enter]

    Pick a point on the object in viewport 3.

    .X [Enter]

    ENDPOINT [Enter]

    Pick the corresponding point on the object in viewport 4.

    Pick any point above viewport 4.

23. To line up viewport JJJ with viewport 3, move JJJ on top of 3, then use polar coordinates to position it 20° above and to the right of 3.

    MOVE [Enter]

    Pick viewport JJJ. [Enter]

    ENDPOINT [Enter]

    Pick a point on the object in viewport JJJ.

    ENDPOINT [Enter]

    Pick the corresponding point on the object in viewport 3.

    MOVE [Enter]

    Pick viewport JJJ. [Enter]

    Pick any point.

    @2.5<20 [Enter]

    This auxiliary viewport can be repositioned any time and still keep its alignment, if you use polar coordinates and the correct angle to move it.

24. Use a similar procedure to line up KKK with JJJ. (KKK is oriented at -105° from JJJ.)

25. Finally, dimension the views in Model Space. Remember to restore the appropriate UCS and the appropriate layer for each viewport before you begin dimensioning in that viewport. For example, when you dimension in the lower left viewport (handle 4), restore UCS Front and layer DIM4. As you add dimensions, you'll probably find that you need to return occasionally to Paper Space in order to stretch the edges of the viewports to make room for the dimensions.

26. When you're done dimensioning, return to Paper Space and freeze layer VPBORDER. Now your drawing is ready to plot.

Project 13B-Alternate: Another Way to Create & Align Viewports & Extract Views

In order to do this project, you must have completed Project 13B (at least the first twelve steps). In this project we set up new viewports for three orthographic views, two auxiliary views and an isometric view of the Clip. These viewports will be positioned the same as they were in Project 13B (see Figure 13-6). We will use the SOLVIEW command to create the new paper space viewports from scratch, and the SOLDRAW command to extract the profile views in each viewport. Both SOLVIEW and SOLDRAW are contained in the Solview program that is loaded after you enter the drawing editor.

To prepare for this project, make a copy of your PCLIP.DWG file named PCLIP-A. At the DOS prompt, enter

```
COPY  PCLIP.DWG  PCLIP-A.DWG
```

Next, start AutoCAD, edit PCLIP-A, and follow the steps listed below.

First, we need to make a few modifications to the drawing.

1. Thaw layers SM and VPBORDER.

2. In Model Space, establish a UCS by rotating the WCS around Z by 45°, then around X by 35°. Save this UCS under the name "ISO," then return to the WCS.

3. Switch to Paper Space and erase all of the viewports.

4. Load AME (Release 11 only).

5. Load SOLVIEW by entering

```
(xload "solview")
```

Next, we use SOLVIEW to set up the viewports.

6. Use SOLVIEW to establish a top view in the upper left quadrant of the drawing.

```
SOLVIEW [Enter]
U [Enter]
W [Enter]
1 [Enter]
```

Pick a point in the middle of the upper left quadrant of the drawing. If needed, adjust the location by picking another point. [Enter]

Pick the two opposite points to define the limits of this viewport.

`TOP [Enter]` (do not exit the SOLVIEW command)

7. Use SOLVIEW to establish a front view below the top view.

```
O [Enter]
```

Pick the bottom edge of the top viewport.

Pick a point in the middle of the lower left quadrant of the drawing. If needed, adjust the location by picking another point. [Enter]

Pick the two opposite points to define the limits of this viewport.

`FRONT [Enter]` (do not exit the SOLVIEW command)

8. Use a similar procedure to establish a side view called "Right" to the right of the front view.

9. Use SOLVIEW to establish the primary auxiliary view to the right of the top view. Establishing an auxiliary view requires that you indicate an edge view of an inclined plane within the top view by locating two points.

    ```
    A [Enter]
    ```

    Make the top viewport current.

    To establish the inclined plane, pick any point within this viewport, then pick a second point by entering @1<110. (You could also establish this inclined plane by osnapping to two points on the right edge of the upper portion of the clip.)

    Pick a point to the right of this line (within the viewport).

    Pick a point to the right of the top view to locate the new viewport. If needed, adjust its location by picking another point. [Enter]

    Pick the two opposite points to define the limits of this viewport.

    ```
    AUX1 [Enter]
    ```
    (do not exit the SOLVIEW command)

10. Use a similar procedure to establish a view called "Aux2" as a secondary auxiliary view below the primary auxiliary view. The two points defining the edge of the inclined plane can be located by picking any point, then entering @1<165.

11. Use a procedure similar to step 6 above to establish the isometric view in the upper right corner. Use the "ISO" UCS that you created in step 2. Exit the SOLVIEW command.

    Finally, use SOLDRAW to automatically extract the views.

12. Use SOLDRAW to extract the profile views in each viewport.

    ```
    SOLDRAW [Enter]
    ```

    Pick all viewports (you can use a crossing window). [Enter]

If you had set up any section views with SOLVIEW, SOLDRAW would automatically extract a section view in that viewport.

SOLDRAW freezes the SM layer in each viewport after it extracts the profile. The only thing remaining is to erase unneeded portions of the profile in the secondary auxiliary view and dimension the views.

You should examine the layers generated by the SOLVIEW command. You could assign different colors to the various layers for visible lines, hidden lines, dimensioning and hatching. You should also experiment with the Section option of the SOLVIEW command.

If you like the SOLVIEW and SOLDRAW commands, you may want to set up your prototype drawing so it includes the appropriate layers with their colors and linetypes. Remember, however, not to place permanent information on any -VIS, -HID or -HAT layers, since this information will be erased if you decide to re-extract a view with SOLDRAW.

Project 13C: Step Stool Assembly

In this project, we'll use an extremely simple assembly, since our purpose is to illustrate the process of creating an assembly using xrefs and blocks rather than to illustrate complex modeling.

We'll create the Child's Step Stool Assembly. The overall height of this stool is 7.00 inches. It's made up of two different solids—the disk (which serves as both bottom and top) and the peg. (See color illustration C-12 on page 172.)

This project illustrates assembly with blocks and xrefs, checking for interference, altering an externally referenced part and producing a three-quarter section view.

Create the three drawings, PEG, DISK and STOOL, using the SMB prototype drawing, scaling each viewport at one-quarter scale (.25xp).

First, we create the peg and the disk.

I. In a drawing called PEG, on layer 0, create the peg (cylinder) according to the dimensions on the detail drawing below, placing the center of the base of the cylinder at 0,0,0 in the WCS. In order to illustrate interference checking, make the height of the cylinder 6.75 instead of 6.25. Save the drawing.

CHILD'S STEP STOOL

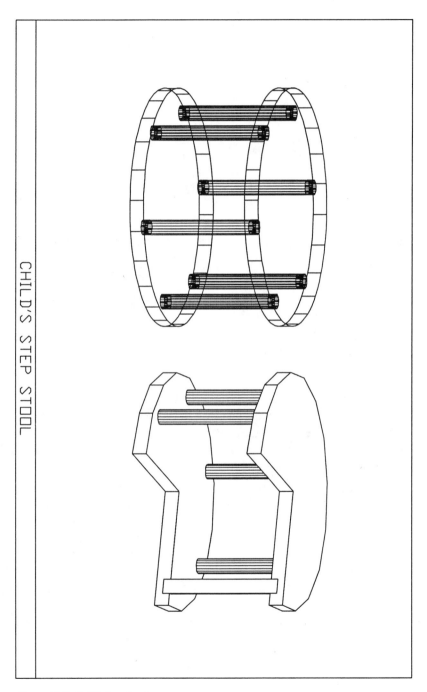

Figure 13-7: Child's Step Stool.

2.   In a separate drawing called DISK, on layer 0, create the disk (one large cylinder minus six small cylinders) according to the dimensions on the detail drawing below. Place the center of the base of the large cylinder at 0,0,0 in the WCS. This disk can be created from a region. Save the drawing.

Now we build the assembly by importing the disk and peg into an assembly drawing.

3.   In a drawing called STOOL, create a layer for the Peg and another for the Disk, each with a different color. Use INSERT to import the disk, placing it on its own layer at 0,0,0. (This will be the bottom of the stool.) Then rotate the UCS around the Y axis 180° and insert the disk again at 0,0,-7. (This will be the top of the stool and should appear above the base because of the UCS we've set up.) Return to WCS.

4.   Use the Attach option of the XREF command to import the peg, placing it on its own layer at 5,0,.375. Save the drawing.

If you try to use SOLLIST on the imported parts, you'll find they're not yet functioning as solids. The inserted disks must be exploded (only once) before AutoCAD will consider them solids. The attached pegs (xrefs) must be bound, using the Bind option of the XREF command, then exploded in order to function as solids. After exploding, return them to their appropriate layers with CHPROP.

   You explode an imported block to get a solid. If you explode it again, you destroy the solid and are left with only the lines, circles, etc., that are used by AutoCAD to display the solid. So make sure you explode imported blocks only once.

In a side view of the stool, you can easily see that the peg is too long. If the amount of interference were very small, you wouldn't be able to see it and would have to use the SOLINTERF command to detect it.

5.   Bind the peg and explode the disk and peg.

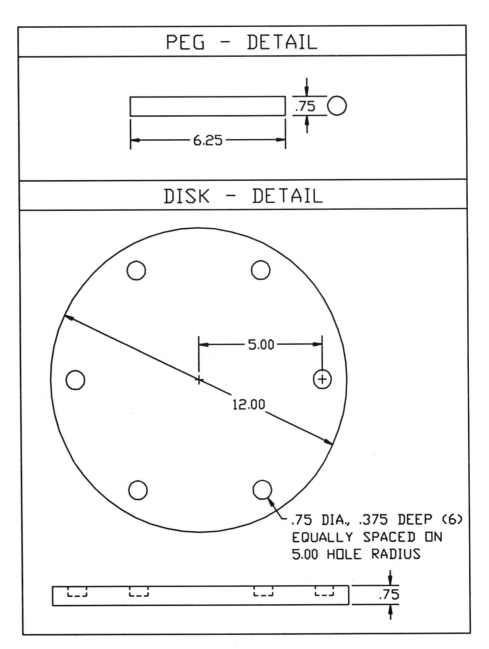

Figure 13-8: Peg and disk details.

6. Check for interference.

   > SOLINTERF [Enter]
   >
   > Pick top disk and peg. [Enter][Enter]
   >
   > N [Enter]

7. Quit the STOOL drawing (so the binding and exploding will not be saved.) Edit the PEG drawing and use SOLCHP to change the height of the cylinder to its correct dimension, 6.25.

8. Edit the STOOL drawing so the peg will be the proper length. Array the peg to fill in the five other locations.

9. Convert the imported blocks into solids by binding the xrefs, then exploding all blocks and return them to their appropriate layers. Use SOLLIST to list each one to make sure it is now a solid.

   Finally, we'll create a three-quarter cutaway view of the assembly.

10. Create a large box at 0,0,0 that is 8 x -8 x 8. Subtract this box from the assembly in order to create the three-quarter view. Save your drawing.

Moving On

One advantage of solid modeling becomes obvious when you need to produce dimensioned secondary auxiliary views, as we did in this chapter. And that advantage is even more striking if irregular shapes are found on an oblique surface.

Another advantage of solid modeling shows up when we consider the uses of solid modeling outside AutoCAD, as we do in the next chapter.

DOWNSTREAM
APPLICATIONS OF
AutoCAD AME

14

Downstream Applications of AutoCAD AME

The solid model you just created with the AME solid modeler can be only the beginning of a downstream application. The end product of your AutoCAD AME solid model, in whatever file form you choose (DWG, DXF or IGES), is more than an actual working engineering drawing; it is data.

Solid modeling data is used for one or more types of post-processing. Some of the more common types are illustrated in the following diagram.

Downstream Applications of AutoCAD AME

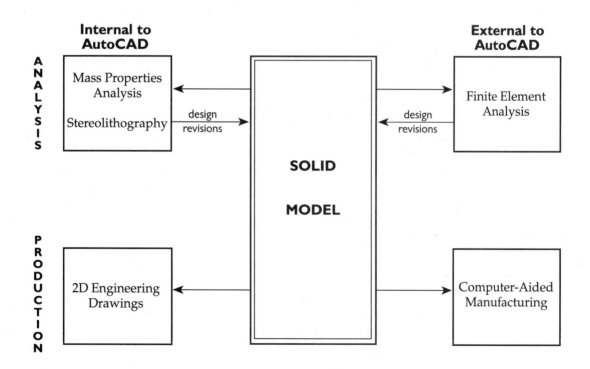

On the left side of the diagram, you can see that three of the types of post-processing are included within AutoCAD AME—mass properties analysis, the extraction of 2D engineering drawings and stereolithography. On the right side of the diagram, Finite Element Analysis and Computer-Aided Manufacturing rely on external (3rd-party) software.

On the top of the diagram are the types of post-processing that can generally be classified as analysis. These types are important in the design process because they provide feedback geared specifically for the revision of the solid model.

We have already described the mass properties commands and the 2D extraction commands in Chapters 10 and 12, so we will limit our discussion here to Finite Element Analysis, Computer-Aided Manufacturing and Stereolithography.

Finite Element Analysis

Finite element analysis (FEA) involves the division of the model into a finite number of elements. These elements provide a means of analyzing such things as stress or heat transfer.

Once the model is completed, everything that is needed to make such an analysis is known—the exact shape of the solid; the location, size and shape of each individual element, based on the division of the object by the FEA software; and the solid's material. Thus, each element can be analyzed mathematically in relation to its neighboring elements, and points of high stress or high temperature can be displayed in different colors.

Such information can be extremely valuable for modifying the shape of the object. The solid model serves as a prototype, and it may be modified and re-analyzed several times before the final design is adopted.

Computer-Aided Manufacturing

Computer-Aided Manufacturing (CAM) involves the creation of tool-path programs (M-code/G-code files) and is used to create parts and components on CNC equipment, such as a CNC milling machine, lathe or wire EDM. The specific data generated by the CAD system can be directly utilized in a Computer-Aided Manufacturing setup. Enough information is contained in a solid model drawing for the automatic or semi-automatic creation of these tool-path files.

Various CAM software manufacturers take different approaches to the use of solid modeling information. Some require the manual application of meshes to the solid model before tool-path information is extracted. Others use information contained either in the solid model itself or in the display blocks composed of line, circle, arc and polyline entities that AME builds. In either case, the creation of the basic tool-path file is relatively straightforward. Setup, tooling and fixture information is added to the file, and the file is formatted for a specific CNC controller.

Stereolithography

The SOLSTLOUT command is a built-in AME command, but it is classified (in AME R2) as a "bonus feature." This means that it is still under development and not fully tested or supported by Autodesk.

The SOLSTLOUT command places information about a solid in an ASCII or binary file. This file is in a format that can be used by Stereolithography Apparatus (SLA) for the creation of a physical prototype. AME applies a mesh that breaks the surface of the solid into triangles and outputs this information to the file. The SLA converts this information into stratum contours for the layer-by-layer creation of the actual shape.

To use SOLSTLOUT, follow these steps:

1. Create a support structure for the solid (see STLSUP.LSP in Chapter 15). Union the support to the solid.

2. Make sure the solid, including its support, is entirely in positive space in the WCS (all X, Y and Z locations on the solid and the support must be positive).

3. Set SOLWDENS to a medium-high setting, perhaps 8 or 10. The solid will be re-meshed for this command. The finer the mesh the more accurate the surfaces (and, of course, the larger the output file).

4. Enter the SOLSTLOUT command, pick a single solid, and indicate binary or non-binary (ASCII) output. After the mesh is created, you are asked for the name of the output file. An extension of ".STL" will be added automatically. SOLSTLOUT will display the number of triangles in the mesh.

SOLSTLOUT may have problems when generating a mesh to represent double-curved (non-developable) surfaces, small features on large objects, thin shells and shallow cones.

DXF Files

Beware using DXFIN and DXFOUT with drawings containing solids. If you use DXFOUT, set the accuracy at 16 decimal places and do not use the Entities option, because block-definition information will be omitted. Also, use DXFIN only in a new, blank drawing, or the block definitions will not be imported.

Communication With External Software

Some external software is written in AutoLISP or C language, so it can run inside AutoCAD. Other external software requires the use of interchange files to access information from AutoCAD. AutoCAD can produce both DXF and IGES files for this purpose.

The AME Reference Manual states that DXF files (produced with the DXFOUT command) include all solid modeling information but IGES files (produced with the IGESOUT command) do not contain solid modeling information. This needs some clarification.

It is true that DXFOUT/DXFIN will re-create solid models whereas IGESOUT/IGESIN will not. However, some software packages do not require the direct solid modeling information in order to work properly. For example, some CAM software creates its own surface or tool-path information from the regular AutoCAD entities (lines, circles, arcs and polylines) which AME creates to display the solid model. Of course, this information is contained in both DXF and IGES files.

This aspect of solid modeling with AME is still developing. It is beyond the scope of this book to provide a description of the various external software packages that post-process AutoCAD's solid models. Nevertheless, in some situations, post-processing may be one of the principal reasons for creating solid models.

Moving On

If you've stayed with us throughout this book, you've explored all the major aspects of solid modeling with AutoCAD AME. We hope you feel you've become acquainted with it well enough to appreciate both its usefulness and its limitations. If so, you're in a good position to determine whether it is appropriate for your design situation.

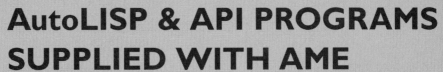

AutoLISP & API PROGRAMS SUPPLIED WITH AME

15

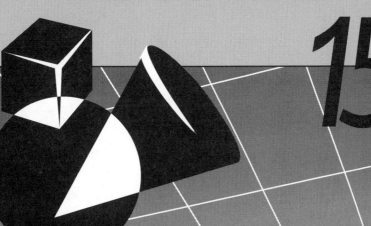

• •

AutoLISP & API Programs Supplied With AME

AutoLISP Programs

n order to run any of these AutoLISP programs, the program file must be installed on your hard disk (probably in directory C:\ACAD\SAMPLE), and you must load the program into the drawing editor by entering the following at the Command prompt:

```
(load "xxxxxx")
```

where xxxxxx is the primary name of the program file. Include the parentheses and the quotation marks. To run the program after it is loaded, enter the name of the program.

SOLMAINT.LSP

SOLMAINT is intended for drawings containing AME R1 solids. It removes intermediate wireframe blocks and thus reduces the size of the drawing. Do not use this program in AME R2 drawings.

WBLKSOL.LSP

WBLOCK used with the asterisk ("*") retains handles, but WBLOCK used with a block name does not retain handles. If you have several composite solids in your drawing, how can you write one of them to file? You cannot use the WBLOCK command to do this because a composite solid depends on handles for the identification of its primitives.

WBLKSOL will write the solid blocks to file and retain handles. It does so by temporarily deleting all other drawing entities, writing the selected blocks to file (using WBLOCK with the asterisk) and then restoring the deleted drawing entities. This may take considerable time. You may want to save your drawing before using WBLKSOL.

Without WBLKSOL you would have to use the following steps to accomplish the same thing:

- End your drawing.

- Switch to the File Utilities menu and copy the drawing to another drawing file.

- Return to the Main Menu, edit the new drawing and delete unwanted entities.

- This drawing file will be considerably larger than one produced with WBLKSOL, so you may want to use SOLPURGE on the Erased items and END the drawing once or twice to reduce its size.

HOLE.LSP

HOLE allows you to add counterbore and countersink features to existing holes. You must create the basic hole first, then run HOLE. First, indicate CSink or CBore. Then, select the flat face on which the feature will be placed; select the edge of the hole; enter the included angle for countersink, or radius and depth for counterbore.

The CBORE and CSINK programs on the companion diskette for this book (described in Appendix A) use an alternate approach. They create the hole and the countersink or counterbore together, but leave the placement and subtraction up to you. This approach is quicker when you have multiple holes of the same size to place in your drawing.

STLSUP.LSP

STLSUP creates two different kinds of support structures used in Stereolithography: the "star" (radial) and "eggcrate" (grid). These supports are placed under the composite and unioned to it before using the STLOUT command.

API Programs Files

These are C language applications accessible through AutoLISP. The application file must be installed on your hard disk (probably in directory C:\ACAD\API\SAMPLE), and you must load the file by entering something like the following at the Command prompt:

```
(xload "c:\\acad\\api\\sample\\xxxxxx")
```

where xxxxxx is the primary name of the application file. Include the parentheses and the quotation marks. In most cases the command (program that you run at the Command prompt) differs from the general application name, as listed below.

TUTOR.C

TUTOR includes seven programs: SOLPIPE, SOLTOPOL, SOLTRACE, SOLNORM, SOLTAN, SOLCLASS and SOLUCSPD.

These programs are intended to illustrate various capabilities of the Application Programming Interface (API) for the beginning user of API. For the general AME user, only the first program, SOLPIPE, is of interest. It creates a pipe (hollow tube) when you specify the outside and inside diameters and the beginning and ending points of the pipe.

ASM.C

ASM includes two programs: SOLCONTACT and SOLALIGN. Both programs assist you in moving one or more solids in relation to a fixed solid by making use of the flat-face features or axis/edge features of the solids.

SOLCONTACT allows you to move solids so that the flat surface of one solid ends up in contact with the flat surface of another solid.

SOLALIGN allows you to move solids so that the axis or edge feature of one solid lines up with the axis or edge feature of another solid.

DRILL.C

DRILL includes a single program, SOLDRILL. It allows you to create a drilled hole, blind or thru. The blind hole has no drill point on the end.

DESIGN.C

DESIGN includes six programs: SOLSHAFT, SOLWHEEL, SOLGEAR, SOLBEAR, SOLBOLT and SOLNUT.

SOLSHAFT creates a shaft with a keyway. The keyway includes no runout or other indication of machining.

SOLWHEEL creates a wheel with a hub and keyway.

SOLGEAR creates a gear. There is no hole in the gear. Since AutoCAD does not have an involute curve, the gear teeth have a half-profile consisting of a line near the root diameter and an arc near the outside diameter.

SOLBEAR creates a generic bearing mount having uniform thickness.

SOLBOLT creates a hexagonal extrusion and a cylinder to represent a hex-head cap screw.

SOLNUT creates a hexagonal extrusion minus a cylinder to represent a hex nut.

LAYOUT.C

LAYOUT includes three programs: GEAR, SHEET and LAYOUT. All three of these programs create regions.

GEAR creates a gear profile. The gear profile is identical to SOLGEAR above.

SHEET creates a rectangular region located by its center.

LAYOUT creates an array of one small region within another large region (a sheet) in order to find the maximum number of regions that can be fabricated from that sheet and the percent usage. By using different rotations for the small region, various totals can result. However, no nesting is done, so the program is impractical for die strip layout. (The bounding box of rotated shapes determines how close one instance comes to the next.)

SYMMETRY.C

SYMMETRY includes a single program, SYMMETRY, which determines whether a region has symmetry. The command notes symmetry about an axis parallel to the X axis, an axis parallel to the Y axis, or circular (radially repeated) symmetry.

OFFSOL.C

OFFSOL includes two programs: SOLOFF and SOLMAC. Both programs work with polylines that have straight segments only.

SOLOFF offsets a polyline a given distance. It handles some corners differently than AutoCAD's OFFSET command.

SOLMAC creates a tool path for milling a surface, the boundaries of which are represented by a polyline. The tool diameter is used as the pass offset. Each pass is a stand-alone loop with no connections to previous or subsequent passes. The resulting tool path, if actually used, would not machine the entire surface but would leave many "stumps" unmachined at toolpath corners.

List of Files on the Companion Diskette

The *Solid Modeling With AutoCAD* Companion Diskette contains batch files, pausing scripts, prototype drawings, sample solid drawings and AutoLISP programs. Each file is described briefly below. The diskette also includes a comprehensive manual explaining each program in detail. The instructions can be printed out for handy reference.

Batch Files

KEYSET.BAT assigns 19 solid modeling, viewing and osnap commands to certain keys, for single-keystroke operation.

KEYRESET.BAT resets the keyboard to its original condition.

Pausing Scripts

PROJ2A.SCR, Project 2A

PROJ2B.SCR, Project 2B

PROJ5A.SCR, Project 5A

PROJ5B.SCR, Project 5B

These scripts are called pausing scripts because they inform you what the next operation will be, then stop and wait for you to press a key to continue. The script files are written to match the numbered steps in the specific projects.

Prototype Drawings

SMA.DWG

SMB.DWG

These prototype drawings are identical to the drawings produced by Project 2A and Project 7D. SMA is for solid modeling on an A-size sheet; SMB is for a B-size sheet. These drawings contain the appropriate layers and viewport setups (including correct freeze-thaw status of viewport-specific layers) for doing solid modeling.

Sample Solid Drawings

CLAMP.DWG

SKULLY.DWG

COVER.DWG

LEVEL.DWG

CADDY.DWG

PCLIP.DWG

STOOL.DWG

These are samples of selected projects in the book.

AutoLISP Programs

The AutoLISP programs are designed to streamline certain operations that are repeated often in solid modeling. The programs pertain to solid construction, working with Paper Space viewports and extracting 2D views. These AutoLISP programs can be loaded in the usual fashion by entering

```
(load "file name")
```

Solid Construction

BX.LSP   A better box command (can be used in place of SOLBOX).

WDG.LSP   A better wedge command (can be used in place of SOLWEDGE).

SSWEEP.LSP   Creates a spline sweep of a selected profile along a selected polyline.

ESLOT.LSP   Creates a solid entity in the shape of a slot.

DRILL.LSP   Creates a solid entity in the shape of a drilled hole.

CBORE.LSP   Creates a solid entity in the shape of a counterbore hole.

CSINK.LSP   Creates a solid entity in the shape of a countersink hole.

PIERCE.LSP   Extends a line to the piercing point of the line and a selected plane.

COMPOUND.LSP   Provides the compound angles used for setting up compound sine plates.

Working With Paper Space Viewports

VP.LSP   Displays both the number and handle of a selected viewport.

CVIEW.LSP   Centers view around given point and scales view in relation to paper space in selected viewports.

C.LSP   Allows user to snap to the center of a viewport. Handy in the middle of a move or copy operation.

FS.LSP   Fills screen with current viewport.

ADDVP.LSP   Adds one or more viewports, establishing proper VISDEFAULT setting and viewport-specific layers.

ZAVP.LSP   Sets ZOOM XP all viewports.

ALIGN.LSP   Aligns one viewport with another, orthogonally or at any angle.

DIMVP.LSP   Sets up for dimensioning in a selected viewport (switches to appropriate UCS and layer).

Extracting 2D Views

AUTOPROF.LSP   Automatically creates profiles in all selected view ports.

PROCLEAN   Cleans up profiles by erasing redundant hidden lines and lines appearing as points.

INDEX

T o order additional copies of *Solid Modeling With AutoCAD* or any of the other books in our AutoCAD Reference Library, please fill out this order form and return it to us for quick shipment.

	Quantity		Price		Total
Solid Modeling With AutoCAD	_____	x	$29.95	=	_____
Solid Modeling With AutoCAD Diskette	_____	x	$49.95	=	_____
The AutoCAD Productivity Book	_____	x	$27.95	=	_____
The AutoCAD Productivity Book Diskette	_____	x	$49.95	=	_____
AutoCAD: A Concise Guide	_____	x	$23.95	=	_____
AutoCAD: A Concise Guide Diskette	_____	x	$19.95	=	_____
1,000 AutoCAD Tips & Tricks	_____	x	$27.95	=	_____
1,000 AutoCAD Tips & Tricks Diskette	_____	x	$49.95	=	_____
AutoLISP in Plain English	_____	x	$23.95	=	_____
AutoLISP in Plain English Diskette	_____	x	$19.95	=	_____

All five books & five diskettes
  (30% off! Shipping included.) _____ x $226.00 = _____

Please specify disk size: _____ 3 1/2" _____ 5 1/4"

Shipping: Please add $4.20/first book for standard UPS, $1.35/book thereafter;
  $7.50/book UPS "two-day air," $2.25/book thereafter.
  For Canada, add $8.10/book = _____

Send C.O.D. (add $4.20 to shipping charges) = _____

North Carolina residents add 6% sales tax = _____

Total = _____

Name _____

Company _____

Address (no P.O. Box) _____

City _____ State _____ Zip _____

Daytime telephone _____

_____ Payment enclosed (check or money order; no cash please)

_____ VISA _____ MC   Acct.# _____ - _____ - _____ - _____

Expiration date _____ Signature _____

Please mail, phone or fax order to:

Ventana Press, P.O. Box 2468, Chapel Hill, NC 27515
919/942-0220, FAX: 800/877-7955

To order additional copies of *Solid Modeling With AutoCAD* or any of the other books in our AutoCAD Reference Library, please fill out this order form and return it to us for quick shipment.

	Quantity		Price		Total
Solid Modeling With AutoCAD	_____	x	$29.95	=	_____
Solid Modeling With AutoCAD Diskette	_____	x	$49.95	=	_____
The AutoCAD Productivity Book	_____	x	$27.95	=	_____
The AutoCAD Productivity Book Diskette	_____	x	$49.95	=	_____
AutoCAD: A Concise Guide	_____	x	$23.95	=	_____
AutoCAD: A Concise Guide Diskette	_____	x	$19.95	=	_____
1,000 AutoCAD Tips & Tricks	_____	x	$27.95	=	_____
1,000 AutoCAD Tips & Tricks Diskette	_____	x	$49.95	=	_____
AutoLISP in Plain English	_____	x	$23.95	=	_____
AutoLISP in Plain English Diskette	_____	x	$19.95	=	_____

All five books & five diskettes
 (30% off! Shipping included.)   _____ x $226.00 = _____

Please specify disk size: _____ 3 1/2"   _____ 5 1/4"

Shipping: Please add $4.20/first book for standard UPS, $1.35/book thereafter; $7.50/book UPS "two-day air," $2.25/book thereafter. For Canada, add $8.10/book   = _____

Send C.O.D. (add $4.20 to shipping charges)   = _____

North Carolina residents add 6% sales tax   = _____

Total = _____

Name _____

Company_____

Address (no P.O. Box) _____

City _____ State _____ Zip _____

Daytime telephone _____

_____ Payment enclosed (check or money order; no cash please)

_____ VISA _____ MC   Acct.# _____ - _____ - _____ - _____

Expiration date _____ Signature _____

Please mail, phone or fax order to:

Ventana Press, P.O. Box 2468, Chapel Hill, NC 27515
919/942-0220, FAX: 800/877-7955